THE
GRAD STUDENT'S
GUIDE TO
GETTING
PUBLISHED

THE
GRAD STUDENT'S
GUIDE TO
GETTING
PUBLISHED

Alida Allison
Terri Frongia

PRENTICE HALL

NEW YORK • LONDON • TORONTO • SYDNEY • TOKYO • SINGAPORE

Prentice Hall General Reference
15 Columbus Circle
New York, NY 10023

An Arco Book

Arco, Prentice Hall and colophons are
registered trademarks of Simon & Schuster, Inc.

Library of Congress Cataloging-in-Publication Data

   The Grad student's guide to getting published / (edited by) Alida Allison,
Terri Frongia
   p. cm.
   Includes bibliographical references.
ISBN 0-13-352972-X
1. Scholarly publishing 2. Learning and scholarship--Authorship--
Marketing. 3. College teaching--Vocational guidance. 4. Authors and
publishers. 5. Graduate students. I. Allison, Alida. II. Frongia, Terri
Z286.S37G7   1992   92-19639
070.5—dc20   CIP

Manufactured in the United States of America

1 2 3 4 5 6 7 8 9 10

CONTENTS

ACKNOWLEDGMENTS

The history of *The Grad Student's Guide to Getting Published* demonstrates how networking works. The editors have had a long academic relationship with many of those who contributed essays or interview time to this book; some of these contributors recommended others; still others are recent professional acquaintances. We thank them all.

We thank our current editor, Eve Steinberg, at Simon & Schuster, for her fine work, and our former editor there, Diane Eisenberg, now at Harvard Law School; and Diane Buckles, Andrea Saltzman, and Martha-E Razo of San Diego State University's English and Comparative Literature Department. We thank our families: Byron, Brendan, and Steve Allison and Antonio, Davide and Serafina Frongia.

The editors of *The Grad Student's Guide to Getting Published* spent their years of doctoral study together, enduring whirlwind seminars, increasingly demanding exams, obdurate dissertations, publication pressure, and job-search shock. In addition to demonstrating the benefits of networking, we have held to one goal in writing this book: to endorse the all-too-infrequent practice of scholarly collaboration and to exemplify it as well.

Acknowledgment is hereby given to Joan Baum, author and editor, and to the City University of New York's Professional Staff Congress for permission to excerpt from their 1990 booklet *Publishing in the Academy*; to Theodore Ziolkowski, author of "The Shape of the PhD: Present, Past, and Future," excerpts from whose essay are reprinted with permission from the Modern Language Association from *ADE Bulletin* 97:12–17; to Bill Gladstone of Waterside Productions for permission to reprint the "Author's Guidelines"; to Linda

Nilson for permission to excerpt from her curriculum vitae; and to Princeton University Press, Johns Hopkins University Press, and *Critique* for permission to reprint their reader's report forms.

Finally, Alida Allison would like to thank her former professor, now colleague, Peter Neumeyer of San Diego State University, for his generous and consistent support; it's made all the difference. And Terri Frongia would like to thank her mentor, Jean-Pierre Barricelli, for his unflagging dedication in imparting his own enthusiasm wisdom, and humanistic ideals to his students—*ora siamo disposti a salire a le stelle.*

INTRODUCTION

The Grad Student's Guide to Getting Published began with a focus on a specific population—graduate students in the humanities and social sciences—and on a specific issue—our need for practical information on academic publication. Yet as the book metamorphosed from original conception to finished manuscript, the editors realized that it offers to anyone concerned with the workings of the scholarly community a comprehensive critique of the place of publication within the profession, especially as the primary measure of excellence for hiring and promotion, as is currently the case.

The Grad Student's Guide to Getting Published is intended to:

- explain the processes of academic publishing and to provide examples of its workings from a variety of functional vantages and pedagogical perspectives;
- save graduate students the wasted time and effort of naive approaches to publishing such as the submission of unrevised seminar papers;
- highlight the importance of relationships between student and mentor, among peers, and within networks for the exchange of ideas and for publication;
- encourage confidence, dialogue, and collaboration beginning in graduate school and extending through the professional years;
- promote a standard of quality in writing, both in content and in style.

The editors solicited contributors to fit into the book format in the same way that guest speakers would fit into a seminar. The contributors come from the humanities, social sciences, and publishing communities. New assistant professors' concerns naturally overlap in most cases with those of advanced graduate students, and we have given attention to these concerns throughout the book. Graduate students in women's studies, rhetoric and composition, and Spanish contributed essays that assess and rank journals in their fields, demonstrating skills that are transferable to other fields. They discuss transforming dissertations into books and describe their experiences working with professors. Professors from several disciplines contributed essays or were interviewed; these disciplines include economics, French, political science, philosophy, comparative literature, Spanish, English, and sociology. The professors range from first-year assistant professors to luminaries. They describe what they do as readers for or editors of journals; as mentors; and as submitters to journals or as collaborators with students. Administrators from three campuses explain the hiring process and suggest ways to maximize graduate study and the early years of teaching. Academic publishers offer advice on writing well and on approaching publishing houses.

Although much of the same advice—for example, to begin publishing as soon as possible—reappears, differences of opinion did emerge and were left intact by the editors so that readers could assess them and decide for themselves. For example, Susan Cayleff, Larry McCaffery, and Jack Zupko recommend writing book reviews, whereas for Jonathan Turner the amount of time required to do them is not justified by the credit book reviews receive when their writer is considered for reappointment, tenure, or promotion. Such differences may occur for several reasons, such as individual preference, the needs of the academic discipline, or the appraisal system of the campus. In any case, it is ultimately up to each graduate student, job seeker, or new tenure-track professor to be well-informed about the expectations for satisfactory progress that pertain to his or her own specific environment.

1

Acknowledging the Need to Publish: Training and Hiring

The Need for Academic Training in Publication
Alida Allison, PhD

Gates of Ivory and Gates of Horn: Teaching the Craft and
the Art of Scholarly Publishing in the University
George Slusser, PhD

Assessing Academic Standards for Excellence
The Benefits of Publishing in Graduate School
Alida Allison, PhD

Getting Jobs and Getting Published
Brian Copenhaver, PhD

Publication, Hiring, and Retention
Patricia Huckle, PhD

Assessing Candidates
Max Neiman, PhD

Getting Hands-on Experience in Publication and Hiring
Alida Allison, PhD

The Need for Academic Training in Publishing

If you are in graduate school, you need this book. You especially
need it if your graduate department is not offering you sufficient
and appropriate career training: training in academic publishing.

1

Graduate students increasingly face the same fact as do faculty: publishing is essential. Ask almost any graduate student and you will be told, "I need to publish." You will also be told, "I don't have the time. I don't know how. And what with classwork, I don't have a chance to read the journals."

It's all true.

Yet few universities provide an education in submission to professional journals and presses or in the ancillary information and skills that aid in building publishing credits and securing a teaching job. And if you haven't been educated in the processes of submission and revision, haven't practiced reading journals or haven't exercised your abilities at conferences, then the publication expectations that accompany your first tenure-track job may seem more intimidating than they actually are. A course on scholarly presses and journals would explain that publication is 10 percent inspiration, 40 percent organization, and 50 percent determination. We offer four essential pieces of advice:

Get your department or your college to offer a course in scholarly publishing. We, as graduate students in literatures and languages at the University of California, Riverside (UCR), petitioned as follows:

> Publication is increasingly emphasized as a requirement for academic hiring. Yet the critical response to most of the writing done in seminars is necessarily limited by time to brief comments from professors. Papers are filed away without being critiqued or revised with a larger audience in mind. To provide a training course in academic writing comparable to classroom-teaching courses for teaching assistants (TAs) would be to recognize the real career needs of students to follow through from research to publication.
>
> Graduate students would benefit as well from the opportunity to familiarize themselves with periodicals in their fields; such in-depth study is usually not feasible in addition to the reading required by most seminars. Thus, well in advance of seeking a job and then seeking to hold on to it, graduates from UCR would be experienced in the publication skills crucial to success.

Our faculty responded with the first "Publication Workshop" offered for credit the following quarter. Notably, the workshop was the direct outcome of communal graduate student effort combined with a receptive faculty. Though we agree with Dean Theodore Ziolkowski, whose comments conclude this book, that doctoral work is already needlessly protracted, this one particular course is an exception that should be available for credit at all universities.

Get as much out of the publication course as you can. Work at investigating journals hands-on in the stacks; focus on actually revising and submitting a paper; contribute energetically to the class. The seminar setting should provide an arena for the discussion of ideas for papers, the development of clear and compelling expression, and the exchange of information, such as assessments of journals and experience with conferences.

Get as many people as you can to register. More people yield more information to be pooled, more ideas to ponder and shape into topics for journal essays and conference presentations, and more papers to critique and edit. Solid enrollment also ensures the continuation of the course.

Get an actively publishing professor to run it, preferably one with a sense of humor. Don't wait for faculty to initiate the course; one reason for the scarcity of academic writing seminars on university campuses is the difficulty in teaching them.

The professor for our workshop, Dr. George Slusser, fit the job description. His comments on the course and on the state of academic publishing follow.

Gates of Ivory and Gates of Horn: Teaching the Craft and the Art of Scholarly Publishing in the University

GEORGE SLUSSER, Associate Professor
Director, Comparative Literature Program
Curator, Eaton Collection in Science Fiction and Fantasy
University of California, Riverside

I am old enough to have glimpsed the genteel world that graduate school in the American university once was. This, in fact, was the world I entered as a graduate student in comparative literature in the late 1960s. Professors were seen as people of vast, cumulative erudition. Students sat in their seminars and wrote papers that, in such august presence, could only be acts of apprenticeship. They advanced to candidacy, then wrote the dissertation. But never did the thought cross their minds of trying to publish one of these graduate papers before getting the PhD. Such hubris was unthinkable. Anyway, there was plenty of time to acquire the necessary erudition. Time had to move slowly in academia; slow time was the nature of the profession.

That was the world I entered. The world I left was radically different. The bottom dropped out of the academic "market" (did knowledge really have markets after all?) in the 1970s. I received my PhD in 1975 and stepped not through ivory gates but through gates of horn. In this new academia, publications were suddenly a vital necessity. It was no longer quality but quantity, and perhaps, impossibly, both. It was no longer simply publish or perish but, desperately, publish and publish and publish, faced always with the grim reality of perishing nonetheless.

Almost overnight, this situation created a new graduate student and a new breed of humanist and literary scholar. The immediate need for an avenue of publication led to the current proliferation of contending "theoretical" approaches. The rapid mastery of a "methodology," and its attendant jargon, allowed students to produce articles. They flooded the new journals springing up to take the essays and the old ones that were rapidly converting to these more "relevant" aspects of study. A dissertation was no longer apprentice work; it was a career plan carefully mapped out to lead, on the strength of its methodological maneuvers, to rapid book publication and, hopefully, to a position as spokesperson (tenured, of course) for this new orthodoxy.

This deep and confused sense of the task of scholarly publishing, which the graduate student in the humanities faces today, makes it necessary that the nature and modalities of this task be confronted in a course. Such a course belongs to a generation suddenly aware of the necessity of publication but again asking questions of value.

The entire thrust of the graduate course in scholarly publishing I created in the Comparative Literature Program at UC Riverside is that this needn't be an either/or situation, that even when the realities of publication, as graduate student or as fully sanctioned academic, are faced head on, there still remains a possibility of combining craft and art, of making pragmatism and idealism function together in order to create new avenues of scholarly discourse.

Thus far, this course has not been designated a required course nor has its potential been recognized as a general course on graduate publishing. The problems of scholarly publishing in all the disciplines are fundamentally the same, and with slight accommodations for differences in methods and modes of discourse, students from other departments could be incorporated into the class framework. The course has, over a period of two years, attracted a large number of graduate students in comparative literature and in various national literatures.

Furthermore, it has, by shaping itself around the input of each of these students, been quite successful in deriving a sense of how graduate students, today and tomorrow, can contribute effectively and creatively to scholarly publishing.

The best way to explain this course is to describe how it has worked, presenting first the plan or syllabus as originally conceived and then relating the changes that organically occurred as the plan encountered the needs and skills of successive groups of students. These transformations were, to me, quite fascinating. What began as a pragmatic look at the different areas of scholarly publishing, aiming at an assessment of the availability of each to the graduate student, gradually evolved into a very cogent mixture of cultural analysis and ethical self-examination. As possibilities for publication unfolded, so did assumptions about and prejudices toward certain kinds of scholarly endeavors; students began to see the academic world for what it is. They came to articulate its hidden assumptions, and by doing so learned to seek out its broad opportunities for creative expression. Traditional canons fell, and we found ourselves face to face with the information age and its vast opportunities for multicultural exchange. Given the fact that increasing numbers of my students were not only non-U.S. citizens but came from non-Western cultures, the necessity of getting beyond the parochial structure of American academic publishing became obvious.

The initial course was designed to link process with product and research with publication by taking a hands-on approach to the various media of scholarly discourse. The introductory lecture stressed practical and ethical problems alike. It emphasized that publication for the scholar is an activity surrounded by tremendous and often vicious power plays; that there is nonetheless a vastness and variety of opportunities; that if one looks hard enough, there will always be a potential outlet for his or her writings. Thus, once a topic is hit upon, one must do thorough research in order to find the likely journal or press. I stressed, however, that the best way of learning how is to find a possibly compatible journal (or line of books) and to study published works in these sources as models to follow. This means not simply aping jargon, but understanding the deep structure and argumentative strategies of the pieces.

I began by asking the students to choose a term paper or some other writing project they had on hand and which they felt good about, and to imagine they were going to submit it for publication. Instead of their revising this paper in a vacuum, I asked them to locate a series of journals that publish in the area of their choice and to find among these the one or two most likely to accept the paper such as they conceived it. I then took the students down to the area of the UCR library where recent issues of scholarly and semischolarly journals, some 800 titles, are shelved. Here I simply walked the group through the rows, randomly pulling issues and doing spot analyses of each journal's format, publishing parameters, and where relevant, ideological orientation. I pointed out the editorial statement that tells what kind of submissions are desired and what length they should be, and what style sheet to use. The editorial information also states how many copies of the submission to send and whether electronic as well as hard copy is required, and whether a stamped, self-addressed envelope should be enclosed with the submission. I showed them how to decipher an editorial board to determine the breadth or narrowness of the journal's focus. Is the board international? Are the names intimidatingly famous? Do all the names, in a journal ostensibly open to all modes of sociocultural analysis, belong to well-known ideologues? Students at the graduate level may not have acquired the savvy to read all these codes, but mere exposure to this kind of analysis opens eyes to the hidden agendas in journal publishing.

Once their choice of possible journal(s) had been made, I asked the students to read sample articles in several issues and to present an analysis to the class. Aspects they addressed included the configuration of topics in a single issue (were topics organized by theme, or randomly presented?), the style or "tone" of the articles, and the effect achieved by them and by the journal as a whole (did theoretical prowess or studied casualness characterize the articles, or was erudition, with myriad citations, references, and notes, the general characteristic?). This was a useful exercise; it got students to profile journals in hopes of finding the right match for their work and, at the same time, exposed them to a diversity of academic writing, calling on them to develop personal preferences.

Having gotten that far, students wanted to know more about how academic journals operate. What happens, for instance, after submission? What are the early signs of success or failure? How long should one wait until inquiring as to acceptance or rejection? To answer such questions, I invited one of my colleagues who is active as reader (or referee) on several scholarly journals. The seminar period was devoted to his experiences, covering the ground from neatly typed manuscripts to questions of preferred length and format. The personal nature of this typical reader's standards was an eye-opener. The potential submitter learned that along with matters of originality of scholarship and clear logical argument there are subjective factors as well. This reader, for instance, told the class he rejects all manuscripts over twenty-five pages without reading them. In the face of such "standards," the prospective published author is more willing to accept rejection notices without taking them personally.

The next topic was that other immediate avenue to publication open to the graduate student: the conference. The bulletin board of every department is festooned with calls for papers. Increasingly, graduate students are answering these calls, and increasingly they are being accepted. Many of these conferences announce the intention to publish "selected papers." In many cases this is wishful thinking. But some gatherings have promise. How to spot them? In class, I took a random sampling of conference calls and analyzed them. If publication is sought, the student should look for certain things: Is it a one-shot or occasional conference? If so, is it sponsored by an organization likely to have funds to produce a volume? (Beware of conferences sponsored only by universities, as these are often impecunious these days.) If it is an ongoing conference, is there a "track record" of publications? And if so, what sort are they? (You can look them up in the library.) I held up UCR's Eaton Conference as a model of the latter. It has now published twelve volumes of selected essays for twelve conferences. And a glance at the contributors' notes in these volumes reveals that there are essays by a number of graduate students. Working with editors of volumes like this to prepare a conference paper for publication is an invaluable professional experience for a graduate student. It is worth a host of seminars.

I appended to my discussion of journals and conferences a mention of the dissertation as a source of possible publishable articles. Today's student tends to see the dissertation as a potential "quick" book. I exposed the pitfalls of such logic: overhasty publication in almost all cases not only adds little to job attractiveness, but may "blow" an idea that could with patience and revision become a good book. But I did stress that a carefully chosen and organized dissertation can often yield at least one pre-PhD publication. Because most students in the class had next to no idea of what a dissertation might be, I brought samples to class for analysis. These, taken from other institutions (University Microfilm puts many on library shelves), we looked at less for content than for strategy.

In many, even where the topic was original and well-formulated, organization into chapters effectively acted to obscure publication possibilities.

Dissertations and book publication raised the question of university and scholarly presses. These are for after graduate school. But knowledge of how they operate is essential for the future professional. To give students a sense of the submission process, I invited colleagues with both successful publishing careers and experience on the University of California Press editorial committee to speak to the class. As with my journal-reader guest, such live testimony was invaluable. In this case, each scholar could speak from both sides of the fence. Each had gone through the agony and ecstasy of submitting book-length work. And each had had to judge the submissions of others.

As was the case with journals, there was a need to show the student the great variety of presses available. I spread fifty or so dust jackets, in all sizes and formats, on the seminar table and led the students to classify and analyze the nature of the books from their presentation, jacket copy, etc. There are trendy books and "plain brown wrapper" scholarship; there are essay collections, translations, books on state and local culture, biographies. It becomes clear that scholarly publishers are publishing offerings that are deemed uncommercial by the corporate publishing houses. But it is also clear that these presses, pushed by economic necessity, are increasingly sensitive to sales, and one finds among the pile more "coffee-table" projects, albeit for the more selective "intellectual" audience. Market pressures are good to the extent that they open these presses to work on those (shamefully misnamed) "popular" forms of literature and culture. And students immediately saw, from this profusion of jackets, that there is a press for about any project imaginable.

Graduate students see university presses as (mostly) off limits to the fledgling scholar. But these presses also control the journal and anthology market, as taking note of journals' publishers—as opposed to their editors—reveals; or at least they have until now. Increasingly, graduate students want to set up their own journals or edit their own collections of essays. These often come from in-house "study groups" or from locally generated conferences or seminars. And today, with desktop publishing programs everywhere, such books are easy to produce. The problem lies in distributing them so as to gain academic currency for the work contained within them. To address this, I invited two colleagues who have created their own press. They produce and distribute books that have real academic merit, but which serve areas of scholarship too specialized even for university presses or too controversial to pass the often conservative editorial boards at such presses. These speakers brought books they had published and walked the students step by step through the production and distribution process.

This alternate- and self-publishing raises the question of academic legitimacy, a concern in a world where most students, despite altruistic postures, really see publishing as the way to a good job in a so-called top institution. I portrayed the reality and its hierarchy of "values" as bluntly as possible. But I also pointed out the excitement of the new information explosion that is quietly sweeping academia despite the (perhaps fatal) inertia of university presses and established journals. Disciplines are changing so fast that presses cannot adapt. New, self-produced journals are springing up that, even defying the hallowed "refereed" format, are eminently successful, both in disseminating information and in building careers. I brought to class a colleague who co-edits a nonrefereed journal on feminist film theory. No traditional outlet would touch the topic, so she and a talented group of scholars simply wrote and published. The essence here was speed, and the result is exciting readings. My colleagues with their desktop press have had the same experience of being timely. They produced works of scholarship that, to the establishment presses, seemed to have little interest. But these presses miscalculated audience changes. Desktop academic publishers have produced bilingual translations of little-known poets and have found renewed interest in these figures in the light of today's increasing multicultural emphasis. And they have done bibliographies of science fiction and mystery writers. Both genres are prime examples of today's mass-market literature, something that has proliferated so fast and in so many interesting directions that the current scholarly press apparatus has no hope of keeping abreast. The primary writers go unmapped: will Oxford University Press do a bibliography of Jack Vance, or of Clifford Simak? Increasing numbers of PhD candidates are doing such bibliographies, even for dissertations. Their sole publication outlet, for now, is the small desktop operation. And I advise those interested to publish in this way. The world of academic hiring may still be snobby, but this is rapidly changing. And the traditional presses are fiddling while Rome burns.

To end my class, I invited a series of speakers to share their experiences in a number of neglected disciplines. First, a textual editor described the historical importance of providing accurate texts and outlined his personal experience with the multivolume California Dryden Project, a genuine "variorum" text. He bridged past and future by showing how computer technology has revolutionized conventional textual editing. He also told of how "deconstruction" and other structuralist theories have stimulated (often by reaction) new philosophies and methods of editing and in a sense have revitalized the field.

Next, a noted 18th-century scholar described to the class in great detail how he compiled a large bibliographic essay on "this year's work" in 18th-century studies. Such an essay involved reading some 150 monographs and editions (scholarship in all fields is proliferating wildly) in several languages and then placing them in the context of changing trends. He explained that this task took a year of his time, and that, though scholars in most fields avoid such work because they see it paying so little reward in terms of promotion ("Why don't you write a book instead?"), it is vital to the profession. Also vital is the unsung work of those who edit the volumes of essays without which most scholars would never get into print. He saw the profession top-heavy in prima donna exercises and told students to follow their instincts and not be afraid to do bibliographic and editing jobs.

Finally, a person who has made a career of literary translations told his story and gave his sense of the nobility of this task, which is the only way cultures can make real communicational gestures toward each other. Translation, he stated, is not a reductive process but a coming to realize the intricacies and complexities of one culture by another. He displayed his ten or so book-length translations which, along with their critical notes and apparatus, represent a herculean task, one that over the years has had an impact on his field (Soviet literature) far greater than any academic reward received. Again, he urged the students to follow the heart and the ways of art.

To me this class seems absolutely fundamental to the graduate school experience. It is a forum where pragmatic concerns and ethical needs interact and shed mutual light on each other. It makes a nice antidote both to hidebound traditionalism—the "genteel" mode that is still alive and well with all its canonical snobbery and prejudice—on the one hand, and to the legion of "theory" courses where method serves to mask ideological intolerance and (worse yet) rampant careerism on the other. I find that students learn more about how to write when they have a stake in the results. The attention they pay to matters of organization and style in the journal essays they examine is worth a hundred seminar papers written in the limbo of "candidacy." They also learn what a dissertation is and what it might be. In short, they learn to think ahead, as far in fact as their total careers. They learn that craft and art can, on occasion, work together.

Assessing Academic Standards for Excellence

The ethical concerns Dr. Slusser raises are key to your own exercise of the knowledge and skills you have acquired through years of intense, and expensive, study. To what audience do you want to direct the fruit of your intellectual training? There is no question but that current academic practice favors the peer-reviewed journal article and the university press monograph over any other form of tangible achievement. Significantly, these are two of the most specialized and inaccessible forms of writing, both in level of discourse and availability. Many academic journals have circulations of less than 2,000 subscribers, though they may have greater readership where available in libraries. Still, publication in one of these outweighs writing a textbook or a chapter of a reference series, or a practical book (like this one) or syndicating book reviews, or organizing a conference. Even though more people might benefit from these latter outlets, new professors are cautioned against unwise expenditures of energy. Yet university people at many levels have expressed dissatisfaction with, and cynicism about, this narrow emphasis on certain kinds of publication as the main basis for tenure and promotion and as the standard of excellence in the profession.

When you become a faculty member, an administrator, or an independent scholar, you may also question the narrow definition of the scholar's role and responsibilities—if you haven't already questioned them as a graduate student. Is it truly a less significant use of education to write for or speak to a wider audience? How will you differentiate between your value as a professional and your value as a person? The kind of publication you rank high and the kind of activities you consider valuable when promotion time comes—both for yourself and for your colleagues—define your professional standards and shape your field and scholarship in general.

Graduate school is the ideal place to observe, question, and discuss the professional activities expressed through the various interests and styles of faculty and administrators. Note the possibilities: the grants professors receive; the projects they undertake; the way they work with their graduate assistants. One of the least pleasant aspects of the profession is the attitude that an impressive curriculum vitae (cv) excuses rudeness, egotism, and exploitation. Some of your professors may have demonstrated or even expressed this philosophy: "Being treated shabbily is part of grad school. I was treated shabbily. I'm treating you shabbily, but then, when you're a professor, you will treat your graduate students shabbily. It's the way of the academic world." It is obvious, however, that you needn't perpetuate this unenlightened attitude. When you become a professor, don't do unto graduate students as you may have been done unto.

Cooperative effort in graduate school can result in the establishment on your campus of the kind of publication seminar we benefitted from at UC Riverside. In the absence of a publication seminar on your campus, *form your own reading group to critique each others' essays with a focus on publication.* Invite professors as speakers; they may be impressed enough by the attendance to expedite approval of a regular course. Furthermore, by drawing upon the strengths of a like-minded peer group, you can begin to establish a network of colleagues to correspond with and seek out at conferences for years to come. You may indeed remain a writing group long after you have gone your separate geographical ways; you might, at some point, even desktop publish collectively. The assortment and eccentricities of your graduate school colleagues mirror the diverse temperaments and capabilities you'll have to live with among your professional colleagues. Establishing ties early on in graduate school is one example of many practical and foresightful means available to maximize your years of study. However, with returning students, part-time students, commuting students, working students, teaching assistants, and student parents, it's hard to keep a group together. The group, while useful, is not your main concern.

Beyond networking, even beyond publishing, our paramount advice is: *Never lose sight of completing your degree.* If your graduate school achievements are outstanding, you may be hired while you are still ABD. If you actually begin your new teaching job while still finishing your dissertation, you are stretching the limits of stress. Regardless, you won't be "secure" in a tenure track until you have your PhD.

The Benefits of Publishing in Graduate School

The best way by far for you to study publication is for academic credit rather than in any extracurricular format. Persuade your faculty to act on the common knowledge that publication training is as important an aspect of your education as is teacher training. American higher education has been faulted for being overly theoretical and abstract; as future colleagues, graduate students should request and should receive education in the practical realities of their profession: being published, teaching, presenting at conferences, and interviewing for jobs.

Jobs are scarce; outstanding letters of recommendation, 4.0 GPAs, and good teaching records are not. As search committees wade through applications, candidates who have published stand out. Publication is a solid indication that you are capable of being a professional scholar. Thus, a publication class that might actually lead to vitae credits for you is a class worth petitioning for.

There are more immediate advantages to publishing in graduate school than the benefits during the job search. Since composition is a process of thinking on paper, the attempt to create a journal-quality essay sharpens your mind. Your attention to the questions of logic, clarity, and accuracy in shaping and making your point benefits your overall academic performance. Increased integration of your various projects is a sophisticated streamlining that will serve you well throughout your career. And, of course, your enjoyment of the exercise of scholarship is at the core of your choice of vocation.

Furthermore, graduate students who publish make their professors, departments, and universities look good; for this there are rewards. Status within your academic enclave is satisfying, as is the pleasure of publication itself. Letters of recommendation in your behalf will mention your accomplishment; professors may well recommend you for other writing projects. More tangibly, there are the fellowships and grants graduate of which students should always be aware. Not only your department, but your graduate division will notice the publication added to your cv and will view you as a good investment for university funds, one likely to reflect well on your alma mater in years to come.

The truth is, you're going to have to start writing for publication sometime. Whether you wind up at a research institution where expectations for publication are high, at a comprehensive state-system campus where expectations can nonetheless approximate those of research universities, or at a community college or small private school, sooner or later publication will be a factor in your career. Even if you have only attempted publication in graduate school but haven't had an acceptance, academic logic will nonetheless interpret this as an indicator of potential success. The more publication-oriented you are in graduate school, the sooner you understand the range of journals in your field. The sooner you send your work out beyond the microcosm of your campus, the sooner you understand the processes of professional publishing. You will have learned the basics while still under the closest guidance you will ever get—that of your particular mentor and faculty friends. They can clarify a great deal for you in regard to editorial correspondence, journal requirements, and readers' responses. You will have learned this and will have worked at your writing before the pressure to publish is acute—as it can be when you haven't published and your tenure time approaches or as it can be during the underemployed or over-exploited years following completion of the degree if you don't get a job quickly. Obtaining and exercising knowledge about scholarly publishing should be one of your main objectives while you are in graduate school.

The value of the publishing course at UC Riverside immediately proved itself. Being able to enroll in a legitimate three-unit course made it possible for us graduate students to delve into the most current literature in our field. Since the journals themselves were subjects of study, methodology reports on profitable perusal in the stacks were required and, along with the journals they described, were shared in class. In terms of actual writing, students selected one of their own seminar papers, and, at minimum, devised a method for transforming it into an article, including the selection of appropriate journals for submission. Editorial guidance in terms of developing ideas and of revising seminar papers was provided during in-class workshops and individualized editing sessions. Guest speakers expanded upon the information exchanged with the professor and the other students. All aspects of the class combined to stimulate and encourage thinking, writing, aspiration, and action.

Clearly, in the humanities and social sciences, graduate students' need for information about publishing begins with the most basic questions: What makes a good article? How can I get help from my professors? Throughout this book, the focus is on graduate students and on the questions and concerns raised in our publication workshop.

However, as total and intense an experience as graduate school is, the purpose is to finish it and get on with your career—certainly most of us hope to be professors much longer than we will have been graduate students. The transience of graduate school becomes apparent once you have unpacked your books at the university where you hope to get tenure. From then on, you draw upon your cumulative resources to survive—or, better yet, to thrive—in an environment that privileges the printed word. The practical knowledge and experience we gained in our publication workshop is invaluable, for publications are academic coin for hiring, for tenure, and for promotion.

No matter how much technical skill you pick up, though, there is no shortcut to publication. Nor indeed is there any guarantee of publication. <u>We can't overemphasize that it is ultimately up to each individual author to decide (1) what he or she wants to say and to whom, (2) what kind of article would best express it, and (3) what kind of journal would provide the best vehicle for it.</u>

In the next two essays, two deans address the question of publication and hiring from administrators' perspectives, to which graduate students are usually not privy. Dean Brian Copenhaver of UC Riverside speaks about the relative importance of publication in hiring junior faculty. Associate Dean Patricia Huckle of San Diego State University discusses publication, retention, and expectations. In the final essay, Professor Max Neiman adds the departmental point of view.

Getting Jobs and Getting Published

BRIAN COPENHAVER
Professor of Philosophy and History
Dean, College of Humanities and Social Sciences
UC Riverside

Almost all universities in North America evaluate faculty for promotion, tenure, and merit raises by judging their records against three criteria:

- Teaching
- Scholarship, research, and creative activity
- Public, professional, and university service

Naturally, when universities hire new faculty, they have these same criteria in mind. The best people to hire will be those who have the best prospects for successful careers as defined in terms of these three criteria. In practice, the service criterion matters least for faculty newly hired into beginning positions; service, especially university service, becomes more important with increased seniority and experience. In general, new assistant professors—especially those who have worked as teaching assistants (TAs)—will have had more direct experience as teachers than as participants in faculty governance or in professional organizations or in public service roles. Hence, teaching and research will be the leading issues in the minds of most people who have something to say about hiring you. If you've done a good job in the classroom, if your record as a TA argues that you'll do an even better job of teaching as a professor, what can you do to give the best possible impression on the other key issue: your future as a researcher or as a scholar or as a creative artist? And what's the competition like? What's the "normal" publication record for a newly hired assistant professor?

The competition is tough and will likely stay tough for some time to come. In some fields, it's not uncommon to see several hundred applicants for an entry-level job. And there's no universal formula for success in this contest. Some people get hired as assistant professors with no publication at all; in fact, some get hired without a completed terminal degree, although in this case most universities use lower-status titles for the appointment and take other steps to motivate speedy completion of the degree. Others arrive for assistant professor appointments with several or, in rare cases, many publications. In almost all cases, whatever the initial record of publication, what matters most is, first, the *quality of the research*—usually, a dissertation—required for the terminal degree and, second, the *goals of the department* responsible for the hiring.

The question of publication is really the simplest: in general, the more the better, as a *necessary*, though not *sufficient*, condition of professional advancement and, therefore, of hiring. All other things being equal, someone who has published *more* will be more attractive than someone who has published *less*, but all other things are rarely equal. In faculty personnel systems everywhere, quantity of publication is a basic requirement in the sense that failure is possible just because some minimal amount of publication is wanting. But such minima are rarely precise or explicit, and issues of quality—both positive and negative—frequently and rightly outweigh considerations of quantity. In this situation, obviously, the most prudent thing is to have published as much as possible by the time you enter the job market, as long as the effort to publish does no harm to the general quality of your academic record. Such harm might come in two ways. First, a lot of low-grade publication can make your record weaker than a resumé with no publication at all. Copious publication in obscure outlets without rigorous review procedures or in places dependent on personal or institutional contacts may give the impression of misunderstanding the norms of the field or of having been badly taught or advised. Second, publication of any kind is hard work, and if doing that work detracts substantially from the effort required to present an excellent record overall—in teaching as well as research—then your labor may turn out to be self-destructive.

As a graduate student, your front and center goal in research should be to write the best dissertation you can: "best" in two senses. To begin, your dissertation should convince your faculty advisers, the wise and kindly people who will write your letters of recommendation, that your work is the best thing they've seen since the invention of sliced bread or, in the case of younger faculty, the microwave oven. Your dissertation should move your advisers to write very strong and credible letters about your importance . . . nay, your indispensability, to the future of your field. Next, your dissertation should be good enough to form the basis for publication, whether in article or in book form, shortly after you finish it. These goals are paramount. If other ambitions for publication prevent or impede your attaining them, you've planned poorly. On the other hand, if you can write a first-rate dissertation and produce other publications as well, you're ahead of the game and more competitive for the extra effort that you've made. Remember, however, that publication in addition to your dissertation won't do much good unless it's high-quality publication. If you can place articles in good journals, by all means do so. If you can get a book contract on your dissertation before it's accepted or shortly after, go for it. But don't lose sight of the fundamentals. Your dissertation research and writing should come first.

Speaking of *writing* (for writing of speaking, see below), your prose is something that can give you a real edge. You may have noticed that not all academic writing is clear and forceful. If you work hard at writing clearly and persuasively while beavering away with equal diligence on one topic or another, your work may catch the attention of editors or other readers just because it's intelligible and enjoyable. Dissertations seldom have these qualities, alas, so you may want to do some rewriting for specific purposes or special audiences. Practicing *speaking* as you're sharpening your prose is another good idea. Remember that one of the hiring rituals on almost any campus will be a talk, more or less formal, to the department weighing you in its balance. Your future colleagues will be listening for all manner of things, some of them inscrutable, and all will be held against you. But you can be sure that your learned auditors will be asking themselves at least some of these questions: Can this person become a good teacher? Is she articulate and intelligent? Can he think on his feet? Can she in short compass present a lucid account of a complex issue to vaguely well-informed people who probably know nothing in particular about it? This last question, and the sixty minutes or so that you'll have to answer it, may shape the most important presentation of your research that you'll make for purposes of getting a job. I have no doubt at all that the number of beginners who fail to be hired because of oral presentations is larger than the number who get jobs because they've published one article or another. For my money, the marginal value of a strong talk is greater than that of a published article.

Finally, all of this depends very much on the aims of the department to which you've applied. In general, departments or individuals in departments may be more interested in the general quality of applicants for a job than in the proximity of any applicant's research to a subfield—or the reverse. Call these two conditions F for field specificity and Q for general quality, recognizing them as crude shorthand for points on a spectrum, not precise and distinct realities. In some searches, whether for purposes of teaching or research or both, people who are stronger on Q may finish behind people who are stronger on F, but in other searches the reverse may be true. Probably, but not infallibly, a greater quantity of publication will focus your professional identity and, with it, your F qualities. On the other hand, a mature department that is confident about its own research strengths may be more interested in your Q than in your F, and this may be represented better by your dissertation and the opinions of your advisers than by any particular publication.

Publication is important, both pragmatically and in principle. In principle, people who don't stay in touch with their fields, who aren't engaged in the constant debate with their colleagues and themselves that publication requires, who don't regularly enjoy the open scrutiny implicit in the word *publication*, are unlikely to remain competent and effective as teachers at the university level.

Pragmatically, university faculty who don't publish do perish. Clearly, a quick, strong start as an active publisher can give your whole career a big boost and can greatly improve your prospects for a first job. So do the right thing: start publishing. But remember to do the right thing in the right way, so that publishing enhances the overall quality of your work and doesn't diminish it.

Publication, Hiring, and Retention

An Interview with PATRICIA HUCKLE
Professor of Women's Studies
Associate Dean, College of Arts and Letters
San Diego State University

Q: What happens behind the scenes in hiring? When administration looks over files and applications, what is being looked at?

Huckle: The hiring process is very heavily invested in the faculty of the college. By that I mean it is the responsibility of the departments to do the search and the recruiting because they are the specialists.

However, before the actual search there is a lot of general discussion between the department and the dean about the needs and priorities of the department as well as the resources within the broader context of the college, such as concerns for diversity. So, by the time the application comes to the dean's office and we become directly involved, the top candidates have been selected and are already coming to campus.

At that point the dean's office looks at the candidate's vitae and analyzes whether this person seems to have a reasonable background for a faculty member at this particular kind of institution and whether this person has the qualifications to survive the tenure and promotion process.

Q: Within that context, what role in general does having been published play?

Huckle: Publication is always a part of the professional background for academics. In a comprehensive public institution like San Diego State University, where the model of the teacher/scholar recognizes the importance of publication, it always plays a part.

How large a part publication plays depends not only on the kind of institution but also on the level for which the hiring is made. If we are hiring a junior person, and the department is recommending candidates who have not yet finished the PhD or who are new graduates, then we try to assess the *potential* for publication, as well as the potential for teaching.

And we assess whether the candidate would be a good colleague, to the extent to which we can pick that up through the vitae and through interviews with the candidate.

If we are hiring a senior person, then the publications are part of what we take into account. But it never would be enough, let's say, to look at a publication record and have no other information or to have information that the person is not a teacher. This is not an institution in which someone who only publishes would be hired.

What we look at is that balance: evidence that the person is an active, alive scholar, and that his or her scholarship is related to the teaching profession.

Q: What kinds of activities might people who are just finishing a PhD be doing in advance of being published, if possible, to indicate they have this potential? What activities bolster a candidate who is in print?

Huckle: If we are looking at somebody who has not finished yet, we would depend on the department to demonstrate that this is a graduate student who, for example, has completed the process in a "reasonable time." Whatever the average completion time for dissertations is, this candidate is within that range. If there were extenuating circumstances that caused a break in the candidate's graduate career, that would be part of what the department should know.

On the vitae itself, evidence of participation in conferences is a good sign. Sometimes the departments will ask for a writing sample and, if the department feels the quality of that work indicates promise, we can get affirmative signs that way. If the candidate has not already published as a graduate student, then the references are crucial.

Q: How does an administration looking at reappointment evaluate publications? Is quantity as important as quality? How is quality assessed?

Huckle: That varies tremendously. I can't speak of it as if every administration were the same. And then you have more than one layer of administration in that whole process. Typically, the dean's office provides the first administrative evaluation, then there is a university committee, and then the vice-president directly under the president. Plus you usually have more than one committee of peers, usually at the college level and sometimes at the university level. All are trying to provide a balanced assessment.

I am aware that junior faculty are very concerned with the question of how many articles are enough for reappointment and eventually tenure. The answer is that being a professional academic is a blended activity. We do not weigh publication by the pound, though sometimes it feels as if that's the basis for our assessment. There isn't any one answer; it is impossible to say definitively that you need ten or you need fifty.

The amount and kind of publication also varies by discipline. For example, if your field is classical languages, it is very difficult to get published because there are fewer outlets available to you. And the amount of new knowledge that can be generated in the field may be somewhat limited.

The university usually communicates general policy in guidelines for successful progress. Because there is tremendous variation, your department chair and department colleagues are important. You should know your college, know what your department is like, know with whom you are working.

Junior faculty members should take the initiative to say to their colleagues, "Help me to understand what is required here, and what balance is appropriate. If I'm teaching 200 students, how do I measure that against the expectations that I'll have a research plan?"

In a university like ours that has a relatively high teaching load, most faculty do substantial research during breaks and during the summer. That's the only way I was able to survive.

The Professional Portfolio

The move toward the concept of a professional portfolio for academics is one of the good things that has happened in the last few years. The portfolio is a way of putting together a record of what kinds of things you are doing in teaching, of what methods you use, and so on. It is also a publication research plan. The science people all have five-year plans. I'm not saying that everybody should have to stick to a five-year plan, but I think that the concept of a research strategy leading to publication is terribly important as a means of organizing your professional life. Saying that you need to have a clear idea doesn't mean you can't change it as you go along, but at least candidates should be conscious of where they want to go with the new tools they have acquired in graduate school. Graduate students should formulate and discuss their plans with their dissertation chair or advisers.

Picking Your Advisers Well Is Crucial

I tell graduate students that the most important decision they make in graduate school is picking an adviser who (1) is compatible, (2) has a record of getting people through in a reasonable period of time, and (3) can guide them toward what professional life is about, including publications. For graduate students the active scholars/ teachers they are working with are modeling for them what the appropriate publications are.

Ask Questions and Establish Networks

There is no place like graduate school. After all, that is where every pore of your body is soaked with the literature of your field. You are learning how to research; you are learning how to find resources; and you are learning what the journals and outlets are for publication of your kind of work . . . or you should be learning. One of the historical problems, certainly from when I was a graduate student, was that it never occurred to me that one of the things I wanted to know about was publishing. I never asked how to get there from here, and nobody taught me.

Additionally, professional connections with your national associations and regional associations are important. The kind of networking they offer is very helpful. You might find a colleague at a conference who is working on something that you are working on, and it is wonderful to have that sort of exchange.

However, you should never let one person be your only source of information. Universities are big places, departments are run quite differently, and there are various ways to survive in the institution, both as a graduate student and as a professional.

Assessing Candidates

An Interview with MAX NEIMAN
Professor of Political Science
UC Riverside

Q: How do you rate the importance of publishing for new PhDs looking for jobs?

Neiman: That's very, very important. My experience on search committees is that you can always say, "All other things being equal," but that never happens. You rarely get a situation where the only things you're looking at are GPAs of candidates from, let's call it, the University of the Ivy League (UIL) as compared to candidates from a Public State University (PSU). Sometimes you get an Ivy League file where the applicant has no publications but has incredible letters from faculty. You've got to take that seriously. On the other hand, if you get someone from an Ivy League campus who has sort of routine letters, I'd pretty much rank that candidate the same as someone from a public university with routine letters. I don't place that much credence on the place itself apart from all other factors.

What happens is that most emphasis is usually given to letters from faculty and to publications. <u>Publication in mainstream journals overwhelms everything else. That's the great equalizer.</u> Speaking only for my department, I don't think I have ever seen someone from PSU with two or three mainstream publications turned down in favor of an Ivy League PhD with strong letters—ever. In this example the UIL candidate perhaps has incredible things written about him or her to make up for his or her having been—except for the dissertation—professionally inactive. But if this person from the UIL has been presenting papers at conventions and has submitted things for publication, then you look at him or her a little differently. You ask, "How long has this other person who has published three things been in the doctoral program?" If, for example, your UIL person is truly working through the program with dispatch, and it looks as if he or she is really taking off, that goes into the overall judgment. But publication is still the great equalizer.

Q: If a graduate student has submitted work but hasn't heard back, should that be put on the cv?

Neiman: Sure, especially if a copy is attached to the other material when the application is sent in.

Q: How does your department assess candidates' research plans?

Neiman: If they have a research agenda, it's something to talk about. If candidates come and all they talk about is the movies they'd like to see and how they'd like to spend their weekends, they don't make a strong impression.

Q: In addition to the publications record or research plans, how important are the presentations candidates make when they come to be interviewed?

Neiman: Presentations are very important because by the time the department has narrowed the applicants down to three people, all the candidates have strengths and all have weaknesses. By this time the search committee is starting to look for reasons *not* to pick one, so the choice often comes down to how the candidates come across when they present their material.

Presenting is a nerve-racking experience. But generally you're more knowledgeable about your own research and your own ideas than anybody else at that particular time. You just need to be prepared to have a decent conversation. Whether it's a presentation at a conference or at a job interview, most everyone is sympathetic with the candidate.

I spend a lot of time working with students before they go out for interviews. If I have a student who is introspective and shy I say, "If there's one time in your life when you've got to be other than introspective and shy, this is it. Or please tell me right now that you're not going to go." We have graduate students do oral presentations in our seminars. The other students are expected to respond, and I try to keep the interchange civilized.

At least in my field, it's very important that you keep the time you use to make your formal presentations to a minimum during job interviews. If you are allotted an hour, your formal talk should be no more than a half hour. Leave a half hour for discussion. Be prepared to expand on the comments you made in your talk, or to discuss your dissertation, research plans, or publications, if you have them.

Getting Hands-on Experience in Publication and Hiring

For first-hand experience of how publication fits into the search, recruitment, interview, and hiring process, look to your own department. If you serve as graduate student representative, for example, you will get a valuable preview of how department committees function, the same kinds of committees you will later serve on yourself. Of even more direct relevance to gaining firsthand experience on the role publication plays in the hiring process is that many campuses require graduate students to serve as nonvoting members of search committees. All you have to do is volunteer.

Whether the search is for a full professor or a temporary lecturer, participating gives you experience in:

- reading candidates' applications, letters of recommendation, and cvs and seeing how academic job seekers present themselves on paper. This exposure is valuable background to your own job applications;
- debating, and hearing professors debate, the relative merits of candidates. This reveals to you the complexity, possible capriciousness, and consensus politics that are part of the hiring process;
- deciding who will be called to your campus for interviews and presentations;
- voicing an opinion about the candidates' merits and how well they match the department's and campus's needs.

When candidates do come to campus, sit in on several presentations to observe not only the lecture but the question-and-answer period. This open-question period, whether at a job interview or at a conference, is often the most feared event in a graduate student's journey to professorship—short of forgetting everything in oral exams except your own name. Defuse the fear by watching others in action. Notice positive strategies presenters adopt. A key strategy is, no matter what the question, to move their answer into some discussion of what they've already written, are writing, or plan to write about. Observe what happens when they're confronted by the rare hostile questioner: sympathy is usually for the candidate, unless the antagonism is somehow genuinely merited. Composure and a measured response work to the candidates' favor.

The Modern Language Association (MLA) publishes a *Career Guide*, a fine book which, though addressed directly to teachers of English and foreign languages, is applicable in all fields. Your department should offer special sessions concentrating on hiring procedure. Seek counsel and practice in making presentations, either from individual professors or from within a cooperative group. Once again, these practical activities yield the side benefit of establishing and reinforcing network connections.

The first links in your network are your professors, most important of whom is your mentor. They see your written work in seminars, and once they become aware of your commitment to publishing, they can begin to guide you in the most effective uses of your research, class time, and interests. More advanced graduate students can also be important sources of information. But not all information is equally reliable—you and you alone can decide to whom you will listen.

The most efficient method of using your graduate research is to write seminar papers that either contribute to the subject of your dissertation or can be revised for submission to journals.

2

Finding Your Prof and Finding Your Focus

The Graduate School Network

As a graduate student, you have at your disposal a highly organized, richly diversified network of thought, experience, and opportunity. In your own best interest, therefore, you should familiarize yourself

27

<u>quickly and thoroughly with the complex structure in which you are immersed.</u>

Although graduate school is a place of simultaneous demands, multiple obligations, high stress, and frequent personal overload, you don't need to stumble or succumb. Nearly all the mechanisms you need to cope—*and* to succeed—are already in place, built right into the very process that has you running from due date to deadline to No-Doz.®

However, in your present situation, <u>knowledge not acted upon is useless.</u> For your understanding of the built-in advantages available to you *now*, in graduate school—to make a real difference in your academic life—you must apply what you learn. That is, <u>you must take the time to use the information, networks, and resources surrounding you as strategically as possible.</u>

Your department as a whole and your classes in particular offer you a ready-made pool of "significant others" to further your academic and professional progress. Get to know your peers. The widely varying perspectives and expertise they bring may surprise you, especially given the growing diversity in the student population. Find out about—*and introduce yourself to*—as many professors as you can, at least in your own department. They are your prospective sponsors. It is also extremely helpful to become friendly with department secretaries and other staff members; this is one way you can keep up on future course offerings, deadlines for grants and fellowships, and availability of teaching or research assistantships, and maybe get a dash of extra help once in a while. Campus personnel know a great deal about how your department and the university really work.

<u>We cannot overemphasize the importance of acquainting yourself with staff in the reference room of your library and in the offices of your graduate division.</u> Act on your own behalf so that you don't merely get by in grad school, but actually prosper. Remember, though, it takes time to establish contacts; blatant self-interest and lack of reciprocity will disenchant many of the people who could benefit you, whether they are faculty or staff.

Like the creation of a campus network, the definition of your own best interest should be viewed as an ongoing process; neither is formed or established over the course of a quarter or a semester or two. Unexpected—perhaps even once-in-a-lifetime—opportunities may pop up to alter both your perceptions and your priorities. Your concept of your best interests will also be affected by stages and changes in your situation within the graduate school process itself, as well as in your private life. <u>Just keep in mind that *what* you do, *how* you do it, and *whom* you meet at this early point in your career can have a deep and lasting impact on your life, both personal and professional.</u>

The Mentor: Your Most Important Contact in Graduate School

A refrain echoed throughout this book is: Mentors are the single most important influence in graduate school. The reason for this is basic. Your mentor is the living link between you, the student, and the inextricably connected worlds of your discipline and the academic community as a whole. In his or her hands many of the possibilities for your own development may be held, for your mentor is your teacher and your advocate, your sounding board and your editor, as well as your primary role model for the profession. Above all, he or she is your major, and visible, contact within the greater community you have chosen to join. Mentors may or may not develop into personal friends, but the relationship between you can continue long after you have left graduate school behind.

It stands to reason, then, that one of the most important choices you will make in your graduate career is to select your mentor. Some students go for the undeniable attractions of a "big name," while others prefer the more sedate appeal of an intellectual or spiritual kinship—though these are not necessarily exclusive. Some students want a hard-driving, demanding person who will "force" them to achieve; others function best with an individual who has a less prescriptive, more supportive style. Neither is inherently better, for it doesn't really matter *how* you settle upon the professor or other professional role model you choose. You may find too that your mentor or mentors, in one way or another, choose you. What does matter, however, is that the relationship be mutually positive, professional, and productive.

Jean-Pierre Barricelli, Chair of UC Riverside's Literatures and Languages Department, has guided dozens of students, including both the author-editors of this book. We therefore asked Dr. Barricelli to share his philosophy of mentoring: its meaning, significance, and ethics.

The Role of the Mentor

JEAN-PIERRE BARRICELLI
Professor of Romance Languages and Comparative Literature
Chair, Department of Literatures and Languages, UC Riverside

The dictionary defines a mentor as a wise and trusted teacher or guide. In the academy, this generic definition means nothing. Every professor sees himself axiomatically as a teacher, surely as a guide because he is a good teacher, obviously as trusted, and most unarguably as wise. But will he act accordingly? Will he, that is, behave in accordance with the professional academic duties and expectations of mentorship? I mean, practical career guidance.

First, let me differentiate between two uses of the term "mentor" with reference to some institutional practices. At some universities, you, as a graduate school applicant, may be accepted not by a department (acting in conjunction with the graduate division) but by an individual professor in your desired department. That is to say, you are recruited by a professor who appreciates your file and usually harbors some hope that you will specialize in the area of his own interests. Such a person is referred to as a mentor, toward whom you necessarily feel beholden, even if, as your residence unfolds, your academic interests and circumstances may change. I am not talking about this kind of mentor.

I am addressing the more usual practice whereby you are admitted to a department's graduate program and in time find a compatible professor whose intellectual interests and philosophy are consistent with, or reasonably close to, your own and under whom you would like to work. This person becomes the wise and trusted teacher and guide. And in turn, this person comes to regard "his" student as his "protégé"; he looks after your interests and concerns, intellectual or even administrative (though the latter are more a function of the graduate advisor). In this sense, a mentor is pedagogue, protector, and promoter.

Usually, a graduate advisor's responsibilities, while overlapping inevitably with the mentor's, are quite different. The advisor oversees your curricular program, advises you on courses, requirements, administrative procedures, examination preparation, and units or credits needed to fulfill residence. On the other hand, the mentor stands, in the truest academic sense, *in loco parentis*.

You identify a potential mentor only after taking a variety of courses, "getting the academic lay of the land," as it were, and after consulting with this professor on any number of issues. An intellectual friendship is formed by which he comes to share academic concerns with you, taking you under his wing as a research assistant, for example, or supervising you as a teaching assistant. You come to respect and depend on him, to cultivate his interests in association with yours, and to explore ideas through him.

Since, together with your dissertation director—and they are frequently one and the same person—the mentor represents the most important contact in your budding academic career, you should not hesitate to seek one out long before you embark on your dissertation. Granted, some professors are loners or haughty because they see themselves in superhuman terms, and because of this they feel uneasy, or unwilling, to engage in any kind of intellectual proximity. Patience; such anomalies, however regrettable, come with the territory. But most professors—the accountable kind—will see the enhancement of students' academic experience as their duty or indeed will feel flattered by the interest students show in them. Most of the time, then, a professor who knows he can be of help in your career will welcome you as a protégé. Idealism and pragmatism may commingle in such a situation: many more professors than our cynical natures might think are idealistic, and besides, they can only feel pride in sending their "products" out into the world if they feel confident they can bask justifiably in their glory. The "mentor" you should avoid is the one whose standing in the profession is not one that might promote your goals, or, worse still, who may lure you into his academic confidence out of eccentricity. Please understand: this does not mean that you should limit your intellectual contacts only to the "useful"; some of your finest intellectual experiences may come in discourse with people who are unequipped to be your mentor. But the mentor, ideally, has stature, contacts, and an altruistic desire to help before and after you receive your doctorate.

Of course, a student may be a loner, too—may believe he can make his way without backing. And he may be right. In general, though, it is advisable to have a mentor, someone on whom you can rely during your residence years, who can go beyond your graduate advisor in sorting out job options and publication sites for both articles and books, and with whom you can communicate as a friend after you leave the campus. If he respects your work on the dissertation, he should push you toward publication (the publishing of dissertations—minus the "dissertationese"—was not customary in my day [the 50s] but is more so today [the 90s]); you have a right to expect this. You also have a right to expect him to suggest publication of excellent term papers which, under his guidance, you may convert into articles, and to this end he should steer you in the direction of journals proper for the topics. Again, you should expect from him practical advice and honest encouragement, counsel on job opportunities, and recommendations other than in the form of placement file letters. And during the early years after your doctorate, a true mentor stays in touch, for your first years in the academic world outside are usually characterized by hesitations and trepidations (like tenure anxieties), confusions and even possibly disappointments, not to mention publication queries and teaching surprises. This is where the former supervising professor becomes a professional friend. You should not hesitate to think of your mentor in these terms.

If a mentor is distinguished in his field—and this means that more often than not he is invited to contribute to scholarly journals—he should ask superior graduate students to join him in collaborating on an article or other piece of research destined for print. His protégé thereby gets "a leg up" on the job market, let alone on his career. This is done quite commonly in the sciences, after all, and to some extent in the more "scientifically" oriented social sciences that rely on the objectification and quantification of measurable data. Unfortunately, particularly in the humanities, such joint ventures far from represent a practice. If invited, make the most of the opportunity.

Remember that while you are entitled, not by law but by professional civility, to use your relationship with your mentor, you must not abuse it. It is one thing to ask for guidance; it is quite another to demand it as a constitutional right. Some professors, for reasons better known to them, may become negligent in their career assistance (not management) of current or former students; some students tend to exaggerate a mentor's role, appropriating their usually limited time through repeated requests that suggest that they are not assuming primary responsibility for their own advancement. The mentor may open doors, promote manuscripts, and otherwise provide. But discretion and respect are the rule, the other side of the same coin of civility and consideration. In this context: aggressiveness gains far less than circumspection. A mentor is not in a position—or should not place himself in the position—to get your article or your book accepted through private contact, unless your work is refereed by professional, objective readers. He may influence your invitation to give a paper at a learned conference (and many such papers are published in the meeting's proceedings or are otherwise selected for publication), but he will not maneuver it. Professionalism eschews politics. Or at least it should. And if it does not, you are still better off if you rely on scholarly quality rather than on ideological popularity. The biases of today have never established themselves as central values tomorrow, and your assessment of a mentor will necessarily involve his ultimate wisdom in steering you through a forest of fads. Do not expect him, however, to make up your mind for you and to sculpt your philosophy the way he may have affected your research methodology. A true mentor does not proselytize, and you would be selling yourself short if you assumed the posture of a disciple.

Clearly, as there are professors and professors or methodologies and methodologies, there are mentors and mentors. Each sees his role differently, and much depends on the depth of his commitment, on his intellectual relationship with you, and his and your personalities, to say nothing of the perennial nemesis of time constraints. Yet the function of a mentor can be crucial in that it may shape a lifetime. The success of Dante's journey was facilitated by the presence of his mentor Virgil, and by the time the teacher left the pupil, the latter, Dante, was prepared to assume the responsibilities of mentorship over others.

Getting the Most Out of Your Mentor/Student Relationship

When considered from an intellectual and philosophical standpoint, as Dr. Barricelli does in his essay, the potential significance of mentorship over your professional future is evident. But transforming potentiality into reality is what mentorship is really all about; practically speaking, a constructive mentor/student relationship is even more important when you contemplate the long, hard haul the graduate school process represents in itself.

Theodore Ziolkowski, Dean of Princeton's Graduate School, discusses the duration of this process in the following excerpt from "The Shape of the PhD: Present, Past, and Future":

... [D]octoral education in the United States takes too long and suffers from excessive attrition. As we know from the NRC's [National Research Council] *Summary Report 1988*, the registered time to earn the PhD is 6.9 years, while the total time is 10.5 years. And sad to say, within these averages the times are the longest in the humanities: 8.5 and 12.2 years. This means that the average student in the humanities who graduates from college at twenty-one receives the PhD at thirty-three. . . . Moreover, most of those who enter PhD programs in 1990 will never obtain that degree. While attrition figures are notoriously difficult to ascertain, the estimates nationwide range from an institutional low of 30% to a high of 70%.

Because of its length and potential intensity, the relationship you establish with your mentor will likely affect your attitudes and performance in any number of personal and professional areas. Maintaining frequent contact with your mentor—especially to discuss concrete matters like research development, editorial guidance, and your own particular interests—makes it more likely that you will enjoy the tangible results of his or her personal interest in you. For example, mentors can help you to identify and vector your own strengths and interests, rectify or balance your weaknesses, and guide you toward formulating a realistic strategy for the coming years. Also, while you are engaged in all those countless hours of coursework, they may be able to direct your attention to significant but obscure sources, or provide new perspectives on the issues you're grappling with, or comment on your critical and expressive abilities.

Office hours and appointments are precisely for this kind of concentrated, individualized help, so be sure to take advantage of them. But remember: *do not monopolize your mentor.* Your relationship can be adversely affected if you make excessive demands of time and energy; your mentor has other obligations to students, colleagues, and him- or herself as well.

Using Seminar Research for Publication

For each graduate seminar, you will probably write a substantial paper. If the professor for whom you are writing it is conscientiously student-oriented, he or she will help you get the most out of what you have written. For example, your professor should be able to lead you not only to important literature about your subject, but should also know about upcoming conferences or special journal issues dealing with your topic or interests. Professors can provide you with important editorial feedback and begin to show you at what level you need to write in order to transform your seminar paper into an article a professional journal would consider. In addition, they can help you understand how certain journals are perceived and valued in your field (that is, how they are "ranked") and how you can begin to assess your own abilities, needs, and goals in relation to publication within these ranks.

Keeping in mind that you are asking them to link their names and reputations to yours makes it easier to see why they want their protégés to succeed. Because they have a better grasp of professional necessities and options, mentors may suggest endeavors to you for which you think you are unprepared. Think twice before you decline: more opportunities are lost in graduate school than are bungled.

In short, both your seminar professor and/or your mentor are important sources for information regarding publication. While they may not volunteer it automatically, most will help once requested to do so. Remember, *it is up to you to ask.* They can't divine what you really mean or want when you approach them with inadequately articulated or randomly presented questions, ideas, or writing. Take the time to identify, clarify and organize what you want to know—this is not only an intelligent, courteous preliminary, but a telling display of your own professionalism as well. It's both easier and more inviting for most professors to work with a student who has at least something together than to try to pry a sense of purpose or vision from one who doesn't, or from one who apparently hasn't even tried.

Basic Terms in Publishing

Included in these professional preliminaries is the task of familiarizing yourself with the terminology of publication. Mastery of certain terms and concepts reveals that you've done your "homework" before talking to your professor and that you're really serious about publication. Some of the basic vocabulary you'll need to know follows.

COVER LETTERS are informational introductions to what it is they "cover": your article, book proposal, or manuscript. They summarize the topic in a few sentences and note your qualifications or publication credits or research background. Cover letters save everybody time, but only when they're brief. Simply ask yourself what the editor really needs to know about the article or about you, provide that information, and then stop.

QUERY LETTERS are more complex. Query letters are written in advance of submission of actual manuscript material to ascertain whether or not a publisher would be interested in your subject. Unlike cover letters, query letters are not accompanied by samples of your work; therefore, they represent your best shot at presenting your topic, your approach, and your qualifications within the format of a single page or at most two pages. If your query letter succeeds in interesting a publisher, you will be invited at that point to send in more. If the project is unsuitable (or if your query is unorganized, sketchy, sloppy, or ungrammatical), the editor will decline. Query letters save time, paper, and postage for all concerned. Since they are your first contact with potential publishers, they are worth your careful attention. The key again is to judge what you say according to what the editor needs to know at this initial stage; don't get chatty, hyperbolic, or bombastic. If you are querying book publishers about a substantial project, you will find the "Author's Guideline" in Chapter Six to be a useful guide.

Because the slow pace of academic publishing works to the detriment of the author, we recommend that you *use query letters as much as possible*, especially when the journal's stated turnaround time (that is, how long they take to respond) is longer than three or four months. As long as you state openly that you are querying several publishers at the same time about your subject, you can send out several *simultaneous queries*; in fact, it is foolish not to do so.

Similarly, if there is a particular journal you want to be published in, a query letter describing your topic and asking whether the journal would be interested can save you a good deal of time. This is especially true if, for example, you have a conference paper you would have to lengthen to meet the journal's requirements; before you put in the time to expand and revise what you have already written, query to see if the journal would be receptive to your topic and approach.

MULTIPLE SUBMISSION refers to the simultaneous mailing of copies of the same manuscript material to more than one publisher. The purpose, again, is to save the submitter time. In all cases it is expected that you will notify the publishers in your cover letter that you have contacted more than one publisher. Typically this notice goes something like: "Please note this is a simultaneous submission. I look forward to hearing from you at your earliest convenience."

Most trade, that is, commercial, publishers now routinely accept multiple submissions if so informed. However, while query letters are fine for both commercial and academic publishers, *publishers of academic journals do not accept multiple submission of articles.* The reason is obvious: commercial publishers have paid staff to read submissions; academic journals do not. Thus, it is a severe imposition upon the volunteerism that enables scholarly journals to function if you abuse the system. What if Editor X sends your multiply submitted article to two of her readers, and editors Y and Z do the same at their respective journals, and they all want to publish it? This might seem to you as if you've hit the journal jackpot, but in fact only one journal out of the three is actually going to be able to print your article; the editors of the other two journals have wasted a good deal of precious, unpaid time. They will remember your inconsideration when (and if) you submit work to their journals again.

BLIND SUBMISSION, required by many academic journals, means you use your name and university affiliation only on the cover letter that accompanies your article. When the editor sends your work to be peer-reviewed by specialists in your topic area, they are able to assess your work free of any biases that might otherwise sneak in and report objectively to the editor on its quality. While the procedure does work well, occasionally a writer might subtly identify him- or herself through textual cues, such as citing his or her own work often.

PEER-REVIEWERS, READERS, JURIES, AND REFEREES are terms for the academic specialists who donate their time and who most closely evaluate your submission. Upon their sole judgment often rests the verdict to publish or not to publish your work. If one day you yourself should become one, it is your obligation to return material sent to you in a timely manner. Your editor will also be appreciative if you inform him or her that you do not feel qualified to review a given article, for whatever reason, since editors rely on your expertise and shudder at the thought of publishing shoddy or outdated scholarship. The demands upon the time of a reader can be substantial, so it is not usually wise for junior faculty to undertake such a commitment.

BOARDS OF EDITORS, CONSULTING EDITORS, AND ADVISORY BOARDS can be confusing terms. Editorial boards are comprised of consulting editors; these are specialists who support the journal by reading manuscripts themselves or by recommending to the editors other specialists who are qualified evaluators. In other words, these names can be synonymous with the readers/peer-reviewers defined above, although the actual involvement of any given board of editors varies from journal to journal. Advisory boards are usually well-known specialists or figures in the field who lend their names in establishing the journal and who typically continue to support it. How much more they do, again, varies from journal to journal. They may occasionally recommend an article to the journal's editor.

As you become increasingly familiar with personages in your specialty, looking at these names will provide you with important information regarding the journal's ideological or political perspective, even if such a perspective is not explicit.

SPECIAL OR GUEST EDITORS oversee the production of a single special issue of a journal devoted to a certain topic, theme, theory, or perspective.

DIRECTORIES, GUIDES, AND INDICES are synonyms for reference volumes that are essential sources of information about journals. For each journal in their field of specialty, they provide information that is typically not printed in the journal itself, such as turnaround time (how long it takes for the journal to respond to your submission) and acceptance ratio (the number of articles published annually as compared to the number of submissions). Names and addresses of the journal's editorial staff are also listed, as are circulation figures and submission requirements. Your reference librarian can point you to the most recent directory or guide or index for your specialty; some directories, such as the MLA's *Directory of Periodicals*, are inexpensive and valuable enough to merit your purchase of them.

SASE stands for self-addressed, stamped envelope. Budgets being what they are, you must apply the postage in order to have your work returned. Postage on the return envelope should equal postage affixed to the submission envelope.

In the following interview, Dr. Max Neiman, a professor of political science at UC Riverside and reader for several journals in his discipline, discusses publishing from the pragmatic vantage of his experience as teacher, mentor, and peer reviewer.

Start Being Professional *Now*

An interview with MAX NEIMAN
Professor of Political Science, UC Riverside
Reader, *Journal of Politics*; *Urban Affairs Quarterly*

Neiman: I can't emphasize more the importance of graduate students' writing for publication as quickly as they feel they're capable, even if they begin with "little" things they may not consider to be particularly valuable. They should present papers at meetings as early as possible, write book reviews, and, of course, submit papers for publication in scholarly journals.

All of that seems a lot harder than it really is. The hardest part is getting your work accepted. The point is, you can't get anything accepted if you haven't written it. You have to write and send things out. All it takes is writing a cover letter, putting your material into an envelope, and sending it out.

But for some reason graduate students seem to be incredibly disconnected from the role of professional writer. They must have ten thousand reasons for not sending their work off to publish. Students should realize that most of the student papers I get in seminars are at least not *that* different from the manuscripts I get as a reader for journals. Some student papers are even better.

It's a pervasive problem that grad students don't try to publish their work. When they do, however, it's most often because of a mentor or faculty member who is bringing them into publication as quickly as possible. You know, the best way to get started in publishing is to give one of your best papers to a faculty member to read and comment on; don't be afraid to do it.

Q: Say the professor already read the paper and gave it an "A," but provided very little editorial commentary beyond, "Good paper. You have the nucleus of an article here. Do something with it."

Neiman: If what you do is return immediately to the person who read it, was struck by it, but didn't have much to say about it in writing, and ask that person to read it again, then you're only going to embarrass yourself. With that kind of request you're essentially saying the reader hasn't done a good enough job the first time. He or she is only likely to react with, "Well, I already read it once!"

What you should do first is to make some initial revisions. Make the paper somehow different. Then when you give it back, say, "I was encouraged by what you said about my paper in the seminar, so I went home and I made these changes. Now will you take a look at it?" If you let the professor know that you've already changed it in some way, you establish a more conducive atmosphere for constructive comment.

Also, if you make it known that you want to submit it for publication somewhere, the professor will read it differently. He or she will understand that you're not just interested in the paper's substance, but also in whether you've achieved the accoutrements of professionalism—the proper language, style, approach, and so on. In other words, a reader can appreciate that when you send it off, you don't want the receiver to say, "Aha, another graduate student paper." This is the kind of help you want from your professor.

The other thing that's very important for you is to get to know who in your department is writing and publishing. Unfortunately, that's usually a touchy point. Every department has people who, for one reason or another, are not writing and researching; they may just be out of it for a while. You want to focus on the people who *are* actively publishing because they're the ones who are most current and who can give the most practical help.

Q: Short of going through every journal in your discipline, how do you find out who's active? Do you ask every faculty member? Do you talk to the department chair or the secretaries about it?

Neiman: It really depends on the kinds of rapport you've established. If you have a good connection with the office's staff, such as graduate secretaries, administrative assistants, or management services officers, ask them; they're the ones who would know who the active people are. If you have a good relationship with the department chair, he/she could recommend to you a qualified person to approach.

Of course, finding out about who's publishing and then consulting them for help isn't the only way to get started. You may be an independent type, a self-starter. This type of student just goes off like gangbusters and starts writing more than some of the faculty do. But this type of student is rare.

I must emphasize that simply doing the writing is of itself extremely important. Certainly by the end of the first year your adviser or another faculty member needs to begin trying to get you to become professionally active. Remember, becoming professionally active doesn't only mean publishing. Any piece that you feel is ready can at least be presented at a meeting or conference. And you really should present something at a meeting so you can get the experience and feedback. Then you can rework the paper and, with guidance at first, submit it for publication.

Of course, not all students can be considered novices; certain of them are very advanced, and this is reflected in their writing. But others take a while; they still express themselves awkwardly, or stretch it a little, or tend to become bombastic because they're trying to appear erudite. In essence, what you should be aiming to develop in your writing is a natural professionalism.

To be quite honest, however, this aspect of polish is perhaps the least important of your concerns. I mean, what you *absolutely must* do is make sure that whatever you submit doesn't look like an obvious seminar paper. Make sure, for example, that the paper is cited properly, that the style is appropriate, that you don't have basic grammatical errors, that you've avoided any awkward expressions or incorrect language usage, and so forth. All of these are the kinds of things you just wouldn't expect to find in a scholar's writing.

Most important is to use language and convey competence—a tone of confidence—in the paper so as to project professionalism. If you sound as if you're eighteen or nineteen years old and a little wet behind the ears, that will come through. Rectifying an immature style doesn't mean, however, that your paper has to be jargonistic and opaque. It just has to appear professional. You can get a good idea of the difference from looking at journals and reading articles.

By the way, be *especially* sure to look at articles in the journals in which you're trying to get your article published. Take the time to examine them, see what they look like—their format, length, tone, and so on. Also look at who the authors are, because those are the people most likely to end up reviewing and deciding on *your* article. Try to find articles in some area that's close to your own. You can almost predict that at least one of those authors will be reviewing your article if you send it to that journal.

One of the strategies you can use to get a foot in the door is to check out where the authors of articles in your field are currently located. You can begin to send things out to them, to introduce yourself and your work, and maybe even start up a serious correspondence.

Q: Students are often hesitant to do this for a variety of reasons. One graduate student concern in particular seems to be protecting ideas. They say, "What if my article is rejected, but its being out there provides the basis for another person's piece?"

Neiman: Well, you wouldn't cheat from something you received in the mail, if only because you really have no idea how many other people have already seen it. Things like that are more likely to happen at a cocktail party or some other social setting where an original idea gets presented or developed through the conversation. If someone there suddenly says, "Hey, I've got to leave right now" and walks out, then you might wonder what's up. I wouldn't worry about it, though, at least not as far as sending your work out to key people in your field goes.

You see, what's really important for you to begin is the *networking*. Sure, you can be cynical about it all, and say that this strategy is one roundabout way in which to make contact with potential readers who will then be more sympathetic. But that's not really the main reason why you would be doing it. The reason you send your work out is to get feedback. So naturally you begin to make connections with people in the field, and they get to know who you are.

I do this myself, all the time. I send things out to people, and maybe only two out of ten will respond. But, you know, the two who *do* respond are very appreciative, very interested. They're also the ones who are most likely to give aid when they can. The people who respond are also more likely to be the kind of people you really want to get to know, as professionals and as individuals. That's a great bonus from making these contacts.

Q: How easy is it for graduate students to find out important things about the journal, especially the nonexplicit or "simply understood" things, like ranking?

Neiman: In my field the ranking is pretty explicit. We have one top journal considered all by itself: *American Political Science Review.* Then you have a second level with two journals representing the Southern Political Science Association and the Midwest Political Science Association. Then there's a third tier in which there are quite a few journals—all refereed, very well respected, and so on—which cut across a number of different disciplines. And then I would say in the fourth tier are sort of symposia journals—you know, those that publish conference proceedings or invited symposia and papers and so forth. And finally, of course, there's everything else that is not refereed.

You should always shoot for the very best you possibly can—whatever your field may be and whatever point you're at in your career—*but most especially as a graduate student.* The reason I emphasize this is simple: to enhance your position as a candidate in the field, you must find out about and aim for the very best from the standpoint of promoting yourself professionally. As a graduate student you're aiming high so that when you get your PhD in hand, you'll be in the position of a strong, competitive candidate. That, I think, is your major motivation. And this position could be undermined if you're published in a journal that is sort of questionable, either ideologically or in terms of reputation.

This, of course, is unfortunate, because it suggests that journals that may have been established as proper alternative vehicles for professionals just don't become vehicles for graduate students. Now, there may be other good reasons for your wanting to publish in them; you may want to publish just to disseminate your ideas. But in terms of the payoff for you *professionally*, you've got to deal with the mainstream journals. In doing this, though, remember to take into account the average turnaround time. If there's a decent turnaround time in the best journal, and you feel that your article has certain qualities making it worth some consideration by that journal, then go ahead and send it. Don't worry about whether or not it is going to be published. If you've prepared properly, you won't embarrass yourself, so send your paper off; you never know. . . . At the very *least* you'll get back some good comments for your time and trouble. These comments will help put you in a better position to publish later, perhaps in a journal to which the paper may ultimately be more suited. If the turnaround is only six to eight weeks, why not? It'll be worth it. If the turnaround time is very long, you'll have to weigh alternatives a bit harder.

Q: What about multiple submissions?

Neiman: You must not, under *any* circumstances, submit the same article to more than one journal at a time. This behavior is anathema because somebody from the journal is putting about a two months' investment into your paper. It may seem like a long time for you to wait, but a certain amount of turnaround time is necessary. After all, it's hard to get three reviewers to read and then get their comments back to the editor so that a decision can be reached and relayed to the submitter. To go through all or part of this, and then to have someone say, "Well, I'm sorry, but I got accepted somewhere else. I don't need you"—you can see why editors would get upset. What it will all come down to for you is this: You'll never have anything even considered, much less accepted, at a journal to which you sent a multiple submission, at least while that editor is there.

On the other hand, it is essential for you to understand that the vast majority of submissions—even papers submitted by experienced or well-known people—don't get accepted the first time. In fact, as a reader I generally accept about no more than maybe one out of every seven or eight manuscripts I read. But that doesn't mean that I think only one out of seven should get published. I would say that at least half of them are ultimately publishable. Of all the things I myself have published, maybe only two or three of them hit the first time. You can't expect a manuscript to just go there and score a direct hit.

The categories of response are generally "reject," "revise and resubmit," and "accept." Certainly it's disheartening to have put in the time only to end up with rejection. But if you get a lot of comments and good discussion on your article, then you shouldn't worry about it. Editors have taken the time to comment because your article is worthwhile. Make the changes, and get it off straightaway to another journal.

There really is an element of the crapshoot in getting published in journals. Students don't realize the reality behind the process, so when they get a rejection, they get depressed. They get long critiques on their work, and they think, "Oh gee, you know, forget about it. I can't do this. My work's no good." Students need to understand that's the way it's going to happen ninety percent of the time. The norm is to put in a lot of work and then face disappointment because of a rejection.

Rejection after a resubmission is especially hard. Editors usually send the revised article to one of the original readers and maybe an additional, new one; they then both read it and make a decision. If the readers accept it, the process still may not be over, for even after the second reading some minor problems may remain. These will be worked out between you and the editor; the paper doesn't go out for review again. But if the verdict is "no" on the second round, then it's complete rejection. There isn't a third time. You can usually tell by the readers' comments whether your article was just a piece of junk and you really should forget about it, or whether it is something substantial but unsuited for that journal at that moment.

Since you will have received helpful comments from the review even though your article was rejected, write the editor and ask him or her to thank the readers for you. In other words, be gracious about it because that's the only thing you can do. The editor will think, "Well, that was nice," and you will be remembered sympathetically.

Q: What are the key points you think grad students should keep in mind when they approach publishing?

Neiman: (1) Above all, you must get things written; otherwise, you'll never have any success. That's obvious.

(2) Find out who the important people are in your field. If they're not at your own campus, go ahead and talk to your faculty and peers, but get names from other sources as well and from the journals to which you're interested in submitting.

(3) Send what you're working on out to these specialists. Not only may you get some good feedback, but you're also likely to find a couple of people who might end up being your readers somewhere, someday. These contacts can help.

(4) Be sure the work you send out—whether to people in your network or to journals—is as professional as you can make it. Approach your mentor, your faculty, and your peers to help you with this. Read journals too, so you can recognize good professional writing.

(5) Get to know the journals to which you're going to submit. Try to get some sense of what the journal is doing and what changes, if any, it has in process. This means getting to know (or at least to know *about*) the editor.

(6) Be careful about the journals to which you *do* submit. Shoot for the very best you possibly can, and, at least for now, stay with mainstream journals, because the payoff is better for you professionally.

(7) Don't expect to have your work accepted right away. This is perhaps the most critical point. You've got to remember that *everybody*, even a seasoned and successful professional, has to face rejection as a matter of course.

(8) *Always* be classy—especially about rejection. It never hurts, and it can even help later, often in unexpected ways.

Getting the Most Out of Your Seminars

To help in your endeavor to get as much quality writing and publication-oriented experience out of your seminars as possible, we have compiled a checklist of strategies. It represents the accumulated wisdom of many graduate students and faculty members/journal reviewers in the humanities and social sciences.

Finding Your Focus

The seminar itself no doubt suggested the topic of your paper to you, and you probably consulted a comprehensive reference guide in your field to help in your research. (In the humanities, a volume like the Modern Language Association's *Literary Research Guide: A Guide to Reference Sources for the Study of Literatures in English and Related Topics* is invaluable, for it not only provides guidance in the areas of primary works, scholarship, and criticism, but it offers helpful overviews of pertinent periodicals as well.) Before you decide to revise or submit your seminar paper to a specific journal, however, you should reassess the paper from the standpoint of broad publication as opposed to readership by one professor. In this preliminary process, you simultaneously fulfill a number of important goals: strengthening the paper's content and expression; identifying potential places to submit it to; formulating ways to adapt it into related (but not identical!) articles for concurrent submission to several different journals; and preparing the foundation of new articles in the future. To write articles concurrently is to efficiently use the same basic research to produce and submit one or more articles. Each article, needless to say, needs to be sufficiently different from the others so that if they were to be published simultaneously, neither you nor the journals in which the articles were published would be in any way embarrassed.

If you don't already have a seminar paper you are trying to transform but are simply trying to come up with an idea, these suggestions will serve you equally well.

Look for journals dedicated to a particular aspect of your seminar and read articles from their most recent issues. Note significant items such as names of authors, critics, and texts. Identify methodologies used and any evidence of ideologies. Look for any ongoing debates or "hot" topics.

Unfortunately, many students, especially in the humanities, still rely almost exclusively on books for their research: *Don't fall into this trap.* You're shortchanging yourself if you do. At the very least, going to the journals expands your awareness of the most current research on your topic. In addition, you learn about the journals in your discipline, thus broadening your understanding of options open for submitting and placing your work. Once you're a professional, it's going to be assumed that you have this knowledge.

Pay attention to postings about upcoming conferences, calls for papers, professional seminars, activities sponsored by other institutions, etc., in your field. The theme or focus of one of these may mean a chance for you to present, get feedback on, and perhaps even publish your paper, or some version of it. Moreover, such announcements may give you ideas for new papers or the recycling of old ones. If you really want to keep current about conferences in your specialty, you should join a professional organization or two early on in your career. If you need help in deciding which one(s) would be most beneficial, you may want to consult your discipline's equivalent of the MLA's *Guide to Professional Organizations for Teachers of Language and Literature in the United States and Canada*. Guides like these provide essential information about organizations, such as necessary addresses, size of membership, and—most importantly—names of periodicals and publications sponsored by the organization. Additional benefits from checking postings include:

- exposure to the kind and extent of professional activity in your field;
- garnering of important information such as deadlines, potential funds, and opportunities for correspondence and networking that you can act upon now or in the future;
- help in structuring your own professional schedule and goals, either for the short or long term;
- subject matter for informed conversation, whether it be small talk or serious assessment of what you have discovered.

Remember: Share whatever you learn with your peers, mentor, and faculty. It's a sensible policy that may pay off later on.

Doing (Additional) Research

The same strategies you use to find your focus can also help you to identify additional research that will strengthen your paper or better tailor it for publication in a specific journal. One avenue you might consider is taking full advantage of *all* the libraries to which you have access (department, college, university, local, interlibrary loan). Get to know the reference librarians *well* and find out about the special resources available at the libraries you will be using most.

If you live near other universities, research centers or institutes, or public facilities like museums, consider visiting them to discover what they have to offer. Even if you don't stumble onto new sources for your dissertation (or even a paper or an article or two), you will establish contacts with other professionals—both in and out of academia—who may provide you with useful information or opportunities.

Doing the Writing

Even the very *best* seminar paper does not necessarily make a journal article. You will probably have to do extensive revisions before you want to have others read it in a journal.

The following is a list of items or areas you should pay special attention to when rewriting (or just assessing) your seminar paper for submission:

- Illogical structure or faulty reasoning
- Derivative ideas and lack of a distinctive, individual voice (after all, this is *your* article, not anyone else's)
- Inaccessible style and presentation
- Overextensive citation and excessive length
- Insufficient or irrelevant samples
- Colloquial, obscure, sexually or racially discriminatory, grammatically incorrect, or otherwise unprofessional language

While it may be true that felicity of phrase is more a factor in the humanities than in the social sciences (one of the professors we interviewed in the social sciences referred to such humanities-oriented considerations as "rutti-tutti"), clear and uncluttered writing is a desirable goal in any discipline. Most readers recommend the following: a title that is interesting or provocative (but *not* inappropriate or flip); a "grabber" opening sentence; a first page or introduction that succinctly but appealingly states the purpose and focus of the article; and a tone that is more "intellectually conversational" than stodgily academic and/or jargon-laden. A final important injunction: Be *very* selective with your footnotes—use them *sparingly*. Make sure that they are necessary and relevant. A perfunctory or disorganized catalogue of the background research you have done is the principal giveaway that your submission was (and to a large extent still is) a seminar paper by a graduate student.

Finding Other Uses for Your Essay

Perhaps, for whatever reason, you just can't transform your seminar paper into an article for submission to a professional journal right now. What else can you do with it to salvage at least some, if not all, of that effort?

A lot depends on the paper itself, and a lot depends on you, your schedule, and your long-term plans. But here are a few suggestions:

- Abbreviate the piece and work it into a short "Note," rather than a full-fledged article, depending on the content and on the needs of the target journal.
- Submit it for presentation at a suitable conference, if it is either relatively short (up to fifteen pages) or long but easy to revise into more-or-less freestanding parts. You should especially try to present *anything* related to your dissertation—even if it's just "work in progress." Since the dissertation represents your specialty, you want as many people to know about it as possible— and a conference is an excellent means to that end.
- Consider using your seminar article as the basis of, or your contribution to, a collaborative effort with a colleague.
- Go back to the paper you most enjoyed doing—it may be a clue to what you should focus on in your dissertation. As a matter of fact, there should be at least *one* (if not several) papers you could work on as a chapter or part of a chapter for your dissertation.
- Check to see if there's a journal in your discipline dedicated to publishing work by graduate students or new junior faculty and try sending it there, more or less as is.
- Submit it to one of your home campus publications, such as your department's newsletter. Such newsletters are distributed beyond the department to administrators on your campus and to other campuses, providing networking possibilities.
- Investigate other avenues for publication, such as desktop publishing.

The suggestions above can help you capitalize on the extensive education you now have and will eventually accumulate in graduate school. This includes your experience as a graduate student instructor (teaching assistant). Yes, there are methods of translating aspects of your *teaching* experience into publications, as we shall show you.

Remember, every seminar offers you three different areas—participants, research, writing—from which you should try to derive the greatest benefit:

Participants. Both faculty *and* fellow students comprise your single most significant resource within the seminar, presenting you with opportunities for mutual support, guidance, networking, collaboration, and perhaps one day, even a job.

Research. All seminars force you to read, discuss, present, analyze, synthesize, and write up research and its results. While you already know how to do these, keep mindful of maximizing your efforts. For example, when you give an oral presentation, do so as if you were at a conference; time yourself, attempt a lively delivery, X [and don't read from your paper.] Also, remember to note which publishers are cited when you consult recent journals and compile the bibliography for your dissertation. These may well be the very publishers you want to approach later about publishing *your* book.

Writing. Try to produce a paper that will not only get a good grade but will also help you formulate a conference presentation, obtain a publication credit, make progress on your dissertation, or, at the very least, acquire a respectable writing sample to send to network contacts and search committees.

Occasionally, your first publication is the result of someone else's intercession—usually a professor's. Don't count on it. It's much more likely that connections you have made yourself somewhere along the line from BA or BS to PhD will develop into concrete publication credits. These credits, remember, can be the edge you bring into the career competition. Such was the case with Jack Zupko, Assistant Professor of Philosophy at San Diego State University, an interview with whom follows.

Graduate School Networks and Getting Published

An Interview with JACK ZUPKO
Assistant Professor of Philosophy
San Diego State University

Q: How did your publications as a graduate student come about?
Zupko: The first thing I published was a book review in *Eidos*, a graduate journal of philosophy published at the University of Waterloo in Canada. This journal is received by university libraries in North America, as well as by graduate philosophy students in Canada and the U.S.

I was an undergraduate major in philosophy at Waterloo when *Eidos* was launched. Waterloo had a rather atypical philosophy program at that time because graduate MA and PhD candidates outnumbered undergraduate majors by about four to one. The impetus for the journal came from graduate students in the department who saw the need for a medium in which to publish work by philosophers who were still studying and in the process of completing their degrees. I had kept in touch with some of them after I graduated in 1982. My guess is that when a book that dealt with medieval logic and semantics arrived at *Eidos* for review, and no interested or qualified reviewers came forward, the editors may have remembered my interest in medieval philosophy as an undergraduate. So they contacted me at Cornell, where I had gone on to do graduate work.

Q: Is the journal still being published?

Zupko: Oh yes, and it now has a very nice format: each issue is devoted to a specific theme such as epistemology, or the works of major philosophers such as Wittgenstein or Derrida. Papers are solicited for each thematic issue a year or so in advance of its actual appearance.

Q: So graduate students in philosophy departments can look for those "Calls for Papers" flyers, or they can look for them in the journal itself?

Zupko: Right. The prospective themes of forthcoming issues are printed on the back of each issue, together with the deadlines for each.

There are other journals of philosophy that have the same format. The foremost example here is *The Monist*, which appoints a special editor to oversee the selection of papers submitted for a particular issue.

Q: Did you have any practical or credited training in graduate school on how to publish?

Zupko: No. Not at all. Nor was I aware of programs of this sort being offered by other departments.

Q: Did it seem that there were expectations that you would somehow publish anyway?

Zupko: Yes and no. Although professors recognized the importance of publication in one's professional life, many seemed to feel that the "how to" of publishing is something best learned on one's own—something any suitably motivated graduate student could figure out for himself. Their main objective was to train you as a philosopher and get you through the program. If you felt the work you produced while under their supervision was good enough for publication, then, I suppose, you would submit it yourself. But there was never any instruction in how this should be done. This may have been because the question hardly ever arose. I know of one or two cases in which a professor actually urged a student to send a course paper off to a journal, but that was extremely rare.

As for the expectation of eventually publishing anyway, some professors are of the opinion that it is easier to publish a philosophy article today than it was twenty or thirty years ago. I think they are right about this. There has been an explosion in the number of new philosophy journals appearing over the past two decades, and along with the proliferation of journals, a much greater opportunity to get one's work into print. This is in many ways bad from the reader's point of view, since there is now a superabundance of philosophy journals containing articles of marginal quality or dubious merit—pieces that never would have been published in the old days. And I think you will find that there has been a corresponding increase in the number of articles dying citationless deaths, as they say. But this is a positive boon from the professional philosopher's point of view, since again, it means a better chance of getting things into print. And everyone knows that publications are not only the main criterion of tenure and promotion, but also—at least in philosophy, anyway—a sorting mechanism in hiring decisions.

Q: What else did you publish as a graduate student?

Zupko: An article in a volume of conference proceedings and a bibliographic article for a book. The former resulted from a talk I gave at the Eighth International Congress of Medieval Philosophy, which met in Helsinki in 1987. I may have seen a poster advertising the Congress, or perhaps it was mentioned to me by other graduate students working in the same area—I don't recall which. In any case, the theme of the Congress interested me, so I sent in an abstract that was accepted. My talk was based on a chapter of my dissertation. A few months later, participants were invited to submit written versions of their presentations for publication, which I did. I believe it finally appeared in print this year.

Q: So you streamlined all that—a conference credit and a publication in a journal—and you used your dissertation to do so.

Zupko: That's right. I was following an important principle of academic survival—that of mining one's dissertation for articles. The fact that I gave the talk at a conference, or that the conference submissions were refereed, is less significant. For professional evaluation purposes, it's the article in print that matters.

Q: Did the bibliographic article relate to your dissertation as well?

Zupko: In a way. The topic of that article, chronicling research developments since 1972 in the study of the fourteenth century Parisian School of Science, happened to tie in with my dissertation, which dealt with the philosophical psychology of a leading figure of the period. Like the book review I mentioned earlier, it was solicited, but the solicitation came about in an indirect way.

The article was part of a much larger project to compile a multi-volumed research guide of annotated, bibliographic essays covering all areas of philosophy. It was begun in the 60s, abandoned in the 70s, and finally taken up again by a different general editor about five or six years ago. Initially, specialists were contacted and asked to write critical surveys of research done in their fields since about 1900. Many of these essays were submitted, but the project was abandoned before they could be published. By the time it was revived, there was a fifteen-year hiatus that needed to be covered in order for the volumes to become current once more. I was asked to write a supplement to the article on the Parisian School of Science, covering research developments between 1972 and 1987.

For the volume on medieval philosophy, the new general editor contacted a Canadian philosopher who had been involved in the project the first time around and who was willing to help see it through to completion. This philosopher, in turn, contacted several other specialists for the names of people who might be willing to write supplements to the original articles. One of the people he contacted was a philosopher at the University of Toronto who has known me for a number of years, and who is acquainted with my research interests. The Toronto colleague recommended me for the supplement on the Parisian School of Science, and I was eventually contacted in this regard by the general editor. I was a graduate student at Cornell at the time, and I remember being concerned that this solicited article might prove too great a distraction from my dissertation. As it turned out, I was able to base the article on sources with which I was already quite familiar, besides uncovering some interesting new items along the way.

Q: Do you think it helped when you went for job interviews that you had that publishing experience?

Zupko: I've no doubt that it made a big difference. Publications help separate you out from the mass of other applicants who also have teaching experience, good letters of recommendation, and all of the other necessary credentials in place.

As in most humanities disciplines, the competition for jobs in philosophy is fierce because the number of openings is far fewer than the number of philosophy PhDs actively seeking academic employment. For example, we received about seventy-five applications a year ago for a tenure-track position in philosophy here at State, even though the search was cut short by the cancellation of the position shortly after it was first advertised in "Jobs for Philosophers" and the *Chronicle of Higher Education*. I was on the search committee. What struck me about the dossiers we did receive was the number that more than qualified the candidate for the position and that also seemed tied as far as teaching experience, strength of letters, and academic presentations were concerned. Although our search did not reach this point, publications would surely have been used as a makeweight in determining which candidates got interviews. This is the general trend, of course, and one reason for it is that members of hiring committees tend to be swamped with academic and other professional duties when these searches are usually conducted (November–January). There is only so much time to devote to a search. When one is faced with a sea of qualified applicants, those who actually have things in print begin to look better than those who don't.

Building Toward Publication

If you have chosen a career in academia, you know that getting your work published will one day become a necessity for your advancement. While you are still in graduate school there are many practical and positive things you can do to actually fulfill or at least prepare for this critical challenge. Although specific strategies to help you while you're still in graduate school have been presented in this chapter, its general recommendations will be useful throughout your professional life. The principles summarized below can provide you with a solid foundation:

- Carefully select a mentor who will facilitate your progress toward the degree and, beyond that, toward your professional goals.

- Establish strong relationships of mutual benefit with your peers, and promote your personal and collective interests.
- Familiarize yourself with (*and* avail yourself of) the inherent, diversified network of individuals and resources offered by your discipline and institution.
- Think and act professionally now, while you are still open and flexible enough to modify your skills, attitudes, and priorities.
- Maximize the research and writing you produce, even if this means reformulating, revising, and adapting it to various purposes.
- Finally, take the responsibility and the initiative to act on your own behalf, both in the pursuit of specific goals *and* in the realization of your own potential.

3

Finding Your Journal

The Unexamined Method Is Rarely the Best

Burgeoning or diminishing demands for your specialty, increasingly competitive job markets, mounting pressures to publish, bewildering arrays of journals—all of these are realities you face both as a graduate student and as a new faculty member. <u>Too much is at stake for you to rely on an unexamined, unstructured method of placing your work for publication.</u>

If you have not had the benefit of a course in academic publishing by the time you are actually ready to select journals to which to submit your work, you will typically resort to the only strategy most graduate students know: you will choose journals because you recognize their names. At best, this strategy should be used only as a kind of "default" system for submission selection. The "knowledge" of particular journals upon which it relies is usually the product of what can only be described as osmosis: everyone assumes you "know" the journals simply because you're so often exposed to them. You see which journals publish the articles you're asked to read for seminars and which journals are referred to repeatedly in your research. You see what your library subscribes to and what your department receives. You see where your own professors are publishing and perhaps note where they are not. You just kind of pick up things that way.

Of course, picking up information and comprehending it so that you can apply it effectively are two very different things. Why assume that you will automatically possess the knowledge you need and be able to utilize it appropriately? Why permit yourself to depend on the vagaries of osmosis or the expertise of others?

What you need to do is to acquire the necessary expertise for yourself. That way, when you ask, "Where should I send my paper?" you'll know better than to wait for someone else to give you an answer. In fact, you'll even understand that there is often no single *answer* to that question at all; rather there is a range of choices representing *a comprehensive response* to the unique configuration of your particular paper and your individual ambitions for it.

Regardless of the stage in your career, an adequate strategy for advancing yourself and your work will always serve you well. Therefore, you need to know not only *why* and *how* to find out everything you can about journals, but also *what* to look for in order to decide to the best of your own ability where and what you should submit. This chapter investigates these questions from a variety of perspectives.

In the next two essays, Assistant Professor Joseph Childers of UC Riverside's English Department and Associate Professor Susan E. Cayleff of San Diego State University's Women's Studies Department offer an overview of important questions you should be asking yourself when you look at journals as a prospective contributor. The general and practical issues considered in Dr. Childers' essay, such as asking yourself what you want from your publication, constitute the critical first step in targeting journals. Dr. Cayleff's article, written in collaboration with two of her graduate students, offers practical strategies that both encourage and empower students to make the passage from passive student to active professional.

Some Considerations in Placing Your Article

JOSEPH CHILDERS
Assistant Professor of English, UC Riverside
Editor, *Critical Texts*

One of the most difficult, and important, decisions facing an author with a publishable essay is deciding where to place it. In the humanities, there are literally thousands of journals that are seeking intelligent, original work by newcomers. While some journals may have a bias against "unknown" authors or graduate students, for the most part all journals that accept unsolicited manuscripts unprejudicially evaluate the essays they receive and choose what they deem the best from that number.

Of course, what one journal may consider to be very good may not even be publishable in another. Consequently, to ensure the most sympathetic reading possible, it is important that you choose as a target journal one that will provide the best venue for your work. At one level this may seem like a relatively easy task. For instance, if you have written an essay on *The Prelude* by William Wordsworth, you may immediately think of *The Wordsworth Circle*, a journal devoted to works about Wordsworth and other Romantic poets. While this indeed may be *one* appropriate place for the *Prelude* essay, it may not reach as wide or diverse an audience as some other journals for which your essay is equally well suited. Thus, you'll need to consider what you want from the publication of your essay. If you merely want a line on your cv, then publication anywhere will do. Few scholars, however, publish *merely* for the institutional rewards that accrue from getting their name in print. Usually, scholars are trying to instigate some sort of change in the way others see the world, or a particular part of the world. Often authors are attempting to disseminate information that will help others teach or that will shed new light on others' research. For this reason, authors usually want to reach as wide an interested audience as possible. Yet placing essays in those journals that cater to an author's "ideal" audience is often time-consuming and always competitive.

Because placing a piece in a top journal is so competitive, you should always be prepared for rejection—not psychologically or emotionally perhaps, but pragmatically. Many journals reject manuscripts with only terse notes and without readers' comments. If this should occur, and you believe your essay to be publishable and important, then you should send it to another journal immediately. One way to be prepared to do this is to keep copies of the piece in a folder with the names of places to send the essay listed on the outside of the folder. List the names of the journals in descending order of placement preference. Any correspondence (receipt, acceptance, rejection, suggestions for revision) should be noted and dated next to the name of the appropriate journal. This allows you to know immediately the status of your piece: if it has been received; if it has been accepted or rejected; how long it has been at any specific journal; how often it has been sent out, etc. Also, it outlines a plan for placing the essay that you can execute quickly and efficiently.

The list of journals on the essay's folder should not read like some sort of birthday or Christmas wish list, whatever you may think of your essay. If you are determined to publish your essay, you should choose prospective journals carefully. This means that you should be familiar with the contents and the agendas, overt and hidden, of those periodicals you are considering as venues for your essay. Nothing is more embarrassing, or discouraging, than getting an essay returned with a curt comment about its inappropriateness for the journal. It pays, therefore, to be aware of exactly what sorts of periodicals might be interested in your work. If you are not a reader of the major journals in your field, you should become one. Not only should you read articles that interest you, but you should consider the "shape" of a number of issues of the journals in which you would like to publish your piece. Ask yourself, "What is the general length of the pieces that are published (number of words)?" If your piece is considerably longer or shorter than most of the essays in a particular journal, you may want to consider either expanding or cutting the piece or finding a different place to send it. Second, "How many pieces on your topic have been published by the journal in the past few issues (say, the last two years)?" If it is a journal that covers a wide range of topics, chances are slim that it will be interested in repeating itself within a two- or three-year period. If it is a more specialized journal, you should consider whether your particular approach to the topic has already been used. If it has, your argument would need to be extremely compelling and, probably, your conclusions different from those of the earlier piece to warrant publication of your essay.

Other issues also may arise when you're choosing a place to send your work. For instance, many journals have methodological, theoretical, or political agendas they are concerned to promote. Sometimes, as in the case of periodicals such as *Critical Inquiry*, which labels itself "pluralistic," these positions are articulated. Just as often, however, they are not, and it is then that the prospective contributor must be able to discern the particular interests promoted by the journal. If a journal seems to follow a particular methodological practice such as "new historicism" or "deconstruction," perusal of a few of its articles should make you aware of its biases and help you to decide if it is a good place for your article.

In my own field (literary studies) one of the best sources of information about journals is the *MLA Directory of Periodicals*. Published every other year by the Modern Language Association, the *Directory of Periodicals* lists the "vital statistics" of every journal cataloged in the *MLA Bibliography*. Be advised, however, that the MLA issues a full edition, which lists all cataloged periodicals, and an American edition, which lists only journals published in the United States. If you are interested in sending an essay to a foreign journal, you should be sure to check the international edition. Included in the listings is information such as how wide a journal's circulation is, restrictions on contributors, the ratio of number of articles received to number of articles published, the journal's scope, and the editorial style (usually either *Chicago* or MLA) that the journal uses. This information can be extremely useful for preparing a manuscript and for making final decisions about where to send an essay. Also, the *Directory of Periodicals* often provides information about a journal that will not be found in the pages of the journal itself. Nevertheless, familiarity with a journal's *Directory of Periodicals* listing is no substitute for knowledge of that journal's character and contents.

Finally, speaking as an editor, I can offer a few suggestions that will help an author make a good impression with a journal. Be aware of the journal's editorial style, and follow it. This may seem like a small issue, but it demonstrates that you have taken the time and care to present your material according to the journal's preferred style; and it indicates that you have done at least enough of your homework to know what that style is. Send the correct number of copies, no more, no fewer. Too many copies of an article, besides being ecologically incorrect, merely clogs things up at the editorial office. Too few means that the editorial office will have to take time to make extra copies to send out to its readers. Do not send long cover letters or curriculum vitae copies. An article should not require a long cover letter to explain it; the essay should speak for itself. I don't know of any article that has ever been accepted on the strength of its cover letter. Also, a copy of your cv is entirely unnecessary. Most journals are not interested in an author's past accomplishments or status in the profession and prefer to consider an essay on its own merits.

It goes without saying that publishing in quality journals is vital to most academics' careers. Certainly, search committees are often impressed by a job candidate who has published in good journals or one who has demonstrated her scholarly activity by accumulating a number of publications as a graduate student. Yet publishing is only one aspect of the profession, and for many positions it is less important than one's commitment to teaching excellence. Also, having a long list of publications in little-known or poorly regarded journals smacks more of desperation than of a true interest in sharing insights and the results of one's scholarship. It is by no means true that the candidate with the most publications always gets the job. For while all departments are interested in hiring productive colleagues, they are not necessarily interested in hiring people who publish articles to the exclusion of their other duties. Most departments in the humanities expect a relatively small output from their junior professors, the idea being that a good part of the first years on the job should be devoted to preparing one's book for publica-

tion and to teaching. Thus, while publishing is important, it should by no means be the sole focus of a young career. Nor should you feel compelled to publish too broadly or without direction. One or two excellent and well-placed articles can do your career a great deal more good than a score of marginal pieces in obscure journals. Quality, not quantity, should be the watchword.

Breaking Into Print: Strategies for Publishing in Women's Studies as a Grad Student

SUSAN E. CAYLEFF, Associate Professor
Women's Studies Department
San Diego State University
ROBERTA A. HOBSON, MA Candidate
Department of History
SDSU
ROBERTA J. SCHMITZ, MA Candidate
Department of History
SDSU

Getting published in graduate school in the area of women's studies must be approached methodically, deliberately, and in a well-organized manner. Because women's studies is by its very definition interdisciplinary, graduate students must aim their publication efforts at both women's studies and their disciplinary specialization: history/literature/sociology/anthropology/law—whichever applies. Although many examples cited here reflect my own bifocal expertise in women's studies/history, the suggestions made may be generalized to all fields. In your effort to enter the world of academic publishing, I encourage you to adopt some or all of the strategies presented.

"Introducing Yourself": Your Vitae and Publications

As your initial step, assemble a thorough, top-quality curriculum vitae. Submit this with all letters of inquiry to journals: since you are not an established scholar whose credentials are generally known, the vitae "introduces" you to your correspondent. Don't be embarrassed that you have no listings to put under "publications" (after all, that's what you're working on); instead, replace it with a category entitled "Major Research Projects," where you can

list particularly strong graduate seminar papers you have authored. This information lets the editor know your experience and interests. (Be sure to have at least two of the seminar papers listed available in professional-looking, complete, "shareable" format, in the event you are asked for a writing sample.)

On the other hand, if you have already published, the publications should be listed in this order: books, articles, book reviews, reference works, works under contract (with projected publication dates), and finally, works in progress (these have no home yet, but are underway).

Make your vitae present you in the most positive, realistic light possible.

Possible Routes for Beginning Publications

Book Reviews. If you choose to offer your services to a journal as a book reviewer, you should do the following:

1. Look on the frontispiece of the journal to get the correct mailing address for "correspondence." It's worth a phone call to the journal to secure the name of the editor-in-chief or, if they have one, the book review editor, because mail addressed to a specific individual, rather than to a generic "Staff," is likely to receive more thoughtful handling.

2. Craft a brief cover letter introducing yourself; for example: "I am a third-year American studies PhD student at Brown University. As you can see from perusal of my enclosed vitae, my primary fields of interest are. . . . I would like to offer to review books in my areas of expertise. . . . I look forward to hearing from you and contributing to the *name of journal* in future issues." Inquiries like these get positive results: don't be discouraged if a few to several months elapse. Remember, you're learning about the vagaries of "academic time." Make sure you place *all* correspondence on your university letterhead.

3. Once you receive the request to review, follow the press's instructions. Use previously published reviews in that journal as models, but remember to rely on your own perspective—knowledge of the field, political interpretations, world view—to make the review distinctively yours.

4. Don't forget to add the review to your vitae *immediately*, and even *before* it comes out in print. This is why you have categories for "works in press" and "works under contract."

Calls for Papers. The foundation of this plan lies in subscriptions to newsletters specific to your own special discipline, such as the

one for the American Association for the History of Medicine or those in women's studies such as the "National Women's Studies Association Newsletter." Be aware that the areas covered by specialized newsletters can overlap, which means the broader the scope of your attention to such announcements, the more likely you are to discover opportunities. These kinds of newsletters are sometimes available in university libraries.

Keep a close eye on "Calls for Papers" for special journal issues and book series volumes that appear regularly in these newsletters; they represent an energy-efficient way for you to get published. Say, for example, you're working on an aspect of women's legal history in California: *Frontiers* happens to be compiling a special issue on women in the West; or, you're working on the biography of a social reformer: Oxford Press has a call out for new and revised entries for an updated volume of *American National Biography.* By intelligently applying your research and getting accepted, you could get a "peer-reviewed" article out of the former and a "reference work" from the latter.

When you see a call appropriate to your work, write the editor in charge of the project, and include an introductory cover letter (similar in content to the one mentioned for the book review) and vitae. Sometimes an editor will want a one-page proposal of your topic. Try to stick with an area on which you've already worked/ are working. Most graduate school course loads do not allow for taking on "new" research. Also, try to build upon and use your expertise by developing research that will enhance your course work (or that you've already done as course work). If the editor responds favorably, be sure to follow carefully the instructions regarding length, focus, questions asked and answered.

"Blind" Journal Submissions. The third and final tack you can choose is to do a "blind submission" to either a women's studies or discipline-specific journal. Set reasonable goals for yourself where you have the greatest likelihood of success. If you're working on an aspect of state history, for example, I suggest you send a letter of inquiry and your vitae to the appropriate state historical journal. Detail your research in the letter, and ask if the journal is interested in receiving a submission on your topic. This saves time. If the answer is "no," you can move on to another publication.

If the answer is "yes," you need to produce a paper to submit. This is where I'd like to make some observations on the subject of "Seminar Papers vs. Academic Publication."

- Eliminate "qualifiers" from your language; you're sharing expertise, not conjecture. This necessitates your thinking of yourself as a scholar/student, a role with which you will become increasingly comfortable.
- Make clear, precise statements and assertions you believe true; avoid "safer," more verbose, circuitous, and/or noncommittal arguments.
- Meet deadlines.
- Respond graciously to reviewers' criticisms through consideration and/or compliance; avoid perceiving the criticisms as personal attacks or indications of your inabilities. Although suggestions for revision are rare for the seminar paper, they are inevitable for the professional article. Remember: comments strengthen a piece; learn to view them as a positive third eye.

While a revised seminar paper submitted for publication in a peer-reviewed journal may not get accepted right away, it's still worth your time to make the attempt: you can at least add it to your vitae while in progress—a clear indication to others that you're on the road to writing for publication. Of course, if it ends up officially accepted one day, then it will "count" as a refereed publication.

In addition to improving and promoting your work, you also need to actively learn about where to send it. The first thing you should do is secure for your permanent files a copy of the most recent edition of *Ulrich's International Periodicals Directory* "Women's Interests" pages. Each entry here lists essential information about the journal, such as editor(s)-in-chief, circulation size, year of founding, former titles, and description. Read this last item carefully—it tells you the journal's audience and agenda. *Frontiers*, for example, describes itself as "bridging the gap between the academy and the community," while *Feminist Studies* declares it has the mission of "presenting scholarly research, essays, art, book reviews, and poetry, fiction and creative narrative pertaining to the feminist experience in the social sciences, history, politics, and literature."

In preparation for this section of the essay, two graduate students of mine, Hobson and Schmitz, surveyed by questionnaire some dozen journals in the areas of women's studies and history, inquiring as to their peer-review process, turnaround time, record of publishing graduate students, style stipulations , emphasis on issues of diversity (gender, race, social class, sexual preference, region, etc.), and policies for selecting book reviewers. They also queried as to where each is indexed and its frequency of publishing thematic issues.

While all of the results of their findings cannot be presented in any detail here, I would like to offer a few examples of important information they uncovered. For instance, while none of the journals prohibited graduate student submissions, we noticed that their emphases varied greatly; it is therefore crucial that you consider the journals' needs in deciding where you send your work.

Turning to more specific sample responses from their questionnaire, I would like to share some interesting insights into several of the journals queried:

Signs puts all published articles through a peer review process consisting of two distinct stages: in the first, the submission is read by an internal reviewer and then referred to two external reviewers with expertise in areas similar to that of the article's content. If it "passes" stage one, it then goes to the Board of Editors for the second phase of its review. Since the manuscript can be sent back to the author for revisions at any time during this process, turnaround time is impossible to calculate. While *Signs* does publish submissions by graduate students, the actual percentage is unknown. It asks authors to follow the *Chicago Manual of Style* and to "address diversity issues ... where appropriate ... and to address their arguments to an interdisciplinary audience." Generally speaking, *Signs* avoids thematic issues, although its occasional special issue on a particular theme is announced about eighteen months ahead of the planned publication date through a "call for papers."

American Historical Review publishes only peer-reviewed articles; submissions pass through three to six reviewers; turnaround time is six months to two years; 1 percent of articles published are by graduate students. *AHR* supplies a style sheet, and occasionally issues are thematic. Book reviewers, who must have published at least one monograph, are selected by the *AHR's* editorial assistants.

Women's Studies International Forum, published in Brighton, England, puts articles through at least three peer reviewers. Publication time varies from three months to one year after submission; it has published graduate students (no numbers are available). Its guidelines stress feminist, nonsexist, nonracist content, and it follows the American Psychological Association (APA) format. Book reviewers are chosen for their knowledge of the field and by their contacting the journal with details of their special interests.

The *Journal of Women's History* stated that 9 percent of its authors were graduate students in their first two years of graduate study.

In addition, some journals, such as *Frontiers, Journal of Women's History*, and *Signs*, give specific and complete manuscript submission instructions in each issue, including examples of footnotes. Many others in the field, like *Women's Studies Quarterly*, also specify that issues involving race, class, and gender are particularly encouraged.

Parting Words

In short: plan ahead, choose a realistic plan, and follow up by writing your contact person to ask the status of your inquiry submission (but not until six months have elapsed in which you've heard nothing). Be patient. You are moving toward becoming a more fully developed scholar.

[The authors of this article would like to thank the following individuals for their detailed responses to our questionnaire: Megan Morrisey, Editorial Assistant, *Signs: Journal of Women in Culture and Society*; Christine Zmroczek, Managing Editor, *Women's Studies International Forum*; Margaret L. Andersen, Editor, *Gender and Society*; Beth Olson, Managing Editor, *Journal of Women's History* Marlene Smith-Baranzini, Associate Editor, *California History*; Virginia D. Hollis, Secretary to the Editors, *American Historical Review*; and an anonymous respondent, *Feminist Studies*.]

Stages in the Process of Targeting Journals

By addressing the issues professors Childers and Cayleff raise *before* you actually start corresponding with journals, you will save yourself both time and emotional energy—two resources graduate students have in short supply. In addition, the preliminary consideration and practical strategies they propose can go far in helping you to "shape" your career—*and* your cv—into the form most professionally productive and personally expressive of your own unique abilities and interests.

Only after completing the first stage of the process—determining the kind of publication you're aiming for and what you want it to do for you—should you begin the second: identifying potential target journals. This stage consists of two phases: surveying the paper itself, and prospecting for other sources that will increase and/or refine your list. The real heart of the targeting process, however, is contained in the third stage: when you actually go into the stacks with your list to handle the journals themselves. Your collection of possibilities should shrink dramatically during this "hands-on" stage, providing you with a manageable basis for your ranking, in order of preference, of the journals remaining. This final identification and prioritization of the journal(s) to which you will actually submit constitutes the fourth stage. Although assessing the journals is effectively over at this point, there remains a fifth and final step to the whole process: submission and follow-through. Since this stage represents the end goal of the whole process, it is *essential* that here you perform the following tasks: double-check that your paper conforms to the format of your Number One choice, actually send it off and keep track of the progress of your paper once it's submitted, and prepare to implement another submission (if necessary) to one of your back-up targets.

Assessing Journals and Alternatives to Journal Articles

DIANE BUCKLES, MA Candidate
Department of English and Comparative Literature
San Diego State University
JACKIE SENTENEY, MA Candidate
Department of English and Comparative Literature
SDSU

Assessing Journals

However you define "English," and wherever you draw the line between "literary studies" and "composition and rhetoric," journals can provide at least one fairly well-established demarcation.

Chris M. Anson's 1986 "A Computerized List of Journals Publishing Articles in Composition" numbered seventy-four publications, including a number of small regionals, and more journals have emerged since then. While many journals listed here publish work both in literary and composition studies, there are a number that focus specifically on issues in composition.

The "Big Two" are *College English* (CE) and *College Composi-*

tion and Communication (CCC). Both journals are published by the National Council of Teachers of English (NCTE). *CE* has a much wider audience because it publishes work in both literature and composition, while the quarterly *CCC* focuses entirely on the more specific concerns of composition specialists.

Although both *CE* and *CCC* are juried and the editorial boards do not know who wrote an article until it is accepted for publication, it is unlikely that you can look forward to being published as a student in one of these unless your graduate work is of quality on par with the best in the field. Because big names vie to publish in big-name journals, it makes sense that it would be more difficult for a graduate student to gain access as an author. That's why it is perhaps more realistic to try for other journals. Between spring 1990 and spring 1991, five articles by graduate students were published in *CCC*; all but one were written in collaboration with a professor. In this same period, only one essay by a graduate student not writing collaboratively appeared in *CE*, and it was on a literary topic [52.7 (November 1990): 743].

Aside from the two major journals, there are a number of other journals, some very prestigious, others minor, all focusing on different aspects of composition and rhetoric. Some publish theory and pedagogy, some just pedagogy, some just empirical research. Others focus on the history of rhetoric from classical to modern times. Still others cross disciplinary lines. You should not send an article on pedagogy to a journal that publishes only research or an empirical study to a journal that is only interested in classical rhetoric.

Some journals will give you very specific guidelines. For instance, the editorial statement of *Research in the Teaching of English* (*RTE*), which publishes results of empirical studies, says that submissions will be evaluated according to:

- originality of the study;
- quality of its contribution to our understanding of pedagogically relevant issues in language teaching and learning;
- adequacy, clarity, and relevance of the conceptual framework;
- logic and reasonableness of interpretations and conclusions;
- methodological competence and appropriateness for a given question.

Other requirements are also frequently listed on the front pages or the covers of journals. These may include:

- length of articles: *Written Communiciation* allows up to thirty-five pages; other journals provide specifics in numbers of words, 4,000 to 7,000 being common, while some don't specify.
- documentation style: MLA, APA, Chicago. Unlike most journals publishing in composition studies, *RTE* requires APA-style rather than MLA documentation. Be sure to submit your article in the appropriate style.
- number of copies to submit: up to five—or on disk.
- biographical blurb on yourself, though the majority will not require or want this unless your essay is accepted.

The editorial board may express its right (as does *The Writing Instructor*) to edit your article "to conform with the Guidelines for Nonsexist Lanuage in NCTE Publications." Editors of both *CE* and *CCC* also specify use of NCTE guidelines.

Furthermore, some journals specify a particular audience. Some, like the *Journal of Teaching Writing*, take articles on all grade levels (preschool through university). *Language Arts* relates to high school only. *The Writing Instructor* takes articles on secondary school and college, while *Teaching English in the Two-Year College* focuses on two-year colleges and freshmen/sophomores at four-year institutions, and *Writing on the Edge* addresses only issues at the four-year college level.

Even a journal that is not specific to composition and rhetoric could well be an appropriate forum for your article, depending upon its slant. For instance, there has been a convergence in recent years of composition studies and feminism. *Feminist Teacher* addresses pedagogical issues from a feminist perspective and seeks "essays, articles, course descriptions, bibliographies, and letters-to-the-collective" describing how educators address issues on sexism, racism, homophobia, and other forms of oppression in the classroom. *Radical Teacher* is another general-subject journal looking for articles on politically informed pedagogy—feminist, Marxist, or Third World. Authors of articles on the politics of composition pedgagogy might consider such journals for publication possibilities. *Writing on the Edge: A Multiperspective on Writing* also claims a special interest in gender and composition.

Also, realize that some journals are more receptive to submissions by graduate students than are others. The following journals are some examples of this category:

The *Journal of Teaching Writing* (*JTW*), as a refereed journal, is

a good target. Its prefatory statement, "We especially welcome articles written by classroom teachers, whether they are first-time writers or well-established authors" indicates it's a good prospect for
graduate teaching assistants (GTAs). Editors suggest that "contributors should tailor their writing for a diverse readership with interests that are more practical than theoretical." Articles may range
from short descriptions of principles or practices that offer helpful
insights to longer pieces (15 to 20 pages) that explore topics in
greater detail. Appearing semiannually, *JTW* publishes articles on
the theory, practice, and teaching of writing throughout the curriculum. Each issue covers a range of topics, from composition theory
and discourse analysis to curriculum development and innovative
teaching techniques. Submission guidelines: three copies of each
manuscript—typewritten, doublespaced, and conforming to MLA,
1988. A self-addressed stamped envelope (SASE) is required for the
return of one copy of the manuscript. Manuscript length: 12 to 20
pages. From submission to notification of decision: 4 months. From
submission to publication: 12 to 18 months. Acceptance rate: 10
percent. (We present this detailed information here as a sample;
most journals print similar specifics.)

  The Writing Instructor (TWI), published by graduate students
at the University of Southern California, is especially interested in
publishing work by other graduate students and in making this
work available for use by readers of the journal, as it states in its
editorial policy:

> In addition to contributing theoretically grounded discussions, authors
> are also encouraged to submit or to append to their articles, when
> appropriate, classroom-tested exercises, handouts, and classroom tools
> which can be reproduced by photocopying a page from *TWI.*

  Forum in Reading and Language Education is a refereed journal
published by the Language Education Department at Indiana University. Its purpose is to publish scholarly papers by graduate students from around the nation reflecting current theoretical,
instructional, and research concerns in the field of reading and language education. In addition, each edition of the *Forum* will feature
a response by noted scholars in language education. Editors "encourage interested students who have prepared or are preparing a
paper addressing any research, theoretical, or institutional issue in
reading or language education to submit their work to the editorial
board of the *Forum* for review and publication." The journal will

consider any article by a grad student or one in which a grad student's name comes first. An abstract of 50 to 150 words should accompany the submission.

The Writing Lab Newsletter, Purdue University, is an informal monthly publication (ten issues a year, September to June) for those who direct or tutor in writing labs and language-skills centers. Articles, announcements, columns, and reviews of materials focus on topics in tutoring writing. Intended readers are both writing lab directors and tutors. Manuscripts can vary from short (two to four double-spaced pages) to long (six to twelve double-spaced pages).

Assessing Alternatives to Journal Articles

Just as journals vary in their prestige, so that publishing an article in a prestigious one confers more status on the author than publishing in a lesser one, publishing certain kinds of texts also "counts" more than others. Aside from publishing your own full-length journal articles and/or books, there are other, albeit somewhat less noteworthy, alternatives: conference papers, book reviews, shorter articles, and Educational Resources Information Center (ERIC) documents.

The first step toward getting conference papers published is joining the scholarly societies. As a graduate student, joining offers you a number of advantages:

- opportunities for professional development, networking, and collegiality;
- career and scholastic opportunities;
- sharing and disseminating knowledge and learning from others;
- currency with the newest issues.

Furthermore, membership is inexpensive for students. You get the journal(s) sponsored by the society at low student prices, journals that list announcements of upcoming conferences, and calls for papers. Perusing these announcements can often give you ideas for articles and keep you up-to-date in your field. You can be put on mailing lists to receive flyers from publishers. These can acquaint you with the specialties of university presses. Besides, membership in a scholarly society is one more item you can list on your cv.

For example, by joining the NCTE you can subscribe to the following journals at student prices: *College Composition and Communication, College English, English Education, English Journal, Language Arts, Research in the Teaching of English,* and *Teaching English in the Two-Year College*. Membership in the *Rhetoric Society of America*, established in 1968, is very inexpensive for students and includes a subscription to its journal, *Rhetoric Society Quarterly* (*RSQ*). This interdisciplinary society of "teachers, scholars, and students of the history, theory, practice, and teaching of rhetoric and its applications to other areas of thought and knowledge" sponsors a session at the annual Conference on College Composition and Communication (CCCC), as well as one at the annual MLA conference at the end of the year. Regional MLA conferences frequently present sessions and panels on composition issues within the broad interests of the association.

Attending conferences while you are a graduate student is essential on-the-job training, whether or not you are presenting a paper yourself. In fact, it is preferable to attend a conference or two before you actually become a presenter or panel member, just to demystify the event. Most conferences offer special rates to graduate students, and there are many from which to choose.

Another method of accumulating publication credits is by writing reviews. Some journals assign reviews to regular contributors, but others solicit reviews of books and other related published work. For instance, *Computers and Composition: A Journal for Teachers of Writing* and *The Technical Writing Teacher* accept reviews of books and software. *Issues in Writing* accepts reviews of any crossdisciplinary or interdisciplinary work of interest to academic or nonacademic readers. *The Writing Instructor* accepts short textbook reviews and brief notes on practical resources for teachers. *The Writing Lab Newsletter* accepts reviews of materials that focus on topics in tutoring writing. While a review does not count as much as an original scholarly article, it does count. And it indicates not only that you are making the effort to publish but that you are keeping pace with issues and ideas in your field.

Even in the most competitive journals—and for the same reasons as you might write a book review—you can try for something less formal than a full article. For instance, the "Staffroom Interchange" section in *CCC* accepts shorter, more informal pieces of under 3,500 words. Again, such a credit is not as good as a full-length article, but it is a publication.

Since 1966, another way to publish work has been on the Educational Resources Information Center (ERIC), which is sponsored by the U.S. Department of Education. ERIC storehouses information in databases and on microfiche. As a national educational information system, ERIC's separate clearinghouses focus on specific areas in education; the Clearinghouse on Reading and Communication Skills disseminates materials on composition. When you send a document to ERIC for consideration, it will be evaluated by someone from NCTE and/or CCCC. Documents are permanently indexed in *Resources in Education (RIE)*, ERIC's monthly journal indexing abstracts, within three to four months after acceptance. As a contributor, you will receive a complimentary microfiche. Advantages of publishing in ERIC are that approximately 2,500 organizations receive *RIE*, and more than 700 libraries subscribe to the ERIC microfiche collection, providing a wide base for dissemination of your article. ERIC documents never go "out of print." You retain the copyright even after your paper becomes a publication in the ERIC database. Remember, there's the possibility that you may be requested to submit your paper for publication in ERIC after presenting it at a conference. While an ERIC document does not carry as much weight as a journal article or a conference paper, it does expand considerably your audience, thus helping to get your ideas—and your name—noticed.

There was no such thing as an advanced degree in composition and rhetoric before the mid-1970s, but this is now the fastest-growing area of graduate study in many departments of English. Along with this new area of study have come new journals and new publishing opportunities for both faculty and graduate students.

Whether you are a graduate student or a faculty member, publishing is, of course, good for your individual career. But because composition and rhetoric is (in its modern form) such a young field, publishing here can do a larger good, too, by adding knowledge and legitimacy to a new discipline.

Practical Aids To Help You in the Assessment Process

Assessing Your Paper
In order to determine (1) the form of publication—article, note, book review, etc.—to which your paper is most suited, and (2) the kinds of journals potentially receptive to it, look first to your paper's content and structure and ask:

- What is the paper's subject and thesis?
- What specific data, works, authors, texts, etc., does it discuss? Are they traditional, canonical, new, innovative, revolutionary?
- What kind of approach or critical apparatus (e.g., methodological, theoretical, political) is applied, critiqued, modified, or refuted in it?
- Overall, how should the paper be classified? That is, what kind of article does it represent—standard research study, review of the literature with "new" conclusions, evaluative description, close analysis?
- What essential aspects of the paper—such as illustrations, tables, foreign language(s), length—may need special consideration in placement?
- What are the journals, if any, cited in the paper? Note the dates of the citations and if several articles come from the same journal over a period of time: this will give you a good idea if one of these journals may still be receptive to your own topic.

Once you have assessed the characteristics of your paper, brainstorm to identify by particular category *all* the kinds of journals to which you could—at least potentially—submit it. Certain special types of journals to look for include comparative, interdisciplinary, cross-cultural, special interest (such as ideological, political, ethnic, religious), theoretical, popular, historical, "school" or movement, form or genre, thematic, national or territorial, and so on. Also, don't forget to investigate the possibility that your paper may somehow reflect the focal interest of some professional association(s); many of these have their own special publications to which you may be able to submit, whether or not you are a member. Your reference librarian can help you identify these.

Using Other Sources to Brainstorm

Once the paper itself has been more or less exhausted for possible targets, prospect for other journal titles. To do this, you may want to consult the following sources for ideas:

- your personal network of professors, peers, and university staff, such as the reference or acquisitions librarians;
- posters in your department announcing newly launched or recently modified journals;
- appropriate citation indexes, or the principal "directory of periodicals" (a copy of which you will probably want to own) in

your discipline. Some of these, like the one put out by the Modern Language Association, contain several helpful indices (e.g., "to subjects," "to sponsoring organizations," "to languages published");

- sources that will keep you up-to-date on titles of new journals (such as the *Dictionary of Literary Biography Yearbook's* "The Year's New Journals" section) and on the actual contents of new and forthcoming issues of certain journals (you can ask your reference librarian to access this information for you on the library's electronic database);
- stacks in the library, where recent issues of periodicals are displayed.

These techniques will save time; they will also stimulate future endeavors if you make notes about alternative versions of your paper and possibilities for their placement. You may encounter additional possibilities for spinoff uses of your paper, for example, a conference presentation; an essay collected in a volume; a contribution to a reference work or survey; a writing sample for a job, fellowship, or internship application; or even a grant proposal. Place any announcements, ideas, or leads you turn up in a convenient place, like the folder Dr. Childers recommends—one designed to jog your creativity *and* your memory. If you investigate possibilities thoroughly and plan well enough, you may even discover you've prepared the foundation for something major, such as your dissertation topic, your future career specialty, or some other equally substantial contribution to your "professional portfolio."

Under ideal conditions, it's best to consult *both* a directory of periodicals and the actual journals themselves *for every title you have on the list you have brainstormed.* However, you may have uncovered an overwhelmingly large number of possibilities, or you may only be interested in journals with a quick turnaround time or "good" acceptance ratio, or you may have only a limited amount of time. Under these conditions, go either to the directory or to the journals themselves to quickly eliminate the least likely targets, so that you can more carefully assess the titles remaining on your list.

Guides/Indices/Directories of Periodicals. These reference books contain certain essential information you may not find elsewhere, not even in the journals themselves. Look up the titles of prospective journals in the *most recent, most complete* edition of the appropriate reference work in your field, and read everything in the entry. Information here usually includes estimated turnaround time—how long the journal takes to make a decision and how long it may be between acceptance and publication; acceptance ratios—the number of articles or book reviews submitted per year and number actually published; and restrictions, if any, on contributors, as well as fees and charges for which contributors may be responsible. Since such factors may adversely affect your likelihood of success, find out all you can *before* you submit your work.

The Journals Themselves. Purposefully look at the journals you are considering. Handle several recent issues. Evaluate their overall quality, their preferences, expectations, tone, and currency. Note any changes, such as format, approach, scope, editorial board, or publishing institution. If you are *especially* interested in a particular journal, find some older bound issues and study its history. By actually sitting down with the journals, you individualize them and gain a more realistic knowledge of them as physical and conceptual entities.

You will certainly reject immediately a number of journals for a variety of logical reasons: their titles or descriptions may have been misleading; they may be unsubstantial or unprofessional looking; or their contents may reflect beliefs, ideas, or perspectives with which you do not wish to be associated.

Other journals, however, will probably require a more thorough analysis on your part. To do this, you should have three items at hand when you sit down with the journals: a notebook dedicated *exclusively* to this process and its findings; the applicable directory of periodicals; and a copy of the "Assessment Sheet."

This assessment sheet developed out of the publication seminar offered by our department and from our own hours spent in the stacks. In it, we suggest many attributes to consider in selecting the best possible journals for your purposes. The discussion following the assessment sheet will help you interpret what the information you uncover is "saying" about the journal and its status in your discipline. We have also included a graduate student's sample report on applying the assessment sheet to her own focused survey of target journals.

ASSESSMENT SHEET

I. The Journal as "Package": Production Values
   A. Style of cover: slick, modern, sedate, traditional?
   B. Overall "eye appeal": grabs attention? easy to read?
   C. Paper quality: cover and pages?
   D. Illustrations and visual aids?
      1. Photographs, plates, drawings
      2. Tables and graphics
      3. Special typesetting
II. Inside (Cover) Information
   A. The Life of the Journal
      1. How long has it been around?
      2. Any historical variations in title?
      3. What is the sponsoring organization?
      4. Who is the publisher?
   B. The Editorial Board
      1. Instantly recognizable names?
      2. Specializations and magnitude of reputations?
      3. Range of coverage?
      4. Interdisciplinary?
      5. Ideological/political/methodological orientation?
      6. Evidence of a coterie or "closed" network?
      7. Gender distribution?
      8. Regional/institutional preferences?
      9. Big names for "window dressing"?
      10. Special categories/ staff?
   C. Submission Information
      1. General considerations:
         a. juried?
         b. author-anonymous ("blind")?
         c. letter of inquiry or mss.?
         d. statement of non-multiple submission required?
         e. membership in association/institution required?
         f. solicited works only?
         g. where indexed?
         h. who gets the copyright?
      2. Manuscript requirements
         a. style manual
            i must send for journal's own?
            ii. prefers which standard versions?
            iii. particular edition?

      b. specific requests for format
        i. placement of notes?
        ii. list of works cited?
        iii. data presentation?
        iv. margins and line spacing?
      c. additional particulars
        i. number of copies?
        ii. types of copies?
        iii. machine ready/ compatibility?
        iv. SASE or nonreturnable?
        v. abstract?
        vi. cover letter?
        vii. length?
        viii. language/quotation requirements?
        ix. illustrations/tables permitted?
  3. Special journal issues?
    a. accessibility of announcement?
    b. amount of lead time (before deadlines)?
    c. topic/submissions requirements?
    d. guest editor(s)?
    e. connection with conference, other events?
  4. What's in it for the author?
    a. free copies of journal?
    b. offsets of article?
III. The Table of Contents: What's There (And What's Not)
  A. Trends: Checking the Last Several Issues
    1. Strictly canonical or innovative?
    2. Recurrent topical/textual preferences?
    3. Predominant national/regional focus?
    4. Trends in gender of authors accepted?
    5. Theoretical/critical preferences?
    6. Favors interdisciplinary approaches?
  C. Percentage of the "Other"
    1. Scholarly: book reviews, notes, translations?
    2. Creative writing?
    3. Professional announcements
      a. categories represented?
      b. easy to find? clearly presented?
    4. Advertisements?
      a. who's advertising?
      b. what's being advertised?

IV. The Articles Themselves: Discovering the "Norm"
    A. General parameters of length?
    B. Average number of notes?
    C. Implicit expectations of structure, approach?
    D. Tone?
V. Protecting Yourself
    A. READ ALL INFORMATION *CAREFULLY*
    B. Follow Submission Instructions Scrupulously
    C. Keep Accurate and Up-to-date Records
        1. Retain copies of *all* work/information submitted
        2. Maintain current files on what, where, when submitted, and to whom
        3 Record any contact by telephone, modem, etc.

Interpreting the Information You Have Gathered

The assessment sheet is designed to help you gather information more or less explicitly stated in the journal itself. However, in order to make an adequate assessment you must also figure out how to "read" or interpret this information, thereby discovering the journal's implicit content. This often elusive but significant aspect of the journal is a major indicator of the publication's relative value, "rank," or "weight."

While the ranking of journals in certain disciplines is unambiguous, in others it is murky at best. Armed with the information you have gathered from the journal itself and from the appropriate directory of periodicals, you should be able to discern, at the very least, the basic level or rank to which the journal you are considering belongs. You can then fine-tune your judgment as you gather experience and input from other people. Since you are probably just starting out, however, you should pay close attention to the evidence provided in the following categories:

1. Background information: editorial personnel, year first published, sponsoring organization. Overall, the bigger the names, the longer it's been around, and the larger or more prestigious its constituency, the greater the reputation and perceived value of the journal. Top-ranking journals can have very impressive pedigrees, as the following examples illustrate: *Philosophical Review*, founded in 1892, sponsored by Cornell University; *PMLA*, 1884, Modern Language Association of America; *Psychological Bulletin*, 1904, American Psychological Association.

2. Subscription information: circulation, publisher. These categories indicate the level of institutional acceptance and diffusion of the journal. Although the *MLA Directory of Periodicals* indicates that circulation figures for journals in the area of literatures and languages are generally small, with over one-third of them below the 1,000 mark, the *PMLA* itself has a circulation of 32,000. *Child Development*, published by the University of Chicago Press, has a circulation of 8,500, while another periodical put out by the same press, *Signs: Journal of Women in Culture and Society*, is at 7,500.

3. Submission requirements. This is perhaps the most important category of all, for it is through the information presented here that you will be able to discern just how rigorous that journal's publication process really is.

Restrictions on contributors. If publication is contingent on the contributors' belonging to a certain association, society, or institution, then the journal may be perceived at a somewhat lower rank than others. Because it has the agenda of furthering only its own, it will likely be viewed as a not-too-critical organ for "in-house" advancement or as one practicing favoritism.

Number of reviewers. This figure is *particularly important*, because it indicates whether or not the journal is "juried" or peer reviewed. A peer-reviewed publication is especially desirable for several reasons: the greater the number of reviewers the harder it is for them to reach a consensus and, therefore, the more stringent the criteria for acceptance. In addition, since peer reviewers are usually experts in the field of that particular article, their judgment about it carries particular weight.

Articles/Book Reviews/Notes submitted per year. The numbers here are singularly revealing of the "popularity" or relative worth of the journal: the greater its significance to the discipline, the greater its recognition factor, and the more professionals seek—and need—to publish there.

Articles/Book Reviews/Notes published per year. The relationship of these numbers to the number of submissions provides you not only with a realistic idea of your own odds for success, but with an insight into the journal's eminence as well. Perhaps ironically, the fewer works a journal publishes, the more eager people seem to publish there: the smaller the acceptance rate, the more competition published pieces have had to beat out; the more articles they successfully surpass, the higher their assumed quality and, therefore, their prestige. For example, a top-ranked journal like the *PMLA* publishes only 24 of the some 500 articles it receives every year, an acceptance rate of only 4.8 percent; the *Philosophical Review* accepts some 15 out of 425, a rate just over 3.5 percent. While such odds are inescapably daunting, they may nonetheless be worth chancing. The "free" professional feedback such an apparatus may provide can greatly improve your article. <u>An acceptance in one of these can make your career.</u>

4. Instructions to submitters. An author-anonymous or "blind" submission policy is always valued more highly than one that lets reviewers know whose work they're reading; the reasons for this are self-evident. As a graduate student you may especially appreciate this policy, for it places you, an unknown, on "equal" footing with the "names" in your field. It also protects your identity, in case you submit something prematurely that you hope won't be remembered by others.

5. Scope or mission. Most journals state their focal interests and how these fit into their discipline or vision of their own larger purpose. A mission statement helps you identify the agenda of the specific journal and the values it seeks to promote. Sometimes, however, the journal will just let its name speak for itself; this can mean the editors perceive the discipline in very open terms and encourage submissions from a variety of fields and perspectives within that discipline. However, make sure this assumption is correct *before* you send your work in by taking a look at the contents of several recent issues. The books reviewed, the languages accepted, the topics discussed, and the methodologies applied are all good clues to the journal's perception of the discipline, as well as to its position and vocation within that larger frame of reference.

Practical aids such as the assessment sheet and your interpretation of the information you gather can provide the basis of an informed, productive decision for your submission. *In no way, however, should they be construed as a sure-fire "prescription" guaranteeing publication.* They are merely tools to apply on your search for the right journal. You may disagree with or disregard altogether the conclusions you reach after using them—the choices are always your own.

Regardless of the methods you use, the assessment process may offer results and choices you did not foresee. The following sample of one student's assessment of journals and the conclusion to which the process led is an example of this kind of unexpected development.

Applied Methodology: Sample Literary Journals Report

A graduate student

Subject: Late 19th-century American fiction.

Material: Revised seminar paper on American southern writer Kate Chopin's novel *The Awakening* and several of her short stories.

Target: Journals in American Literature—general coverage of American literature; 19th-century/late 19th-century literature; literary realism. Also, journals in women's studies.

Method: 1) Check my own bibliography for the paper I wrote for the journals that published the articles I cited. Obviously, these journals are receptive to my subject matter.

2) Check the notes in the articles I cited or used for research to find the journals to which those authors referred.

3) Check the regular sources for topical publications under the standard headings, e.g., the *MLA Directory of Periodicals*, to find other likely journals for my preliminary list of target journals and to inform myself about the requirements, publication history, acceptance ratio, and turnaround time of each. This preliminary list consists of the following titles: *American Literature, American Quarterly, Studies in Short Fiction, Studies in American Fiction, Kenyon Review, Southern Literary Journal, Studies in Literary Imagination, Studies in the Novel, American Literary Realism, Women and Literature*, and *Women's Studies*.

Assessment Process: An initial look at some of the journals' tables of contents narrows the field considerably. For example, I discover the following:

American Literature is a quarterly housed at Duke University and published by the MLA, meaning it is a top journal. On its cover it self-describes as "A Journal of Literary History, Criticism, and Bibliography . . . Notes, Book Reviews, Brief Mention, Current Bibliography." In other words, it prints materials in a variety of lengths and formats. In Volume 60, No. 2 of May 1988, there are articles on Edgar Allan Poe, Emily Dickinson, Robert Frost, and Marianne Moore; that means an article on Kate Chopin would fit into its all-inclusive period and genre coverage. Nine men and one woman serve on the Board of Editors. Though I lack inside information and can therefore conclude no particular gender bias from that fact, I can note that women are even more underrepresented on the board than they are in the academic departments from which the members are drawn; these include Duke, Harvard, SUNY Buffalo, UCLA, the University of Kentucky, the University of Virginia, NYU, and Dartmouth. The sample essay I read from the journal was encouraging in terms of receptivity: "Emily Dickinson's Renunciations and Anorexia Nervosa," by Heather Thomas, 205–225. I note she explains right off what her article will accomplish, that she writes in the first person, and that she uses no jargon.

American Literary Realism 1870–1910, published three times a year out of the University of New Mexico, is substantial but not as thick as *American Literature*. Obvious from both its title and editorial blurb is its more narrowly defined purview: "Criticism, Bibliography, Reviews." In Volume 20, No. 1 of Fall 1987, I note that the Board of Editors was composed of ten men and three women from campuses such as Duke, UC Davis, the University of Missouri, SUNY, Texas A&M. A sample essay, "Monomyth Structure in *The Red Badge of Courage*" by Michael Schneider of the University of Pittsburgh, 45–53, addresses the problem of the novel's ending read via the work of mythographer Joseph Campbell, indicating a receptivity to interdisciplinary approaches. More a close reading than a theoretical piece, the article nonetheless contains many long notes, as do others in the issue.

American Quarterly, published by the American Studies Association and Johns Hopkins University Press, states its goal is to ". . . aid in giving sense of direction to studies of American culture, past and present." The journal is "concerned with relations of American life to the entire American scene and world society." The Board of Editors is unusually large, with the editor-in-chief from the Smithsonian Institute. A sample essay is "The Social and Political Base of Millenial Literature in Late Eighteenth-Century America," 378–393. The author, a history professor from UCLA, uses forty-two notes.

Conclusions:

Of the three journals discussed here, the one likeliest target for my paper is *American Literary Realism*. It specializes in the subject matter of my essay; in contrast, my topic is much too specialized for *American Quarterly*. *American Literature* is highly competitive, and though I might benefit by readers' comments and criticism, my chances of placing my article there are very slim.

The end result of this process of pinpointing placements was that I did not submit the article at all: not because there was no place for it, but because I did not feel that it was ready to go out. In looking it over closely during revision, I realized that, while it was excellent as a seminar survey of contemporary criticism of Chopin's work, the original thinking and interpretation that are the core of a professional piece were still missing. I hadn't yet figured out precisely what it was *I* wanted to say about the text.

Making Final Decisions

By taking the time to assess journals, *whether or not you actually decide to send out that particular work*, you are gaining knowledge about and experience in the demands and expectations of your profession. You are, at the same time, assessing your own unique configuration of abilities, limitations, and desires. As another student observed after going through the assessment process:

> Although my paper was inspired and well-written, it seemed considerably undernourished—even anorexic—in comparison to articles in well-known professional journals; mine would have to be fleshed out considerably to become competitive on that level. But I only came to this realization after spending time in the stacks. So what have I gained from those hours perusing periodicals? I have gained the knowledge that, if I want my paper to get published, I owe it to myself and to my profession to work and rework it until it makes the kind of contribution I want it to make. And, although it's "back to the drawing board" for now, I know that I've finally had the courage to start an enduring, mutually formative relationship with a vital element of my field, and of my professional life.

In a sense, when you go through this twofold process of assessing your work and the journals appropriate for its appearance in print, you are doing much the same thing peer reviewers do when they receive a submission to the journal for which they read. Originality, significance, clarity, professionalism—all of these represent some of the criteria that will be applied to your work. In addition, the "fit" between your intended contribution and the journal—its expected audience, stated mission, implicit and explicit standards and expectations—will also be judged before the journal decides whether to accept it. By subjecting your work to a newly aware critical eye and by carefully weighing options so as to enhance its chances for acceptance, you have completed the preliminary stages of your publication efforts. Last-minute revisions, rationalizing excuses, and outright procrastination must be placed firmly aside; your work is now ready for submission.

4

Submitting Your Work

Submission From the Receiver's Point of View

When all the preparatory work has been done—networking, revising, designating journals—you're on your own in determining that your article is finally ready to be mailed. Because the impetus is strong to seal the envelope and ship it out, this is an important time to step back from your writing.

In submitting your work, you are the initiator of a professional relationship with people who are usually strangers and typically anonymous. What you mail out will be received by people who generally don't get paid for the hours of reading and editing they do. At tenure and promotion time, reading or editing for journals is rated lower than publication, even in the same journal—ironic when you consider that the editor and readers largely determine the quality of what they print (the rest is determined by the quality of what they receive). The writer of the published article gets the credit even if an editor has worked with him or her on an essay for months or years.

At the same time, readers and editors have their own teaching, committee assignments, and research; their own publication credits to work toward; and their own graduate students who see themselves as the professors' primary responsibility. Editors who bargain with academic bureaucracies for funding and time off from teaching to produce the journal are also judged by those bureaucracies. They are expected to assemble a quality journal and see that it is distributed according to schedule. And not all readers are prompt or careful when they accept articles to review for journals, compounding the complications. You are wise, therefore, to make yourself as easy as possible for the editors and readers to work with; this does not mean mindless agreement, but that you submit your work in a professional manner, that you make the revisions you agree to, and that you meet your deadlines.

One of the contributors to *The Grad Student's Guide to Getting Published* commented to us that a fine article would be accepted even if it had been written with a banana. Perhaps—but perhaps not. You'd lose months before your pungent article was returned, as compared to the couple of hours you'd have spent proofing and reprinting your work in the first place.

Still, the banana remark does serve as an overall reminder to lighten up and not to become overly perfectionist. After all, even a banana-stained paper has a better chance of getting published than one that has never been mailed. Graduate students sabotage themselves more often by not even trying to get published than by making mistakes along the way.

As a concrete example of the range of response in the submission process, you will find in this chapter samples of editors' and readers' reports about journal articles received. Included are letters of acceptance, suggestions for revision, and, of course, rejection slips—some excoriating, others vague, a few helpful, and some merely form letters. Chapter Six contains sample correspondence illustrating stages in the publication process of a book. We have used *The Grad Student's Guide to Getting Published* as an example: the proposal guidelines we followed, the cover letter we sent to our targeted publishers, and some sample responses.

The sooner you send your material out, the sooner you'll get your first rejection slip and, with it, the first layer of thick hide required to persevere in the impersonal world of the written word. The sooner, too, you'll get your first acceptance.

The contributors to this book unanimously recommend that you not let rejections deter you from resubmitting your work. However, if rejections are accompanied by excerpts from readers' reports on your article, you should take note of the criticisms and, if you feel they are justified, adjust your work before resubmitting. If the comments make you wish you had never had the temerity to think you were capable of scholarship, be assured your reaction is normal. Only if the criticisms truly seem to indicate your article is worthless should you consider not sending it out again. Serious writers have a list of backup journals in mind, so that rejection does not stall the process of resubmission.

On the topic of being stalled, how long is long enough to wait for a response to your submission? Find out the stated response time for your selected journal by looking the information up in the library or by getting a reference librarian to help you. Once you submit to that journal, you agree to wait that period of time, so wait, but keep a record. Once the time has passed, write politely and provide a specific target date for you to follow up by phone if you still have not heard; three weeks to a month is standard. If no one writes or answers the phone, send another letter informing the editor that if you do not have a response within, say, two weeks, you will withdraw your manuscript and submit it elsewhere. Then you are free to do so.

In this chapter, professors who evaluate articles for journals in French, sociology, and literature speak from the perspective of those who receive your work. Conflicting attitudes toward certain kinds of publications, such as book reviews, have been left in these transcribed interviews so that each reader of *The Grad Student's Guide to Getting Published* can apply the information and advice to his or her own particular opportunities and goals. These conflicting opinions also realistically represent to the reader that academic publishing is not monolithic; just as there are different institutional expectations, there are differences according to individual specialties, interests, and temperaments.

Finally, excerpts are presented from the City University of New York's booklet *Publishing in the Academy*, written and edited by Professor Joan Baum, who in her faculty development seminars counsels sophistication in sending out your work.

Writing for and Submitting to Academic Journals

ROBERT GRIFFIN
Professor of French and Classics
UC Riverside
Assistant Editor, *French Forum* and *French Review*

To tell you how I begin the process of placing my own articles, why don't we create a hypothetical case?

Let's say I want to write on the influence of a certain work of Musset on Baudelaire. This is a restricted area: it's in French; it's nineteenth-century, with maybe a spillover of Romanticism into Symbolism or something like that. My first step is to look under the appropriate headings in the Modern Language Association's *Directory of Periodicals*. Then, to eliminate inappropriate journals, I *absolutely* have to go to the stacks to check the actual issues; that would be my second step. For example, I look into one journal because its name is *Nineteenth Century Studies*. I look through a couple of issues of the journal and find that it's about ninety percent British and American literature. Since I would clearly be working against their focus, the odds would be considerably against me. I won't waste my or the journal's time by sending my work there.

Let's consider another facet of the hypothetical article: say it refers to a number of examples or texts that are visual, and I want to include plates or illustrations. Now, if I send it to a journal that never includes any visual material, such as plates or illustrations, the editors will have to reject my article *even if they love it*, for they don't have the budget or facilities to accept it. I have to watch for that.

Or here's another aspect: say I'm writing something that has a cross-disciplinary, multidimensional approach. Logically I would omit, then, the fairly standard or traditional places because they might not know what to do with an article that is outside their normal bailiwick. I might look at something more innovative and nontraditional, like *Diacritics* or *Modern Language Notes*, or something with a more theoretical or interdisciplinary bent.

In addition, I would want to be aware that certain journals, like *Modern Language Notes*, tend to commission, that is, solicit a lot of their material and are thus much less receptive to unsolicited submissions. Some journals will state this on their inside cover; so I will look there. That way I save myself a lot of time and frustration.

I decide that a journal is not for me, so I pick out another one, one that deals with nineteenth-century French studies; for instance, *Studies in Romanticism*. But let's say my article is some forty pages long. I then go to that journal and look at a few issues. I notice their longest article is only twelve pages long, in print. That means I'm going to have to cut my article in half. Or I'm going to have to forget about placing it there.

Then I notice a similar journal, one that tends to publish lengthy articles. I probably would submit there first because my work would appear as I conceived it. However, I'd also be working on some other, shorter versions of that same material so I could ship them elsewhere.

That's more or less how I function as a submitter; now let me tell you how I read submissions as a member of the editorial boards of *French Forum* and *French Review*.

A very small percentage of articles is accepted: one out of twelve or thirteen for both *French Review* and *French Forum*. That's not a very high acceptance ratio, especially if you're submitting the paper about which your professor enthusiastically said, "This should be published."

One point to remember about the low acceptance ratio is that it cuts both ways. In a positive sense, it means that if you break into a certain journal, say, the *Publications of the Modern Language Association of America (PMLA)*, most people know that you have successfully run a very arduous kind of gamut. So getting into certain mainstream journals is very much to your credit. When you interview for teaching positions, the university will always check out the kinds of journals by which you have been accepted. Later on, however, I think just bulk and numbers sort of take over, so that if you're concerned with advancing your career and obtaining some stability, I would probably recommend to you to go for publication, period. I think it's more important if you're talking about progression through a career just to have some articles, in order to let people know you know what the givens are in this profession.

Publication is the normal expectation anywhere you go. People can always forgive you for not being selective in your choice of journals later on in your career.

On the more negative side, however, no matter where you submit, you want to be prepared for the possibility of rejection. You may not have your article placed the first, third, fifth, or even seventh time around, but that's how the odds work. You should have no fear whatsoever about resubmitting. In a lot of cases, you maybe didn't hit the journal's needs right, or maybe you didn't get the right reader—it's a very subjective thing.

Before I submit a manuscript, I'll have a short list of, say, half a dozen places. I'll have envelopes already made up for them, so that as soon as I have something ready, I'll just ship it right out. If I've gotten a fast reader, I'll be able to quickly submit the piece to the next journal. The last thing you want to do is to dwell on a lack of systematic success.

You should also know that there's almost no relationship between the number of the journal down the line that finally accepts the piece and the article's quality. There are simply too many factors to consider. When you submit to an established journal, you have to have a really thick skin. And you have to hope that you get the kind of reader who will help you out.

It's important that you realize that, while you may be up against a fairly well-organized apparatus, the judgments made are local and subjective and are sometimes thoroughly capricious. For both *French Forum* and *French Review*, which accept about one out of a dozen, it's not that we receive twelve excellent manuscripts, and we members of the editorial board simply pick one for publication for some particular reason. That's not the way it goes at all.

I find that out of the hypothetical dozen, at least half are sloppy and contain things I just wouldn't accept. For example, a journal typically states that it wants double spacing on submissions; one manuscript will be single spaced. Or suppose the journal has certain standards on notes, on quotations, on margins, on the kind of type—dot matrix is often not desired, for example. Papers that don't follow the stated format will be tossed aside. Also, many people submit with terrible typos, or crossings out, and so on. These are all things that obviously detract from the reader's impression of the piece, and yet a large percentage of people continue to submit such shoddy work.

Remember, submitting your article is not unlike presenting a package in the advertising world; you want to send out a neat, clean, sharp-looking copy. At first blush, you want to convince the reader you know at least the basic rules of the game, that you know how to format journal notes, to proofread, and so on.

Thank God for the spell checker on most word processing programs! It makes the copy a lot neater; it helps. Say you submit a tremendous article, and it has three spelling errors; readers aren't going to reject it because of that. But the odds are that if you *are* to write a great article, you won't have those spelling errors. Careless errors like that, on a scale of 100, might each take one point off. They irritate readers after a while. If the person hasn't done any proofreading, my comments tend to become increasingly acerbic as I go along. You should at least reread your own work before sending it to me—that's the least I expect. It's out of line for you to be taking my time if you haven't even given me your best work.

So out of the dozen, say, I can immediately discard a half dozen. Of the rest, three or four are basically unrevised term papers. In some cases, I wouldn't even have accepted them as sophomore papers, much less graduate-level work.

In those seminar papers you write, you'll often find there's a kernel of something really worthwhile, something you can develop into a good essay. But first you have to get rid of the inappropriate, course-oriented apparatus. If *you* don't take the survey or background information out, someone else will suggest you do. It is best to learn how to edit your essays early in your career.

If I were a graduate student, I would certainly not hesitate to ask colleagues or staff members, "Please read this because I'm thinking of submitting it to a journal. I would appreciate it if you would read it in that light." There are many faculty members both willing and qualified to help. It's actually a good idea for you to approach them.

Let's assume you've revised your seminar paper conscientiously, you've had it read by someone experienced, you've checked your journal's submission requirements and proofread carefully. Now you send your article, and wonder what happens.

As a reader, any time I read a journal article, I want to give the author as dead-honest a response as I possibly can. If I think the article is a piece of crap, I won't say it as baldly as that, although a number of readers will. I'll try to issue that judgment backed up in as much detail as I can, pointing out flaws in presentation, in format, in spelling, in scholarship, or in whatever area it seems to me that the individual would actually profit from revising. I will take an afternoon to work with that anonymous individual.

Everyone's ego is on the line when doing virtually anything in the academic world—whether it's taking written exams, or orals, or going out into the big world to break into the publication rat race. If a reader is going to take issue with an article he or she reviews, I feel he or she should do it on a legitimate basis. Readers should let submitters know where the argument is weak or fails and prove they're wrong by citing the evidence. I'll recommend a particular study or article the author ought to know about, if I know of one, and I'll tell the author why it's important to know it to improve the article. I try to be helpful; that's all the more important when a reader is rejecting an article. That's when we really need to give the author a helpful, balanced view of his or her work.

Along with a journal's asking the two fundamental questions about any scholarship, "Is this a contributing idea?" and "Is it well-packaged?" most will ask the reader to provide some sort of a gradation in assessing the piece. The variations range from the most positive to the most negative. "Is this an outstanding contribution?" If the article is outstanding, assessment is pretty much over. But on the next level down is the question, "Is it acceptable or passable?" That would mean the essay is no great shakes, but I as a reader would ultimately come down on the side of publishing it, whenever space is available. "Is it in need of revision?" A "yes" here means I'd have to decide what kind and how much revision and then balance considerations of time and effort. "Should it be submitted elsewhere? If so, please name a journal," is a really helpful question for the submitter. And then, of course, there's the most negative assessment, "Trash it."

I have learned that I can basically tell what my reaction is going to be to virtually any article submitted to me after reading a single page. The first page tells me, in a sense, the whole story. My questions are: "Does this person know how to write? Does this person know how to formulate an argument? Is he or she basically on top of the field?" For the most part, I can tell after reading the first page what's going to happen for the balance of the article. It's very rare that I'm surprised or change my mind on that.

Usually, the reader's reaction has nothing to do with the question, "Does this upset any party lines? Does it offend me personally?" Rather, readers ask, "Does this person know how to deliver a consistent, concise, readable argument?"

What I like is the kind of opening sentence that is really well crafted, so I get an idea of the scope and importance of the particular subject. Even if the writer hasn't yet gotten into the subject itself, I need to feel a certain breadth in the endeavor. You know, "It was the best of times, it was the worst of times": something that would have some kind of ring to it. But *not*, for heaven's sake, *not* something like: "In this article I will attempt to prove...." Like anyone else, what I don't like is "dissertationese." For example, "And in conclusion we can say the following three things...." This is juvenile and must be avoided at all costs! Personally, I find it often helps to write the opening after I've written the article.

I find the most stimulating submissions are the ones that make me think, that make me say, "Well, what about something or other? What about this and this?" What I'm *not* looking for is the article that makes me say, "You know, I've always thought that." I *do* want something that will really get me, that will keep me awake for the afternoon. Good writing does that.

Maybe in four or five percent of the cases I'll get that "Outstanding!" reaction. Most of the time the article is okay; I tend to grade it as passable. In these cases I generally like the author to attend to three or four changes, and sometimes I will even say that I don't need to see it after these are done—I just let the authors take my suggestions under advisement. Usually, however, I want to see how well the author has done with the changes that I have recommended. Has the author read and understood my drift? Were my recommendations seen as merely cosmetic changes, or did the author really rethink what I considered to be a flawed part of the argument? I must say that I'm usually not happy when I get back an article that I've seen before, for the reason that most people do not attempt any kind of substantive change. Yet the fact is that rewriting does help if you approach it in the right spirit.

I've noticed there's an increased tendency these days to cultivate a casualness in style and tone and to make writing as intellectually conversational as possible. The desire is to make academic prose more readable, more "lifelike." A touch of humor is increasingly acceptable, though this may be more true of the humanities than of the social sciences.

If you look at the journal's masthead, at the names of assistant or associate editors, the names and specialties will represent both the fields addressed by the journal, and the kind of readership the journal aims to attract. If you know—or can ask and find out— what areas the journal's board members specialize in, you can fairly accurately predict who will be reading your submission. To some extent, you can tailor your article. For instance, *French Review* and

French Forum will send me articles focusing on the period of my specialty, the Renaissance, and, since I have a book out on Flaubert, I will occasionally be sent articles dealing with the nineteenth century.

Besides tone and usage, the question of notes comes up often. Selectivity is crucial, because ill-conceived footnotes are of no help to the reader whatsoever. Nor are they of much help to the writer aiming for professional publication. Here's a firsthand example: A student submitted an essay that began with his thesis statement. The thesis statement—one sentence long—ended with a footnote. Footnote one listed a dozen articles which, unfortunately, were presented in no particular order: not chronological, not alphabetical, not in terms of their treatments of the subject matter of the essay. What the writer was trying to tell me with this footnote was, "See, I've done my homework. I've done all of the bibliographical research. I've gone to the stacks and looked through all these journals." But a good editor will say, "Look, I don't really see the point in your footnote. What is the list of sources supposed to add to your argument?" That careful criticism speaks well for the editorial eye. *Very* rarely will a reader say, "Maybe it's time to put a footnote here!" Unlike seminar professors, editors of journals assume that you know the secondary material. Would you yourself find it effective when reading along to be distracted by a footnote with nothing in it but journal information? Of course not, and most other people don't either. So avoid the catch-all approach. Clearly, there has to be some real connection between the citation and what you're trying to prove; otherwise a footnote or a name is idle.

In fact, in many of the humanities there's increasingly a tendency to get away from footnoting. In the old days, there may have been more commentary in the footnotes than in the main text, but not any more. Most people who read journal articles don't like gratuitous footnotes. When I make suggestions for revision, I rarely say, "This needs more footnotes." But in many cases I'll say, "You need to pare these notes to a workable minimum."

You can pare by being aware of what is not likely to be superceded in the field and can therefore be used in your footnote as an easily recognizable reference point. You can also use footnotes to convey what is really hot and how whatever it is is important to your own work. I would advise you to be very discriminating. Remember that the journal, and your article, must make some kind of contribution to the field.

Another tough question is that of length, for you often don't really know how long something should be. How short is too short, and how long is too long? I think *in general* fifteen to thirty typed pages is a decent rule of thumb. Anything beyond thirty pages requires a format different from that of most journals or will require publication in some specialized manner, such as a featured essay. Frequently editors will commission people to do longer articles, but an unsolicited submission should be shorter. For American journals, twenty pages of print is fairly long.

In European journals, considerations such as length are politicized or economic. In European publications, you can usually get away with a longer article than you could in an American one. That's very handy for people in certain disciplines, like comparative literature, who need to establish international reputations. The university assumes that all people publish in the United States by preference, so initially one tends to establish a national reputation and then an international one. Yet it's often easier to establish one's reputation in Europe than it is in the United States because of the different standards. So you just might want to consider reversing the traditional process, going from international journals to national ones. The exceptions to the European trend are journals in the U.K., which tend to have an old-fashioned—and I mean this in the good sense—attitude towards scholarship. It's a kind of a no-nonsense attitude that I personally like a lot. They're rather disgusted with this whole elaborate display of erudition, and so on. I find their editors to be the toughest editors of all.

I often use business and production analogies when I talk about academic publishing. Perhaps that's because I tend to think of it as a kind of industry. In a way it is, with all the conditions, and sometimes the mean-spiritedness, of dealing in a commodity—it's a commodity exchange. If you don't look at publishing this way, you might assume that having a good idea will magically result in publication—but that's just not how it goes.

As in industry, there's often not much conscience involved. However, there are rules submitters must accept. Multiple submission of journal articles is *really* taboo. This is changing in other forms of publishing, but you shouldn't submit copies of the same article to six different journals at the same time. What if all six accept? What do you do then? But while there are rules for you, editors of journals (and this applies to presses as well) sometimes don't seem to care about your particular needs. This is where academic publishing really is tough and often unfair, especially when you have tenure or an important promotion hanging in the balance.

One tends to make the assumption that the longer the journal holds an article, the better the prospects are for publication. Contrary to popular opinion, that's often not the case. Sometimes a long waiting period means the journal's editorial process is in disarray. Fast is always best. The sooner you have a response, whether positive or negative, the sooner you can decide what the next step is for all of that hard work.

Publishing is a deadly serious kind of thing, so it's understandable that you want to know everything you possibly can about it. Sooner or later, you develop a kind of survival technique. Part of that comes from experience, part from temperament, part from having some measure of success. No matter what, though, you won't be published unless you get your ideas out there as often as necessary, and you won't succeed unless you submit your work in the most professional form possible.

Writing to Publish in Sociology

An Interview with JONATHAN TURNER
Professor of Sociology
UC Riverside
Reader for *Social Forces*

Q: Would you describe a few of the journals in sociology?

Turner: There is an enormous number, with over 200 published in the United States alone. Most are general, taking a wide mix of articles. A good many, however, are oriented to all the different specialties that constitute sociology. They all pretty much tend to prefer data based articles. Theoretical articles are difficult to get published unless you have a reputation in theory.

It's very important to recognize the hierarchy. Three high-prestige journals are the *American Journal of Sociology (AJS)*, the *American Sociological Review (ASR)*, and the regional journal *Social Forces*. After that, the status of journals drops to a significant degree, and their relative position becomes much more difficult to sort out. The other three regional journals—*Sociological Perspectives*, *Sociological Quarterly*, and *Sociological Forum*, which is relatively new— are about equivalent. These are general journals. On par with those are a wide number of university journals in various specialty areas. *Social Problems* and the *Journal of Marriage and Family* are examples.

Q: Are all of these juried journals?
Turner: Yes. All journals of sociology have referees. At a minimum, they generally use two external readers. If there's a split vote, they get a third or fourth. In fact, I think one of the problems with journals of sociology is that the editors tend to be a conservative lot. They're so concerned with being democratic that they become somewhat shy about taking controversial articles. So when they get split reviews, their reaction is not to say, "This is going to excite a lot of people and get a lot of response." Instead, their reaction is, "Let's get two more reviews." And those tend to be split. And after a while, the editors tend to say, "Well, we don't want to publish this article because it's controversial." So articles that are a little bit deviant, a little bit outrageous, have a hard time landing in sociology journals.

Q: What's the ratio of acceptance for the major journals?
Turner: The top journals reject about 90 percent of the articles. The next level probably rejects about 75 to 80 percent. *ASR*, *AJS*, and *Social Forces* probably receive about 700 or 800 manuscripts a year. And the major regional journals probably receive 300 a year. With the specialty journals, it varies a lot—maybe just 75 to 150. When you get a field like demography, a specialty journal probably receives 700 articles a year. The *Journal of Marriage and Family* probably receives 700 a year. Getting an article in *ASR* and *AJS* really makes a difference in terms of visibility of those ideas because those journals have 5,000 to 8,000 readers while the rest of the journals have 1,500 to 2,000 readers. Graduate students shouldn't even try to crack into *ASR* unless their advisors are wildly enthusiastic.

If I were a graduate student, I would go to a second- or third-level specialty journal or a regional one. They're tough to crack too, but they're still objective.

Q: How did you come to be a reader for some of these journals?
Turner: Initially you are flattered when you're asked to read articles. If you do your work well, the word gets out. Editors are always looking for reviewers because many people either won't do it in a professional way or won't do it at all. Editors typically look for reviewers by checking who's cited in an article; then they send the submissions they've received to those people. Another way is

to approach young people who might consider it prestigious to be plugged into three different articles at the same time, though there's actually a good deal more work than there is prestige or recognition. There's a sucker born with every PhD.

Q: How would you describe the general quality of the ten or so articles you read a month for journals?

Turner: I would say a third are terrible, probably graduate student papers that are okay as term papers, but are not publishable. Another third have major problems, but they're salvageable—maybe not salvageable for a top-ranked journal, but somewhere there's a journal that will take the article if it's worked on. The other third are publishable, most with some revisions. Of these publishable articles, only ten or fifteen percent are publishable in the form in which they are originally submitted.

The quality of writing makes a big difference. We'd like to think it's just the quality of ideas, but that's not true. If an article's well written, whatever other qualities it has come out. If it's badly written, people lose patience trying to figure it out. It's very important to learn how to write in graduate school: you need to be able to express your ideas in a straightforward, worthwhile manner. If you do, you're much more likely to get your articles accepted.

Most bad articles wander all over the map. It's never clear what it is they're trying to do. Some just don't have anything to say. They've got bad data, or they've analyzed incorrectly. The authors don't know the rules of grammar, and they constantly use nonparallel constructions, or they use commas as conjunctions. They make fundamental mechanical errors that are embarrassing—people with PhDs who don't even know the rules of the language. Quite frankly, I lose patience with such articles.

The best articles have an interesting, relevant topic. They have focus. It's clear what the author is trying to do from the very beginning, and the author does it. Articles like that always get accepted, whether they're data articles, theoretical articles, or historical articles. The critical question in reviewing an article is, "Is there a point being made here? And is it being made in a parsimonious, succinct way, bringing in the relevant literatures or data?" You don't have to say all you know in one article, which is what graduate students try to do. You want to say everything you've learned, but then it's cutting, cutting, cutting that's the key.

And then after that, try to develop a nice, straightforward style in which you don't waste words. That's what the social science journals want. You'd be amazed at how difficult that is for many PhD scholars to do.

Q: Do people usually integrate readers' comments when they resubmit their work?

Turner: For the most part, authors try—although I just reviewed one that didn't. The reviewers who read it the first time read it again. All of us felt that the author had made such a perfunctory, mechanical effort to incorporate the comments of the reviewers that the article got rejected.

Q: What do you tell students who want to break into publishing by doing book reviews?

Turner: Book reviews don't count for anything in the publishing game. Sometimes young professors and students think they do, but unless you've had a lot of experience doing them, they take a tremendous amount of time. I limit myself to six a year. As a general way to break into publishing, it's about the worst way. I don't think it does anything except get your name around a bit.

Q: So what does count?

Turner: Publishing a regular article. In sociology, it's really critical these days that you have three or four articles published before you get your PhD. It didn't used to be that way twenty-five years ago, but the world's changed. The students who have published are always at an advantage.

Q: What's the role of conferences in getting published?

Turner: I don't think they really help you get published except indirectly. Going to conferences helps you become more professional. You get people's reactions to your papers, and you get over the initial hump of presenting your ideas in a public forum where you don't know anyone. That's very important because eventually you have to go on job interviews. The more times you can present your ideas in public away from your fellow students, the more those experiences will translate into sophisticated presentations.

Also, meetings can put you in contact with other people who are working on similar issues and problems. So much of getting published depends on networks; it's not just the simple process of submitting and having editors send out articles for review. That's certainly the central mechanism, but a lot of it is knowing editors, knowing when special issues are going to be published, knowing who's editing books—networking so the movers and shakers think of you. The way you start to build networks is going to meetings. You start very modestly in that you know only a few people at first; it's very intimidating. But over time, if you go to enough meetings, if you read enough papers, if you get identified with certain research traditions—you will build networks. Those networks will allow you to publish. That goes not only for graduate students but for new recipients of the PhD who don't have jobs yet.

I didn't go to meetings at all for the first five years of my career because I didn't feel I had anything to do or say. That was a mistake. Though attending conferences is a lonely game at first, there are always a lot of fellow graduate students you can huddle with. You don't have to sit around like a wallflower; there are always sessions to go to. Maybe your mentors can help you along or fellow former students or peers. Over time you develop new friends and network ties, and it gets easier and easier.

I think graduate students are encouraged at conferences. In fact, when you submit your paper, you simply state your name and the institution you're affiliated with; no one knows if you're a graduate student. Of course session organizers try to get big names because those attract people to their sessions. So, oftentimes, they phone around. Requesting papers that way goes against the idea of open submission, but it's done all the time. Short of using their networks, session organizers try to take the best and most interesting papers within the limits of their session. If the papers are written by graduate students, that's not a problem. The best place for graduate students to start submitting their work is to regional meetings and then work up to national ones.

Our association, the Sociological Association, actually has special graduate student sessions. But I don't think that's the way to begin. The same goes for publishing in graduate student journals. Such publications are almost discounted. If you've got a paper that you think is worth publishing, then go for a regular mainstream journal and try to read it as part of a regular conference session, too.

If you want to know about publishing, find out which people are publishing a lot, and talk to them. Those are the ones who know how it's done. Approach people like that in a very professional way, and pick their brains about publishing. Ask if they'll read a paper of yours that's in their particular area. That's perfectly legitimate; in fact, it's part of their job.

Q: Short of asking a professor point-blank, "How long has it been since your last article appeared?" how do you find out who's publishing?

Turner: First of all, a vitae is a sort of public record; ask to see the vitae of faculty in whom you are interested. Second, people at the university will know who in your department is actively publishing. Your career is best served by affiliating with people who have the most visibility. These are busy people who work hard. Yet most professors I know are quite eager to have good graduate students to work with, and they really try to help.

The key is to not let your anxieties and insecurities in graduate school take hold of you so that you gravitate toward the faculty that makes you more secure. It would be nice if you could get a high-voltage but also easy-going person to play all the roles for you from mentor to sponsor to counselor. But that's not always the case.

A lot of what I've just said is true for students in any discipline. The most important things a graduate student can do are to get to know the biggest names in the department, work with them, and try to publish with them. Also, write as many papers as possible. Doing all this is what will make for success in your discipline.

Some Words from the Editor's Perspective

An Interview with LARRY McCAFFERY
Professor of English and Comparative Literature
San Diego State University
Co-Editor of *Critique, Fiction International,*
and the *American Book Review;*
Guest Editor of the *Mississippi Review* and
the *Review of Contemporary Fiction*

Q: Let's say a graduate student wants to publish a piece on contemporary fiction and is considering *Critique.* What can be discerned from looking at the journal?

McCaffery: If you look through a number of back issues, you will see that the editors changed five years ago. Whereas *Critique* has always been significant in publishing articles about writers without established reputations, it used to be that, almost exclusively, the only kind of articles published were individual author essays, usually on individual books. *Critique* would have been the perfect place to submit an essay on, say, Russell Hoban before his novel *Riddley Walker* became well known. *Critique* was the first journal to publish essays on Donald Barthelme and John Barth and John Hawkes. With the change in editorship came a change in emphasis; we now prefer more comparative essays on a number of books and authors.

By way of contrast, *Contemporary Literature* prefers to publish articles on better-known authors. For example, if you had sent an essay about Russell Hoban to *Contemporary Literature* five or six years ago when Hoban was just starting to get a reputation after *Riddley Walker*, it would have been very unlikely that *Contemporary Literature* would have published it. You can see that from reading through the last few years' issues. In fact, if you are working on a paper about contemporary fiction, you will find there are only six or seven journals that specialize. Each has a different bias or slant.

As an editor of *Fiction International* and *Critique*, I would say it's immediately obvious from titles of the submissions that we would never publish at least fifty percent of the essays and pieces of fiction we get. If these authors had even looked at our magazine, they would never have sent their articles to us unless they were completely obtuse. For example, anybody who had looked at *Fiction International* would realize that the material we publish is about ninety percent nonrealism. Yet I would guess that at least fifty or sixty percent of fiction we receive for submission is traditional realism. These writers are wasting their time. They're going to lose at least three months while their work is just sitting here. When I was in graduate school, I wasted much time by sending essays off to journals that obviously would never publish them. Once again we return to the need to look carefully at the journal. Learning how to save time is crucial for graduate students.

Q: What is the evaluation procedure at *Critique*?

McCaffery: Most journals don't explain the editorial submission process; they just state the requirements for submission. *Critique* is a refereed journal, meaning the article is evaluated by peer specialists. Its editorial process is atypical in that you mail your article to the publisher, instead of to the editors. For *Critique*, the publisher is a big conglomerate in Washington, D.C. We've got about fifteen consulting editors or specialists on contemporary fiction who review for us. The publisher mails the submission to an appropriate consulting editor who reads it, makes recommendations, and then sends the article to one of the three editors.

We really do rely on the judgments of our consulting editors. For example, let's say I get an essay on Thomas Pynchon. I've read his books and have read some of the criticism, but I'm not an expert. Several of the people on *Critique*'s board are experts, and when they send me an analysis on, for example, a certain aspect of *Gravity's Rainbow*, I depend on their judgment because it's impossible for me to keep up on everything that's going on. If it were just I, I might look at the essay and think it's original, unaware that what the author is saying has become common knowledge for the last five years. So from the point of view of the journal's editor, consulting editors are crucial. From the consulting editor's point of view, reading for journals is an opportunity to keep up in the field and to know what people are writing about. Serving as a consulting editor for *Critique* looks good on a cv, too.

Q: As you said, the submission process for *Critique* is a little unusual because submissions go first to the publisher. More typically, the editors would receive the article first and look it over. If it's too short, too long, or just not right for the journal, it's rejected and it goes right back to the writer, although that's probably taken two or three months right there. If the essay passes that first screening, and a lot of articles don't, the editor would look at his or her list of readers and try to match up the article with the specialty areas of readers to do the review.

McCaffery: I've done a couple of reader reports for the *PMLA* in the last couple of months, and I think they do exactly what you describe. Somebody initially screens the manuscripts and rejects the ones that are obviously not suitable. Then they send the rest out for reader reports to specialists in the field. That's very common.

Q: What are readers looking for? What do their reports cover?
McCaffery: There are about six categories, among them: "Is this an original contribution to the field? Are the sources well documented? Is it stylistically acceptable?" When I get the essay back from the reader, I have a kind of schematic assessment in hand. There is also a space for specific comments by the reader, who usually writes a paragraph or two. Sometimes a reader will write a couple of pages.

When the consulting editor recommends revision, he or she usually writes a longer analysis. If I agree with the reader either to accept or reject, then I just send it back to the publisher of *Critique* who returns it to the submitter. But if the consulting editor recommends a revision and if I also recommend revision, then I usually write a letter to the writer. I also send along the consulting editor's comments, which are anonymous.

If you get a note from a journal saying, "We would like you to revise this," you should think long and hard before you say, "no." This request means they're definitely interested. My usual advice to submitters is to make the revisions. I loved it early on when I would get a revision request because I felt if I worked on the article, I would probably get it accepted. Usually that was the case.

After all, editors need good material. Basically when I'm asking the author to revise, what I'm saying is, "If you do this, it's likely we're going to publish your work." Or if I have more deeply divided feelings about the essay, I try to make that obvious. I'll say strongly, "We can't guarantee publication of this—there are some major problems you would have to address." On the other hand, revision can be a matter of minor changes. Let's say an article is an essay on Russell Hoban in which the writer is discussing something Hoban said in an interview. I might say, "You make a lot of speculations about this topic, but you should look more closely at the interviews and what is said."

Of course, you have to believe your revisions are actually going to be useful. You should realize that if an editor asks you to revise something along lines that you simply don't agree with—for example, if you're being asked to change your basic position—you gain little by making insincere revisions. It's very obvious to an editor when the revised article is resubmitted that the changes have been made specifically to please the editor.

Speaking now as an author, I have had my own problems with sending revisions to journals. The editors ask for revision; I send it to them. They reject it again. They ask for another revision; I send it back, and then it's not accepted. Much time can be wasted doing that. If you have any questions about the revisions, don't hesitate to consult with the editor.

But never argue with an editor about a rejection. That's just wasting your time and is really irritating. If you were to take the amount of time that editors have to spend on the phone every week with people who tell them why their article shouldn't have been rejected, the poor editors could bring out an extra edition every year.

Q: Some journals in the *MLA Directory of Periodicals* say they take up to a year to make a decision. In a case like that, what about sending a query letter before sending the entire manuscript?

McCaffery: I think that's one way to speed thing up immediately. You are more likely to get a sense from the editors about whether your article has a possibility. And anyway, when you have a journal that's going to take that length of time, you should think carefully before you submit your article unless you have a very strong feeling that it's likely to get published. For example, the *Paris Review* is notoriously slow. I've sent interviews to the *Paris Review* and haven't heard for a year—nothing. So now I always contact the *Paris Review* first to see if there is interest in my proposal.

Graduate students have got to think: "Do I want to attempt to place my article in a very prestigious journal that is going to take a long time to decide and that is unlikely to accept my work anyway?" Students have to get a sense of this. If you're working closely with a professor, talk to the professor and ask, "Honestly, is it likely that the *PMLA* is really going to seriously look at this, or should I try someplace else?"

Naturally, publications in prestigious journals look better on your cv than ones in completely unknown journals. On the other hand, if you can publish two or three articles in middle-line journals, that is pretty good. I think often graduate students would be better off trying to shoot for a journal where they have a realistic opportunity to publish. Again, getting advice from professors who have had experience submitting manuscripts to these journals is the best idea. When I was in graduate school I did this completely on my own, and I wasted ninety percent of my time.

In any of my graduate courses there may be two or three papers that I think actually could be revised and submitted for publication. When I get a graduate paper that looks to me as if it's potentially publishable, I tell the student, "If you're interested in pursuing this, come by my office and we'll talk." I do that routinely, because I think publishing is absolutely crucial; I've had a lot of success helping graduate students to get their work placed. My area of specialization, contemporary fiction, is one in which there are many opportunities to publish. Frequently, graduate students are in touch with new works and new authors who haven't been mined over and researched endlessly. Or a student might come up with a new application of post-structuralist theory to an older text. That kind of new perspective is ideal material for an article.

Q: Was there a publication course where you went to school?

McCaffery: There wasn't a course when I went to the University of Illinois. And I wouldn't have thought to go to a professor. And I now know, for example, that the cover letters I wrote were absurd.

The best cover letter is very simple. When I write cover letters now, I write, "Please consider the enclosed." I usually add a brief paragraph about my background and qualifications: that I'm a professor and I've published widely. Sometimes I send a very short cv.

In graduate school when I was submitting work I didn't have any publications, and I felt intimidated by the whole process. So when I wrote the cover letter, I would spend at least one long paragraph trying to explain and justify what I was trying to do. When editors get a letter like that, they suspect it has been written by a graduate student or by somebody who is not very professional. A graduate student's cover letter should be very direct: "Please consider the enclosed essay for publication." If the student has published, the publications can be mentioned. But instead of explaining what your article is all about and why you've written it, let the editors figure out what you're doing. If they need your help, then they're probably not going to want the essay anyway.

Q: Short of an article in a refereed journal, are there other forms of academic publishing you would recommend as helpful to graduate students looking for jobs?

McCaffery: Book reviews. When I was in graduate school, some of my first publications were review essays in literary journals, and some of them were good literary journals—Chicago Review, for example. I found that if I sent an unsolicited review essay that was not too long, say five to eight pages, to a literary journal that publishes reviews, then I might well find some success.

Q: And that helped you when you went out looking for university positions?

McCaffery: I'm certain that without publications I would not have gotten a job. I tell people who are going on for doctorates that if they want a job they are really not playing the game properly by spending time in graduate school just getting their PhD. They've got to be thinking publication. Otherwise they'll finish their PhD, maybe even do an outstanding job, but then have very little chance of getting a tenure-track position.

That's why I think this book is so significant. Graduate students must think ahead to what their cv is going to look like when they send it out for a job. Even one article helps, something on your vitae to separate you from everybody else who has straight As and outstanding recommendations from professors. It's very difficult to differentiate among all of these outstanding young graduate students. One way to do it is to note that they have already had success presenting papers or publishing articles.

Graduate students can sometimes get firsthand experience of journals right on their own campus. If you're at a university that publishes a journal in your field, you might talk to the professors who operate it. For example, at *Fiction International*, which is housed at San Diego State, we use graduate students to screen manuscripts. First of all, they get three units of graduate credit for their time and effort. Second, they get to find out how a journal runs. They can familiarize themselves with the whole process we've been talking about here. Third, they can feel gratified that they are actually making a significant contribution to something in which they believe. And fourth, it's fun.

Getting involved in some aspect of publishing is part of playing the cv game—learning how to market yourself and present yourself in the best possible way. There is much you can do in graduate school to gain experience and to get noticed when it comes time to look for a job. If you've been making a contribution by assisting in the production of a journal in your specialty, you should ask the professor you've been working with to write a letter of recommendation for you, perhaps emphasizing professional qualities such as your ability to evaluate manuscripts and your competence in a certain field. Of course, it's even better if you put these skills to use by publishing your own work early in your career.

Sample Responses to Journal and Conference Submissions

Some journals acknowledge receipt of your manuscript:

> We wish to acknowledge, with thanks, receipt of two copies of your essay, "Academic Anorexics."

We shall contact you as soon as our readers' reports are in. Usually, the evaluation takes about three months, although occasionally it takes a little longer.

Sincerely,
The Editors
The Post-prandial Review

Of course, you will have already marked or somehow noted in your file or calendar what the approximate date is that you expect a response from this journal based on the turnaround time listed in your specialty area's directory, index, or guide to periodicals.

A standardized form rejection reads more or less as follows:

Dear Professor Darwin,

Many thanks for allowing us to consider your essay "Back to Tortuga" for possible publication. Unfortunately, we must decline it. This need not be taken as reflecting on the quality of your manuscript, since editorial decisions are often based as much on consideration of topic and mode of approach as on overall quality.

Submissions are now being received at a rate that has finally made it impossible to supply individual comments with every manuscript returned. We hope you will understand.

The Editors
Evolutions

In another example, perhaps in an effort to be personable, the harried editor scrawled a note on the bottom of a standarized form. However, it took the recipient over an hour to figure out what this editor's personal note said. The message, in its offhandedness, was hardly worth the effort of deciphering. It read, "Though I enjoyed reading your concise little essay, unfortunately, it is not original enough to merit publication in *Valhalla*."

The following are typical of unforgettable rejections that need to be considered carefully, but not taken as death blows to either one's career or one's ego. Notably, both submissions were "A" seminar papers:

Dear Professor Angstman,

I am regretfully returning your essay, "The Classics in the Contemporary Classroom," as not suitable for publication in *Canon*. Your juxtapostion of plays by Van Hoot, Snodgrass, and Palooza seems to offer little new light on any of the three.

> Ronald McRite
> Editor
> *Canon*

Dear Professor Incognito,

I am returning your manuscript. Following is a comment from one of our readers:

> This piece is seriously flawed by a deeply clichéd vision of epic in general and *Sir Guthrie of Woodstock* in particular . . . . Over the last ten years or so, the major dynamic of criticism on this poem is to suggest its status as cultural critique and its portrayal of heroic ambivalence and questioning . . . .

Thank you for thinking of our journal.

> Sincerely,
> Milo Sprezzatura
> *Epic Studies*

Sometimes rejection is kinder:

Dear Professor Strange,

Unfortunately, the members of the editorial board decided your article "Egonomics" was not suitable for publication, much as they were impressed by the seriousness and thoughtfulness with which you broached your subject. Board members expressed the reservation that the paper tries to do too much in too short a space. As a rule, *Economics and Psychology* does not publish notes.

We wish you well with your project.

> Sincerely,
> Susan Normal
> Executive Editor

Of course, the author would have saved time in the first place by not submitting to a journal that doesn't publish notes.

Following is a sample from *Critique* of a reader's report. Note first the questions the journal asks its readers to assess. Compare these

HELDREF PUBLICATIONS

HELEN DWIGHT REID EDUCATIONAL FOUNDATION
1319 Eighteenth Street, N.W., Washington, D.C. 20036-1802
(202) 296-6267 ▪ (202) 296-5149 Fax ▪ HELDREF@ GWUVM.BITNET

Ms. # _____   Date sent _____

CRITIQUE Manuscript Review

Author _____

Title _____

_____

Consulting Editor _____ Recommendation _____ Date _____
                                (Accept, Reject, Ret. Rev.)

Executive Editor _____ Recommendation _____ Date _____
                                (Accept, Reject, Ret. Rev.)

•••

Please answer each of the questions, note any suggestions for revisions, and write an evaluation that expands at least one of the judgments.

1. Is the topic truly contemporary and does it fall within the scope of the journal? _____
2. Does the critique make an original contribution? _____
3. Are previous commentaries properly identified? _____
4. Is the problem well defined? _____
5. Does the writer present a convincing solution? _____
6. Is the critique of interest to teachers and students of English, American, and/or world literature? _____
7. Is the critique stylistically acceptable _____

SUGGESTED REVISIONS: (Use reverse side or another sheet if necessary.)

OVERALL EVALUATION: (Use reverse side or another sheet if necessary.)

to the questions asked of readers for academic presses such as Johns Hopkins and Princeton University, reprinted in Chapter Six. They are not dissimilar.

Acceptance letters vary, but typically they read something like this:

> We are pleased to inform you that your article "Parsley and Parsnips" has been accepted for publication. Our readers agreed that it makes a fine contribution to the study of alliteration. We have scheduled if for our Spring 19— issue, and will contact you as that time approaches.
>
> Thank you for thinking of our publication.
>
> Sincerely,
> The Editors
> *Figurative Language Journal*

As the publication date approaches, you will be sent page proofs to be proofread. Mistakes not caught at this time will most likely be printed. Since your name is on the article, you will want to check your essay carefully. If the copy or copies of the journal that you are to receive do not arrive on schedule, you should write the editor to see whether there has been a rescheduling of the piece or whether there might be some problem at the editorial end, such as staff turnover or shaky funding. Additionally, your reference librarian can run a computerized check on the journal.

For updating your cv or for other promotional purposes, you can note the progress of your submissions once you begin sending them out. Categorized as "Works in Progress," they will indicate to whoever is reading your cv that you are staying active. Once you have received a letter of acceptance, be sure to upgrade the article's status on your cv from "Work in Progress" to "Publication," according to its type (e.g., book review, refereed article, note, etc.) and to provide the projected publication date. Once the piece has been published, note the publication date and the number of pages.

Getting published even while in graduate school is a feat that sets you apart and serves you well in multiple ways, so don't be shy about it. The accomplishments of their graduate students reflect well on mentors, professors, departments, and colleges alike.

Similarly, having a paper accepted by a conference and reading it there is a feat. The correspondence regarding submissions to conference panels is much like that for submissions to journals. Though the review process may vary, for the larger, more prestigious conferences, more than one person usually reads your submission. A rejection might be a brief form letter, or it might include excerpts of readers' remarks.

The following form letter was used by a conference session organizer to reject papers submitted for her panel. Since, as the rejection concedes, the "Call for Papers" was unclear in the first place, a lot of time was wasted by a lot of people. However, this is not a perfect world, and the best response to such annoyances is to avoid causing them yourself. The rejection letter read:

> I was especially fascinated by your fine and provocative analysis. What I actually had in mind, however, was [something else]. I realize my session title was a bit ambiguous, and unfortunately there was no room for any description explanation on the poster.
>
> I am sure you will find a publisher for your piece . . . .

An acceptance will read something like this:

> We are pleased to inform you that your paper "Popeye as Role Model" has been accepted for presentation at the "Comical Heroes Conference."
>
> Your panel meets May 30 at 10:00 in the Lanai Room. More information is forthcoming.
>
> Sincerely,

Some conferences are well established and well organized, with highly polished introductions by the panel organizer. At other conferences you may be surprised to find you are expected to introduce yourself. Whether you address an audience of eight or eighty, your first experience will be memorable. You might wind up, as one of us did, peering out from the podium far from home on Mother's Day to read a feminist analysis of British fantasy to an audience of six strangers, five of them men, the sole woman being a new acquaintance whose English had proved so minimal at breakfast that she hadn't known the difference between "bread" and "butter." Other graduate students tell first-presentation stories of huge audiences and hellish questions, while others experience relatively placid inaugurations. Everyone has a first time; whether you have a second can depend on *your* ability to reflect upon and learn from experience—and on your sense of humor.

Conference presentations are valuable credits; if you are able to revise and publish what you have written to read for submission to a journal, so much the better. You will want to know whether the conference in which you participate offers publication through conference proceedings; these are not considered to be peer-reviewed since all papers delivered at the conference are published. If there are no conference proceedings, or if you would prefer to submit your work to a refereed journal, remember that you need to reconsider the presentation of your article before you send it to a journal. Just as a seminar paper requires revision before submission for publication, so does a spoken piece require revision.

Therefore, we close this chapter with a reminder of the basic elements of submission. The excerpts below are from *Publishing in the Academy*, a publication of the City University of New York's Professional Staff Congress, under the editorship of Joan Baum.

Preparing Your Manuscript

Excerpts from *Publishing in the Academy* by
JOAN BAUM
Professor of English, York College
City University of New York

It may sound simplistic to say this (it's what we tell our students), but good writing shows immediately in the letter of inquiry, the book prospectus, the introductory paragraph, or the abstract, so take extra time and ensure that first impressions—and the first page especially, speak well for you. Don't repeat the title, don't advertise what's coming, don't apologize or be overconfident. Tone is paramount: be academic, but don't sound that way.

The title shows first; spend time on it. It may be clever or cute, but if it is not clear and informative, forget it. Maybe it's time to avoid the trendy colon-and-subtitle as well. The abstract (if one is required) is next in importance. But even if the journal doesn't require one, an abstract is not a bad way of checking your thesis and rationale. A good abstract has active voice, tight diction, and the right proportional relation to the text. Keep in mind that publishers and editors ask readers on their editorial boards to comment on the importance of your subject, the significance of your thesis, its relation to current trends in the field, its intellectual and scholarly skill, and of course your writing.

... Then there's the matter of tone, significant enough to note here because numerous guest editors told us how annoyed readers get when key terms are unidentified or when theses are announced as "breakthrough." One helpful suggestion, we found, was to read a work aloud, to hear whether it had a commanding style without sounding blustering, or a conversational manner, without being loose (some people like to tape record). Over and over ... when asked to clarify a certain written remark, our colleagues made better sense when they told us what they were trying to do.

In the manuscript itself, double-check details that show you as a careful writer—pagination, typos, integration of text and charts in desired form. Editors ... indicated how put off referees are by sloppiness in these specifics, especially in the age of word processors (and no dot matrix copies, please). Make sure you submit the manuscript exactly as your intended journal or publication wants, which may not necessarily be the way it would appear in print.

Your competence will show in several important ways: in your references, one of the first places editors look to see if you are up-to-date and aware of trends; in your sensitivity to your intended audience; in your effective use of primary and secondary sources in your consideration of when to quote a source and when to paraphrase for the purpose of summary and evaluation; and finally in the overall impression you give of a logical rather than anecdotal presentation.

... Once a manuscript has been sent off, follow up with a letter or phone call if you haven't heard anything after the stated response time. The secret of assertiveness is to demonstrate interest and professional confidence, without sounding anxious or arrogant. Even if your manuscript has been kept an inordinate length of time, don't be insulted ... even the most well-intentioned editors or conference organizers inadvertently lose material or misplace it. Sometimes they get stuck depending upon unreliable readers, or in the throes of unusual personal or professional business, miss deadlines. Inquire. Who knows, some editor wavering in a decision about your piece may be favorably impressed by your polite persistence.

And what if you're rejected? Is it The End? One way to soften the blow is to take advantage of any suggestions to revise and resubmit. Some readers send on comments that, despite stating reasons for rejection, do contain helpful hints for revising. You may be urged to redo your article for the same journal or to send it to another that is more appropriate. If you feel strongly that the rejection was not based on substantive reasons, you might resubmit it when the editorial board changes. Particularly if a journal has a "blind referee" policy (readers and contributors don't know each other's names, and in some cases even the editors don't know), your name will not be known to a new board. Old biases go out with old readers, or perhaps the board the year you submitted received an unusual number of articles on your subject or with your point of view: it happens. Have a "backup" journal or several possibilities in mind, but under no circumstances send copies to all of them at the same time! Euphemistic rationalizations aside, "rejection" sometimes is merely nonacceptance for the moment.

5

Expanding Your Vision

Alternative Kinds of Publication

Although the journal article and scholarly book are accorded the most credit for professional advancement, the traditional hierarchy can be questioned and changed. Nontraditional research materials and procedures, nonmainstream alternatives for publication, and more cooperative approaches to scholarly pursuit are increasingly significant presences in the profession. Your attitude toward and practice of alternative forms of publication will depend upon your own interests, values, and ambitions, upon your career status (graduate student, post-doctoral fellow, junior or senior faculty), and upon the nature of your discipline. Your interests, values, ambitions, and professional needs are open to questioning, too, of course, as is the definition of your discipline. The latter is especially true in this technological age of new research techniques and variable student constituencies. Your contribution may be to speak to a newly identified need within your discipline or across several disciplines. Or it may be to define an emergent specialization within your field, as in the study of testimonial literature or of border cultures. Global communications and electronic databases make currently undervalued scholarly contributions—such as translations, reviews, anthologies, bibliographies, collected papers, conference proceedings, textbooks, and "popularized" scholarship—not only easier to produce and to distribute, but of greater necessity than ever before.

In addition to mainstream presses, a range of specialty presses is also available to which you may submit your work. Technology has also given rise to other, nontraditional means for the publication and dissemination of your work. Either out of choice or necessity, more and more individuals are independently publishing and distributing the results of their endeavors. Books, journals, annotated bibliographies, classroom materials, manuals, guidelines, creative artworks—all of these can now be produced through desktop publishing.

You are not, of course, constrained to do any of this on your own. Pooling resources in a collaborative effort to publish may make personal and professional sense. Several contributors to this chapter advise that you seek out others who share your interests and goals. A good place to start is your own campus. Your university may have grants or other funds available for projects in graduate student research, curriculum development, faculty development, community or professional services, and so forth. Faculty and students within your department or university may be willing to collaborate on a relatively small project, such as a conference presentation, a professional poster, a portfolio, or a journal article, or a more complex long-term undertaking, such as a book. Some might even be truly— to which should be added reliably, intelligently, and professionally— dedicated to mounting and running a journal (Dr. Childers, whose essay appears in Chapter Three, ran *Critical Texts* with fellow graduate students).

But you'll never know if you don't ask. First, you must ask yourself what you would be happiest doing. What do you value personally and professionally? What trajectory do you want your career to take? Realistically, what are the research requirements likely to be at the college or university where you hope to be employed? What kinds of projects do you want to be known for? What kind of people do you want to associate with? To what ends do you want to apply your knowledge and training? Only after asking these kinds of questions of yourself should you ask similar questions of your potential collaborator.

Though we all must respond to the real-world demands of the job search and of tenuring standards, to a large extent your professional development and advancement are up to you. Approached properly, the demands of the profession and your personal desire to make a significant contribution to your field can be unified. If you think that your talent and future lie in producing the traditional scholarly monograph, then you should pursue that to the best of your ability. If you feel that scholarship and your professional goals are best served by alternative kinds of publication, then that should be the avenue into which you begin to direct your efforts. Nor, we state emphatically, does having published one way preclude concurrent or eventual utilization of other routes. You are likely to last a long time as a professor; one way to stay alive is to remain alert to the kinds of possibilities described in the following essays.

Few professors—much less graduate students—approach their teaching as a basis for publication. Yet if you believe that teaching is seriously underrated, then consider contributing to its valorization *outside* of the classroom by utilizing the very apparatus that has often been accused of devaluing it: publishing. In the article that follows, Linda B. Nilson, Director of the Teaching Assistant Development Program at UC Riverside, encourages the use of teaching as a vehicle for research and provides concrete strategies for getting that research published—even in graduate school.

Publishing Research on Teaching

LINDA NILSON, Director
Teaching Assistant Development Program
UC Riverside

It's the classic tug-of-war for the academic's mental time and energy: the conflict between teaching and research. For most scholars, it starts in graduate school with a teaching assistantship, worsens as one grapples with the dissertation on one hand and one or more part-time teaching jobs on the other, and becomes a frenzied struggle as one approaches tenure review. While the balancing act has more room for error after tenure, the conflict is endemic to the academic career.

Or is it?

What really fragments scholarly life is that research topics and course matter barely cross paths. After all, the determinants and impact of fertility change in Brazil will supply little lecture material for a "Social Problems" course, and your multimethod investigation of the role of attention in feature detection won't round out your "Introductory Psychology" classes. What if, however, your teaching becomes the *subject* of your research? Your classroom, in other words, becomes your laboratory: your tests and student evaluations, your data collection, your teaching successes, and your research results.

Unbeknownst to most graduate students (and even to many faculty), there is a rich literature of higher educational research articles, technique pieces, and analytical essays located in many dozens of college teaching journals. This literature offers interesting, genuinely useful reading as well as publication opportunities for the serious college instructor in any discipline and at any academic level, from graduate student on up.

Graduate students at research-oriented universities already may be—and should be—wondering if college teaching publications "count for anything" on a curriculm vita. The answer is "no": if, that is, your job destination is another research-oriented university. But if you hope to get a faculty appointment at a teaching-oriented liberal arts college, state university, or community college, they will most definitely enhance your cv.

In fact, teaching publications vouch for your commitment to *both* teaching and research. In the early years of your career, they also attest to your resourcefulness to conduct research on a shoestring budget. Later, they add to your credibility when you do seek funding, either external or internal, for major instructional improvement projects. These projects, in turn, generate more teaching publications. In short, you can build a research career around teaching.

Where to Publish

What comes first—the selection of the journal for publication or the research and writing of the article? This is more of a chicken-or-the-egg argument than it is in discipline-specific publishing because college teaching journals vary so widely. Some are highly scholarly and formal in tone; others look and read more like magazines. Many print primarily scientifically defensible, quantitative research. Others welcome policy essays, personal commentaries, and how-to descriptions of new techniques. But one rule applies to just about all these journals as well as to academic journals in general: It is easier to publish in a journal when your manuscript contains abundant citations to that journal.

Therefore, *your most promising procedure is to* (1) select a general subject; (2) skim the college teaching journals in your university library to find two, three, or four that publish on subjects similar to yours; (3) search the past several years of those journals to anchor your review of the literature; and (4) then frame and write your manuscript in the style and tone of the journal from which you draw the most literature. Follow the advice for composing cover letters given elsewhere in this book. Of course, be prepared to rewrite your manuscript to fit the style and tone of your #2 journal, should your first choice return a rejection letter. But you needn't prepare yourself for the worst. Teaching journals don't have the 80 to 90 percent rejection rates that the leading discipline-specific journals do. With few exceptions (e.g., scholarly psychology journals), even the refereed publications provide relatively open forums.

Below is a list of over seventy American higher education journals that may furnish literature and/or a publication outlet. (And this list doesn't pretend to be exhaustive.) As you can tell from their titles, several journals are specific to a discipline (e.g., biology, economics, English, sociology, Spanish, or Portuguese) or a disciplinary group (e.g., engineering, medical sciences, or natural and physical sciences), and a few bend in administrative directions (e.g., faculty and staff development). But most are more general and interdisciplinary than their titles may suggest, and *all* publish *college/university* teaching articles.

AAHE Bulletin (American Association for Higher Education)
Academe
American Psychologist
Audio-Visual Communication Review
Behavior Research Methods and Instrumentation
BioScience (Education section)
Change

Chronicle of Higher Education (brief news releases and preapproved opinion articles only)
College Composition and Communication
College English
College Student Journal
College Teaching
Contemporary Educational Psychology

Education
Educational and Psychological Measurements
Educational Broadcasting Review
Educational Evaluation and Policy Analysis
Educational Forum
Educational Leadership
Educational Record
Education Research
Educational Review
Educational Technology
Engineering Education
Exchange: The Organizational Behavior Teaching Journal
Harvard Educational Review
Higher Education
Hispania (American Association of Teachers of Spanish and Portuguese)
Human Development
Human Learning
Human Relations
Improving College and University Teaching
Instructor
Issues in Science and Technology
Journal of Abnormal and Social Psychology
Journal of Applied Behavioral Analysis
Journal of Applied Psychology
Journal of College Science Teaching
Journal of Counseling Psychology
Journal of Curriculum Studies
Journal of Economics Education
Journal of Educational Measurement
Journal of Educational Psychology
Journal of Educational Research

Journal of Engineering Education
Journal of Experimental Education
Journal of Higher Education
Journal of Higher Education Management
Journal of Medical Education
Journal of Research and Development in Education
Journal of Staff, Program and Organization Development
Journal of Teacher Education
Journal of Verbal Learning and Verbal Behavior
Learning and Development
Liberal Education
Memory and Cognition
Programmed Learning and Educational Technology
Psychological Bulletin
Psychological Record
Reading Improvement
Research in Higher Education
Research in the Teaching of English
Review of Educational Research
Review of Research in Education
School and Society
Science
Science Education
Social Education
Teaching Excellence (Newsletter of the Professional and Organizational Development Network in Higher Education)
Teaching Sociology Theory Into Practice
Thought and Action: The NEA Higher Education Journal
Training: The Magazine of Human Resources Development

No university library carries all of these journals; yours may subscribe to one or two not listed here. In any case, there's no use even trying to publish in a journal that you can't locate and peruse.

What to Publish

You have more latitude than you probably think—or at least more than what you're used to as a budding scholar. You can publish a "think piece" without having to rewrite the discipline. You can use your organizational, political, and practical ingenuity to develop policy recommendations. You can describe a successful new course, program, curriculum, classroom activity, teaching tool, or technology, or faculty development strategy that you created, developed, devised, wrote, or implemented—as long as it actually happened and you can report results. You needn't be constrained by strict rules of scientific evidence to evaluate your results—not unless you're either lucky or ambitious enough to get entangled in a noteworthy higher education controversy. The professional literature has featured many such debates: the relative importance of course content vs. instructor expressiveness in student learning and teaching evaluations; the validity and reliability of student teaching evaluations; the effectiveness of programmed learning; what's right and wrong about various interpretations of "diversity." On the whole, however, the literature is a rather friendly, open one that lends itself to *creative* ideas and experimentation.

You can have a wide choice of formats in which to present your ideas and experiments. After studying a broad variety of college teaching journals, I distilled *five classifications of articles* (remember, any given journal typically favors one or two types, so be sure to note any apparent preferences, in order to create a better "fit" between article and journal):

1. *Standard Research Studies.* These follow the standard research article format and most often rely on an experimental, survey, comparative, or longitudinal design. Content analyses and narratives are welcome, but data analyses are more commonly quantitative, and results are usually expressed in statistical terms. Sampling standards are somewhat relaxed, however; the generalizability of findings to specific populations is not a major issue.

One popular theme in the literature is identifying variables that affect student outcomes: student learning/achievement (as measured by a standardized test or final exam); various dimensions of student evaluations of courses and instructors; students' perceptions of their own learning, their interest in the subject matter and the usefulness of course assignments and activities; and students' scores on personality tests and attitudinal surveys. A predictive "variable" may be introducing a study skills unit into a course, reorganizing your course content, or trying out a novel teaching technique or classroom format. The variable can involve differences between students or between instructors. The key is to go a step beyond what has recently been published.

Another research theme examines organizational and institutional variations, such as among departments, programs, and colleges/universities. The chances are good that you can collect "administrative" data for research purposes from many campus offices (e.g., faculty characteristics, admissions criteria and data, scholarship and fellowship data, and degree and program requirements).

The variables and themes listed here are merely suggestive. Don't feel confined to them.

2. *Literature Reviews with "New" Conclusions.* Many college teaching journals are interested in synthetic, evaluative summaries of the research literature on specific topics *if* the author resolves apparent inconsistencies in findings and/or draws useful, valid, and novel generalizations about the literature's overall findings. "Novel" needn't mean unusual or surprising; the object is to be the first scholar to review and summarize the literature in a particular way. The journals have published literature reviews on the validity and reliability of student evaluations; the effect of instructor style on student learning and evaluations; the impact of lecture content on student learning and evaluations; and the effectiveness of various teaching styles, testing methods, instructor development programs, and lecture vs. discussion, among many other topics.

3. *Evaluative Descriptions of Teaching Innovations.* This type of article may or may not include a background literature review. It is primarily a how-to or how-I-did-it piece that focuses on a new and successful teaching technique, classroom activity, or instruction-related program. Only two elements are essential: (1) a detailed description of how the innovation is set up and implemented, and (2) an evaluation of the effectiveness of the innovation (e.g., as compared with a more traditional teaching method, other instructors' or other universities' innovative attempts, or national averages).

Using this format, you can publicize the new classroom simulation or game you invented or the impact of your latest instructional development project. If you play an integral role in revamping your department's curriculum, you can share its success in attracting and retaining majors. If you become involved in setting up and/or administering a new program (e.g., faculty development, minority student recruitment or retention, instructional television), tell the world how well it works. Even if it doesn't have the intended or expected impact, it's worth telling the world so it doesn't try to reinvent a square wheel.

A variation on the innovative program, technique, or activity is the novel setting or application—for instance, teaching a college course in high school, prison, hospital, or retirement community. You can discuss what adjustments you made and didn't make in your instruction; what levels of student interest, motivation, and participation you encountered and generated; and how your "atypical" students performed compared to your more traditional ones back at your college.

4. *Analyses of Current Educational Policies, Procedures, Problems, and Trends.* Like the literature-review type of article, this one takes a broad perspective on issues that extend across departments, disciplines, and campuses. It identifies a specific practice, either traditional or evolving; examines and documents its impact or outcome; and proposes recommendations to enhance its favorable effects, to mitigate its dysfunctional ones, or even to replace the practice with a totally different one. Among the policy analysis topics that have commanded attention recently is how to modify the current faculty incentive, reward, and promotion systems to promote higher quality teaching. How much weight should be given to student evaluations, collegial evaluations, advising duties, instructional improvement projects, etc.? Occasionally, an evaluative description of an innovative program can serve as a springboard for a policy analysis article. A successful new program may serve as a model for solving a common instructional or administrative problem.

5. *Philosophical Statements.* Once you establish a name for yourself in the college teaching field, you can move into more theoretical think pieces. These showcase the insights, ideologies, and personal accounts of established educational sages on general subjects like student motivation, learning environments, teaching styles, professorial roles, the goals of higher education, and the essence of teaching excellence.

Conclusion

Graduate school can be the perfect place to launch your teaching career. If you're one of several teaching assistants who conduct their own sections for the same course and professor, you have an ideal teaching laboratory: all students attending the same lectures, assigned the same readings and homework, and taking the same examinations but randomly distributed across various sections. Here is an opportunity to try out alternative teaching techniques in yours and to assess your students' performance on assignments and exams against those in other sections. Or you can organize your fellow TAs to follow different teaching strategies for an entire quarter or semester, then compare student performance, section evaluations, and any student attitude or personality change that you all agree to measure. You'll get more than a publication for your trouble; you'll learn something you can really use.

Transforming the System from Within

While it is true, as Dr. Nilson states in the opening of her essay, that teaching-based articles will not count for much on the vitae of the professional aiming for a career at a research-oriented university, the rankings of publications and their subject matter—like the rankings of universities—can change. Just as it is an obligation of the university to examine its role in and contribution to society at large, it is an ongoing obligation of the university to practice from within the kind of self-examination that challenges its own status quo: its own rules, rewards, and role models. Educators struggle to balance the needs of their students with their own needs to survive according to the rules of tenure and promotion, which rules devalue excellence in the classroom in favor of publication—and only certain kinds of publication at that. This professional, and personal, crisis permeates all levels of scholarly endeavor—the content and method of instruction, the ethics and praxis of research, the social and political obligations of the professoriate, the encouragement or discouragement of intellectual and academic freedom, and the assessment of one's colleagues and of one's own aspirations. Thus, the profession is—and should be—continuously called to account for the paradigms of success it either consciously or unconsciously conveys to all of those with whom it interacts.

In the following section two perspectives on publishing, values, and the professional experience are offered. The first contribution is an interview with a professor—Dr. Robert Pollin from the Department of Economics at UC Riverside—who speaks from a heterodox scholarly perspective, encouraging publication in nonmainstream journals and collaboration between professors and students. The second contribution is an interview with Robert Apatow, a doctoral candidate in the Department of Philosophy at UC Riverside. He offers strategies for coping with, and benefitting from, conflicts within the basic framework of the educational environment.

What Are You Here For? Questioning the Mainstream

An Interview with ROBERT N. POLLIN
Associate Professor of Economics
UC Riverside

Q: If asked, most professors will tell graduate students they should aim only for mainstream journals. What's your perspective?

Pollin: In my own field, economics, where you publish really depends on your subject and your approach to it. The publications available are pretty segregated, in a sense, because within the discipline and its various specialties there are different schools of thought. For example, there's a predominant school called "neoclassical" economics, in which the *Journal of Money, Credit, and Banking* would be considered about the best in the specialty its title reflects. Although I've read for this journal, my own approach to economics is better reflected by the other journals I often read for, like the *Journal of Post-Keynesian Economics*, the *Review of Radical Political Economics*, and the *Journal of Economic Issues*. These journals are more heterodox. Basically, they are not considered to be in the mainstream. They are, however, top journals *out* of the mainstream. If you asked the majority of economists, especially PhDs from American universities, "Would you say these are the top journals?" they would say "no." For them, the top journals would be only the top neoclassical journals.

Q: How did you become a reader for such various journals, and what have some of your experiences been?

Pollin: I'm not actually on the board of any journal. But I'm often approached to read because of my specialty, which is monetary and financial economics viewed from an unorthodox perspective. For example, the *Journal of Macroeconomics*, a more mainstream journal, heard about me either from my publishing in that journal or by references to my work in articles by others.

The quality of what I'll receive to review will obviously vary quite a bit. But the fact that I've been sent the article at all and that it hasn't been tossed away by the editor means that it's salvageable, somehow or other. Most of the articles I read aren't yet ready for publication. So, as a reader, my professional job is to try to help the anonymous author, the editor, and the journal to bring out what's good in the article and to get it into shape.

I've noticed that authors often don't see what a reader sees as the core contribution of their article. I've experienced this as an author too—my article will come back to me with comments like, "Here's the really good part of it, and the rest we don't need"; or, "Strengthen the core part, and tone down the rest." Criticisms like these are simply part of the process to help improve the article and hopefully make it publishable.

Of course, articles can get negative criticism for other reasons too: sometimes people just disagree. For example, I once submitted an article about which the readers said, "It's well-written, careful, sophisticated, interesting—but it's wrong." I disagreed and showed why. The editor thought my article was good, but he also thought the responses were significant. So he decided to publish my article and the readers' responses (essentially the reader reports) to it together . . . which actually was a good idea.

Another time I submitted a paper, and one of the reviewers said that a technical part of it was wrong. I wrote back, and the reader and I ended up having a long correspondence over it. Once the debate had advanced sufficiently, we invited other people to get involved. Ultimately, the editor reviewed my paper that had sparked the debate, and the article was published. If you're a broadminded editor and the submitter's work is of sufficiently high quality, then there's no reason not to publish articles that provoke debate. Sometimes as a reviewer I'll read an article and I'll think the author is off-base. But maybe *I'm* the one who's off-base. Let the journal's audience figure out for themselves whether the work is right or wrong.

Q: What do you consider to be the most important aspects of a good article?

Pollin: The first is whether there are any worthwhile ideas. The second is whether the ideas are presented adequately. Structuring ideas is probably the single most difficult hurdle for new authors. It's one thing to have an idea; it's another, though, to know how to advance it, how to marshal the evidence in a coherent way. The third is the quality of the writing. Or, if you're working with more technical material as in economics, whether the math is right or the statistics are correct. I think this is less difficult because you approach it in a kind of paragraph-by-paragraph, or sentence-by-sentence, or equation-by-equation way. Getting the technical elements right is less difficult than getting a decent structure. Composition takes a lot of discipline because you have to see how you're going to put the pieces together. As a reader, one of the things I can contribute is helping people improve their structure.

You must be very conscious of structure and work on it very seriously. Reading other people's work is a good way to study structure. So is working on outlines of your article—and by outline I don't mean just Point A, Point B, and so on—I mean sketching out your ideas very roughly but rather completely. Once you have your ideas sketched out, then do a point-by-point outline, and see if it all holds together. Making this kind of effort as an upfront commitment will make you conscious of the structure, which I think then makes the writing easier when you finally sit down to do a draft.

I describe this technique to people all the time, but they often resist it . . . maybe because they realize it's hard work. What good writing amounts to is clarity of thinking, and that's not bought easily. It's difficult. Writing is itself very painful; you have to have self-discipline to make your ideas clear. But if you're not willing to undergo that pain and that discipline, you're in the wrong business.

Q: You've published a number of articles coauthored by graduate students. What are your reflections on collaboration?

Pollin: I don't know how other professors see themselves, but I feel I have an obligation to help students who want to publish; it's part of my job. If a professor says, "I don't have time to help you," then the professor is in the wrong business. If professors are so wrapped up in their own work that they just don't have time for someone who's promising, then they really should just quit.

Collaboration is a good idea, from the perspectives of both the student *and* the professor. For instance, I might come up with an idea, but I might have other things I'm working on. So I approach you, a good graduate student, and say, "Here's my idea. I've sketched it all out. Here are some things you should read, and here are things you should do." You come back to me with drafts or information or whatever, and then we work on it together. Then you do another draft based on that session, and then I sit down and do the final version.

Working together like that is beneficial to me because it would take me much more time to do it alone; this way I have my ideas out there sooner than I would otherwise. Of course, I understand it's not exactly an equal relationship in that I am kind of directing the research and am writing as the senior author. Even so, it's good for you, and it's much easier for you to get published than if you did it all on your own. Also, because you're actually in on the process, collaboration helps to get you involved in being a professional, a scholar. You might get a publication, maybe more than one, from this kind of joint effort. Who knows: if you really like the topic we're working on, you might even get a subject for your dissertation out of it. By the time we're done working together, you'll know what it actually takes to do good, scholarly work—and what it takes to get it published.

Let me give you an example from my own experience. I was serving as graduate adviser when a student mentioned to me that he was looking for research money for the summer. I said, "Here's a paper, a sketch of something I just did. I'm going to develop it. Maybe you'd be interested in being my research assistant?" Well, he was definitely interested; the paper I gave him was only fifteen pages long, and his response was thirty! And he was very critical of some of the things in the paper, which I don't mind at all. At that point I asked, "Why don't we do this together, as a collaboration?" And, with the understanding that my judgment was to be final, we agreed to coauthor the work. I've already published about five papers with graduate students, and I'm working on several more.

Q: If collaboration is so beneficial all around, why isn't it more widespread?

Pollin: I really don't know. I think it's all based on personality. Maybe the professors don't think graduate students are ready, or they just like to work on their own, or they have colleagues with whom they like to work. Personally, I'm open to just about anybody who's obviously interested in what I'm interested in and who is willing to work hard. If the student can't put an article together yet, that's fine—that's what I can do. And the student can learn how I do it. I enjoy collaboration.

One of the problems in academia in general is extreme individualism; I think it's built into the profession. It's very bad because now the expression of that individualism has taken the form of self-promotion. Professors see themselves as solitary entrepreneurs, in a sense; their job is to get their research done and to build up their reputations because these are the bases for promotions, for increased status, and so on. People get very narrow-minded as a result.

Also, many professors just don't see that collaboration can be very beneficial to *them*. While it's useless to collaborate with a weak student, it's extremely beneficial with a good graduate student.

Q: When a collaboration or coauthored article is published, how is it weighed by the profession, and what does it count for the professor and the student?

Pollin: From the perspective of the professor, that depends. Evaluators can get pretty hard-nosed about it; they can say, "Since there are two names on the article, you only have a half a publication here, and we are counting publications to see whether you deserve a promotion." But if I really thought that way myself, I never would have gone into academia. You have to love what you're doing, or it's just not worth it. I see collaboration in a completely different light: that you and I as coauthors got something good out and made a contribution to the field. The collaborative publication certainly can't hurt my vitae. Would it have been better if only my name had appeared on the article? I don't know. Probably marginally better. Much more important, however, is the fact that my collaborator and I did something good together.

From the student's perspective there can be certain professional benefits because a published collaboration indicates a variety of important abilities or qualities. For example, it exhibits an interest in the field and an ability to do research. It also demonstrates an ability to work with other people. Also, it shows that a professor has thought highly enough of your capacities to coauthor with you. However, the publication *is* a collaboration with your professor, so there's going to be some bias. Academics, being cynical, will say that *you* didn't really do the work, your professor did. In order to avoid this perception when students apply for jobs, I usually write a letter that describes what their contribution was, and I *explicitly* state that they weren't just my research assistant. If they had been, I wouldn't have put their names on the article. By making substantial contributions they have coauthored, and I treat them as coauthors by putting their names on the article.

Also, when you go looking for a job it's best if you can back up the collaboration with other things you've done on your own. For example, it may help if you go out and present the paper you've collaborated on at a conference, so that it's clear you know what you're talking about and weren't just doing your professor's bidding. Even better than presenting, however, is publishing an article by yourself, especially if you can do it while still a graduate student.

Q: On the subject of conferences: what function do you think they serve for graduate students?

Pollin: They serve a lot of functions. First, conferences familiarize students with some of the standards and attitudes of the discipline. Because you're a student in a particular department, in a sense you're "protected" on your own campus; you're dealing with people who know you and for the most part wish you well. Presenting papers at conferences is completely different; you have to impress an audience of strangers, which is much more demanding. Second, conferences present a good challenge. You're going to have hostile questions at presentations; that always happens. If you're not willing to stand up and present your ideas and maybe deal with criticism, you've made a wrong career decision. You've got to be willing to do this, and the earlier the better. Third, conferences also present a good opportunity for you to get your name around and create some visibility for yourself for job purposes. Giving a presentation will create an impression, and almost invariably it's the impression that people will remember. These are all good reasons for graduate students to push themselves to participate in conferences.

Of course, to make your presentation a success you *must* be well prepared. When I first started I was overzealous; I would get up at four in the morning to get ready. Although I didn't memorize my paper because that would be too stilted, I did make sure I had a thorough outline in my head. I'd even try to anticipate questions, and their answers. I'd go in to present and I wouldn't even look at any notes. But I found that being so zealous actually didn't help—I'd be so tired I wasn't fresh. I did too much. The best way to present at a conference is simply to be well prepared, especially in terms of your structure—to be clear on what you have to say, and to know it well enough so that you can address hostile questions confidently. If you're a graduate student on the market and you want to look good, showing poise and command of your topic help to make a positive impression. Some people do prefer to read their work, and it really shouldn't matter whether you read off the page or not because all a presentation actually consists of is your talking about the knowledge you have and want to share. Still, I *do* think reading line by line creates a negative impression, especially in terms of people judging your self-confidence and your abilities as a teacher, like whether you could keep a class alive. Why take that chance?

Overall, my advice is this: Don't go into academia unless you really have something to say. Don't publish unless you believe in yourself and you have something you *want* to say. If people publish just to get lines on their vitae, okay. But, really, why work that hard just to say something you don't care about or believe? Because so much work goes into our profession as scholars, you have to have something driving you, something more than money or security. But if you *do* have that drive and ability, you'll do well.

Questioning the Mainstream: A Student's Perspective

An Interview with ROBERT APATOW, PhD Candidate
Department of Philosophy
UC Riverside

Q: Have you had any experience in trying to publish while still in graduate school?

Apatow: Actually, I haven't made any effort to publish yet, for several reasons. I take a philosophical position that few, if any, professional philosophers hold today. I am a Platonist or what scholars would call a Neoplatonist. In other words, I accept the ancient Neoplatonic view of Plato. The problem for me is that most modern philosophers believe Platonism is just plain false, and they don't see the need to discuss the matter. Therefore, most of the issues that are popular in philosophy today begin with assumptions with which I don't agree. The kinds of articles I am most interested in writing are articles that broadly challenge these approaches. However, philosophy journals look for articles that concentrate on specific issues and argue within an accepted approach to a problem. They maintain the analytic ideal that we should work carefully on the parts and then consider the whole. A Platonist or any systematic thinker does not believe that such an approach is reasonable.

At the moment I don't see much room for my interests in modern philosophy. Therefore, like many others, I must do my work in the history of philosophy. The difficulty I have there is that much of the history of philosophy is influenced by modern thinking. In the past century classical scholarship has given little respect to the Neoplatonic view of Plato. In Platonic scholarship I also find that I disagree with many of the fundamental views and methods of interpretation, but here I think the problem is much more manageable.

The challenge of my research in Platonic thought was to discover a way to deal with the larger issues that I am most concerned with in the whole of Plato by carefully examining one of the parts of the corpus. I've done this by deciding to limit my dissertation to the examination of a single dialogue—the *Meno*. Often scholars approach Plato by focusing on a certain theme in Plato or by relating a certain part of a whole dialogue to one of the major themes of scholarship, like the theory of forms. A project that is concerned with something like the theory of forms would have a mountain of literature to contend with, and if one disagreed for the most part with that literature and its approach, one would have an enormous or perhaps impossible task.

My dissertation will focus on this one dialogue on which there is considerably less literature, which is probably because the *Meno* has very little to say about the theory of forms. But this kind of approach doesn't limit me to that one dialogue. By looking at the *Meno* as a unity, I can discuss elements that will support my observations about Plato as a whole, without having to deal in detail with a lot of other scholarly theories with which I disagree. By taking one dialogue that is manageable and less controversial than the other dialogues, I can satisfy the rigorous standards of scholarship and use this scholarly foundation as a solid basis to draw some of the bigger conclusions in which I'm interested. I think this general strategy is one that could be useful to many other students as well.

Q: What are some of your perceptions about the journals in your discipline?

Apatow: Different journals specialize in different topics within the discipline. For example, there are logic journals, philosophy of language journals, metaphysics journals, epistemology journals, and so forth. Each of these journals starts with certain presuppositions about, say, the corpus of authors and works that seem important to them, or how their field should be studied, and so on. That is, they have a distinctive set of principles, books, and articles that are at the foundation of their approach to their topic. It is interesting that often journals don't realize or want to admit that they *have* assumptions and starting points. But you can tell, especially when you carefully study their contents or when you submit your work to them. I mean, if you agree with their basic principles and starting points, they'll be very interested in your work, because you'll be working from common assumptions. If you're a part of that tradition but disagree with some of their assumptions, they may also be interested in your work. However, if you disagree with their entire approach or want to aggressively question it, it's likely they're not going to be interested at all in your work.

People who challenge the basic assumptions of journals can meet with a lot of opposition because the challenge is usually perceived as an attack, not a critical questioning. Even on your own campus, asking challenging questions while you are a graduate student can be very difficult. For example, your department believes its job is to educate you in basic principles. You, however, are not given a chance in graduate school to challenge the presuppositions within those principles. Your department just wants to make sure you understand the basics and can work within your field as it is currently perceived because, presumably, working within the mainstream is the way to get a job. So it's a real challenge to find out how and where you can express your own views.

In order to challenge a field or approach, you have to identify reasons and support your contention that the perspective endorsed or questions posed don't make sense. Then you need to construct an alternative to what you've challenged by saying, for example, "*These* are the questions that make sense." But, of course, it's very hard to convince others that certain questions are interesting because they are so deeply entrenched in their own ways of thinking.

Because of the homogeneity of opinion in my department, I had a hard time believing there was anybody other than I who thought differently. But as I experience more and more exposure to diverse people and their ways of thinking, I'm finding that the world of scholarship is not as uniform or dogmatic as a specific department may lead you to feel it is. Your department will have a certain bent, and there's a certain world that agrees with it. But, to make a philosophy pun, there are many worlds of scholarship out there, and you've got to find the circle of people who share your views.

Q: How can the student discover this group, this world where he or she can fit in?

Apatow: Well, no one's really going to be able to directly tell you where you fit in. The professors in your department can't really tell you, because most of them want you to fit in their world. Still, I've had professors who've told me to read certain books or articles that seem more sympathetic to my own perspective. Speaking from personal experience, I found people outside my department who really opened me up.

Q: Does the department play any part in your making contacts with people from the outside?

Apatow: Yes, it does. Besides making contacts through individual professors, of course, we also get the opportunity to meet other people through what is called the "Distinguished Visitor Series." This is a lecture series sponsored by our department in which the top scholars in every field of philosophy come to UC Riverside. Besides getting to hear and observe the best in the discipline, we also get the chance to hobnob with the "big guys." Needless to say, this kind of contact can be beneficial in a number of ways. I know students whose research assistantships with famous scholars developed from initial contacts made in these lecture series.

Department- and campus-sponsored events are excellent places to make important connections because they give you the opportunity to discuss or show your work to people who are significant in your field. Such encounters also enable you to gather important information. Because these stellar scholars travel around and know everybody, they can tell you where to study or research. They can direct you to other sources of which people in your school may not know. And visitors are usually open about offering help.

Paradigm Shifts and the Profession

A common denominator in the essays in this chapter is a vision of what the profession is or can be—a calling and a career, an integrated expression of life and work, a synergy of self-expression and scholarship. This inclusive paradigm, embraced by many of the contributors to The Grad Student's Guide to Getting Published, is voiced in the following essay by Marina Pianca, Director of the Latin American Studies Program at UC Riverside. Like her colleague Robert Pollin, she highlights the necessity of individualism within the academy while also emphasizing the excitement and effectiveness of collaboration within the academy and beyond it.

Professing Your Commitments: Graduate School and Beyond

An Interview with MARINA PIANCA
Associate Professor of Spanish and Portuguese
Director, Latin American Studies Program, UC Riverside
Editor, *Diógenes: Anuario Crítico del Teatro Latinoamericano*

Q: How would you typify academic journals in your own specialty?

Pianca: We have three distinct journals in Latin American theater in the States. One very long-standing journal, out of the University of Kansas, is *The Latin American Theatre Review*. It's probably the best known. It publishes studies of authors, literary analysis—what may be considered an emphasis on the *genre* of drama. *Gestos*, out of UC Irvine, wishes to expand the theoretical base of Latin American theatre research; it's very interested in the latest theoretical trends. In a sense these journals are complementary. My journal, *Diógenes*, desires to document and research *movements*. Of course, that doesn't mean that in *Diógenes* there are no analyses of plays or that there isn't a theoretical background for the articles that come in; it's just that these approaches are not the objective. The objective of *Diógenes* is the rescue and documentation of cultural and theatrical *processes* that would otherwise be lost to us, buried in history.

Diógenes is very much bound to the history of its subject. As Latin Americans became aware that they had a role in history and in changing their realities, people in theater there realized that their historical practices and theatrical attitudes had to merge in order to create a kind of theater that would hold this historical urgency within the context of artistic practice. Theater festivals, at which debates were held and many theatrical pieces presented, began taking place, with some lasting for weeks. They became the place for dialogue about what the "new theater" was going to be. Working in theater, I realized that I wanted to find a vehicle that would continue the same kind of ongoing transnational dialogue I saw at those festivals. So *Diógenes*, a unique kind of journal, was born. To me, it's a very organic way of continuing to participate in what has been my work in theater from the very beginning.

Q: Once you decided there was this need for an interactional, contemporary journal like *Diógenes*, how did you go about starting it up?

Pianca: When you get involved in a project because you really believe in it, because your existential person and your intellectual person are tied into it, you start getting in touch with people who feel the same way. That's what happened with *Diógenes*. I just said to myself, "I want to do this." I actually requested and received all the articles for the first issue, though I had no funding whatsoever to publish them. The university I was at then in the SUNY system helped me, but there was an enormous crisis in the budget; it wasn't really the time to start a major journal. Then I went to direct an education-abroad program in Spain, and, while there, started getting in touch with different organizations that might be interested in *Diógenes*. Two organizations with interests in Latin America sponsored the first three issues. By that time, the journal had a life, and the university started sponsoring it also. When I came to UC Riverside, I brought it with me; so UC Riverside now sponsors it.

Right now, since it's being published and distributed by one of the major publishing houses in Latin America, the distribution is very good. This assures that the objective of *Diógenes* is in fact being met. You might have a wonderful objective in mind, but if the journal's not distributed, it's useless. *Diógenes* is a journal inasmuch as there are articles submitted and evaluated, but it looks like and is distributed as a book. It fulfills an academic need and is an academic endeavor, but it is also of interest to the publishing house because of its broad scale; it functions as a critical yearbook of Latin American theater. It's unique. The bridging—the creative way of envisioning a project and getting it off the ground—is essential.

Q: How would you typify your contributors?

Pianca: I try to get very well-known people—playwrights, critics, directors, actors—to contribute; at least one per country. Also, my coordinators—I have at least two or three of both genders in each country—help to select submissions that are representative of the ongoing debates about theater within each country, so that we get a heterogeneous image of their process. Our idea is to bring together theater practitioners and theater researchers. It's a new way of participating in the critical process because everyone is involved in the creative process of the journal as much as possible. Along with the contributions selected, I transcribe and introduce a journal-sponsored debate for each issue, a round-table discussion in which people come together and talk about the present situation of theater in their country. The dialogic relationship *Diógenes* seeks is not just among the countries of Latin America: it's also between practitioners and researchers, the academic world and the community, the universities and the community at large. *Diógenes* is interested precisely in the fact that there is not one national theater to rescue but *many* national theaters. *Diógenes* wants to contribute to assuring that diversity of production.

Diógenes also has much to do with how I myself write and publish. To me, these activities have to bring together both existential needs and academic needs. You need to find those research projects in which you can excel as a scholar, but which will also help you to know more about yourself—who you are, where you're coming from, what you value. Because of this, I still feel a great passion for my work.

Q: Being a woman from a multicultural environment, do you feel you have a perspective different from that of many of your academic colleagues?

Pianca: I think I've had more struggles to undertake and more to face because of my approach to the academic world rather than because of my being a woman. There's a very pragmatic reality inherent to being a woman in any job because women do more than one job no matter what they do—that's it. In that sense, it's an enormous effort for us to be "competitive." We have to postpone a lot to achieve success. Still, my greatest effort was spent on having the way I want to function within the academic world accepted. To survive existentially within the academic world without getting burnt out, I had to feel that my work was relevant to what was going on in the world. So, for example, I challenged the notion that literature is the written work alone; I believe that history, politics, and social realities are important factors in cultural production. My major struggle has been having this approach accepted as a valid scholarly endeavor within a literature department. Theater as the study of movements is justified if you're specializing in "history of ideas"; then you might fit into a literature department. But is you want to expand the idea of "text" to include many texts—like the social, the historical, or the performance—that have an influence on the written text and vice versa, with all of this again placed within the context of a dialogic and a dialectic relationship, then that's the struggle. And that's where you start finding the need for interlocutors who believe in the same process and in the same approach as you do. So I would say there are a lot of elements involved besides being a woman, but these are compounded by being a young—and very stubborn—one.

Most of the articles I have published have been solicited because people knew my work: they had listened to papers I presented or had somehow heard of what I was doing. If they were doing a special issue, they'd ask me to write something for them; if they were writing a book and wanted a chapter on something in my specialty, they'd ask me to write it. This is part of what I mean by getting out there. It's not just going to conferences or getting published—it's also carving a niche for yourself that is visible. You should attempt to stand out as an individual who has something to say about something in particular, about something that is very important to you. Then, instead of submitting a generalist perspective to a major journal where you're competing with 600 other submissions, you'll present yourself in such a way that what you have to say stands out. The people who have had the major difficulty are those who've been afraid to choose their own perspective, their own voice. They want so much to "make it" that they act as if they're "walking on eggs." But you can't walk on eggs.

If you are told something like, "Your ideas are unsupported or ill-conceived," and the person saying it deserves your respect, you should certainly look into what that person is saying. I'm not suggesting you should be so hardheaded that you don't accept criticism from anybody; that's not it at all. You should, however, always defend what you're doing if you think it is a significant alternative to what is proposed to you. You have to maintain that even in the face of a pressure or a reality that wants things constructed in a very homogeneous way. I find it ironic that it's easier to be insistent when you're not "homogenized." Of course, not being homogenized doesn't mean simply ignoring the models proposed to you: it just means not adopting a mimetic and unquestioning appropriation of those models. Rules can be questioned. They should be questioned. There's nothing that warrants no doubt.

Q: But what about graduate students, who, by definition, are only learning about many of the possible perspectives, many of the theories and significant voices in the field?

Pianca: I think there's a gap between the words graduate students are learning—words to say things—and what they want to say. It's like the superimposition of a certain theoretical vocabulary. But without the grasp of how theory is useful to understand the object of study itself, it can be very frustrating. Because students cannot express what they have to say with the words that have been privileged within a different context, they start to feel that what they have to say is not valuable, that their thinking has no validity. But theory can only be useful if it's seen as a tool. It's not something that, by simply superimposing it to your thought, makes you more marketable, more glamorous; allowing this to happen to you merely shows that the theory is stronger than your own thought process.

Many times when I was starting out, I would come back from seeing a performance or from reading something and I would start writing, and I would say, "That's not true." I felt a distance between my perceptions and the form in which I transmitted them. Nevertheless, I didn't know how to speak of what I had just experienced in terms that would help me to understand it better. The terms I was using were actually camouflaging the experience. That's what I mean by how the theoretical discourse can be stronger than your thought process: your mind is congested by, instead of being free to work with, those tools. It's very difficult to know what is in fact useful for you to apply and what is useful just to know. That's possibly the most difficult distinction for a graduate student to achieve.

Professors need foremost to transmit to students not their own theories, but rather the need to know, the need to understand, the need to look deeper into reality. My own need to know and understand wasn't only professional, but personal, too. I needed to understand my history—Latin American history; the impact of immigrants on Latin America; the impact of cultural production and how it helps one belong to a culture if one is not a part of it for whatever reason; how my culture kept me from belonging, and at the same time made me belong. Everything else was built on that need. In other words, I was looking for answers, for knowledge. Today the students feel they're not looking for answers, because we have not developed in them that need for critical thinking.

We have made information "God." But real thinking and insight, knowledge, not information, is what we need. There's something Anne Bussis wrote in an article about knowledge formation I would like to share with you; this says exactly what I've been thinking for a long time:

> Only when a person interprets information—however tentatively—does information qualify as knowledge. The interpretation need not be formulated in words: many experiences are represented in nonarticulate form. But an individual must note and interpret a pattern before he or she can be said to know something. In other words, information exists "out there" in the physical/social/cultural world or in physiological sensations arising from the body. *Knowledge* exists in the particular mind . . . an individual could conceivably attend to a particular kind of information for years without ever discerning a pattern that unifies the information or relates it to other meaningful patterns. Such a dismal outcome is not only theoretically possible but also quite probable, if the information an individual heeds consists primarily of isolated fragments of an event. Sufficient attention to information is an important and rather obvious condition of learning, but it guarantees nothing.

And I think this is exactly what's happening to many graduate students. Since they do not think critically about the theories and terminologies employed in their disciplines, they don't know what to do with them—it's all just information that clutters the mind, makes them feel inadequate, and blocks them when they begin to write. They have established no pattern. They have nothing yet that constitutes knowledge to work with.

I'm against this lack of dialogic relationship with reality in our learning process. That's what theory is all about: human beings articulating with the world and how we interpret that articulation. If we don't make that connection and that pattern, then theory is no more than another commodity.

I think a lot of one's development has to do with *not* conforming to trends. In the long run, it's better not to subscribe to the newest theory nor to conform to the cutting edge. But to be questioning, to have the critical thinking pattern that the cutting edge represents—*that* is important.

Let me give you an example: the first material on feminist theory empowered a certain thought process. That it was very challenging explains why it was so readily discredited as non-scholarly and nonacademic. It was a long fight, as we all know, for feminist theory to be accepted and to have the place that it does today. Many of the things I read spoke to me, and I recognized this theory as a valid tool to use for what I wanted to say. Further, the theory was nonshaming in the sense that it empowered my own thought process. Some feminist essays may have questioned what I perceived, but, still, they did not invalidate it; that's what I mean by nonshaming. A lot of writings today invalidate others; that's the whole purpose of it. It's a very conservative approach—maintaining the patrimony of a particular cultural process. This is contrary to what I mean by nonshaming, which has to do with feeling that the perceptions of others can be a contribution. That's what women have done. That's what minorities have done. And I think the whole backlash that is being felt against minorities and against women has to do with the fact that empowerment and the questioning process are very threatening to the status quo.

Our identities are constantly being constructed; this includes our identities as scholars and students. And students especially very much feel the need consciously or unconsciously to construct an identity that will assure them a future. Fear of the future often makes students reject a questioning of the established order within the academic world, because even if on the one hand it can be very interesting, on the other it can do harm. And I totally empathize. It's very easy for me as a tenured professor with my own journal to be very questioning. But personally, I was *always* like that. I remember taking classes that challenged my thought processes, and the more challenging and questioning the professor was, the more fascinated I was by how the course expanded my own mind. I never even thought of getting "a job"; in the sixties and seventies I don't think many of us did. That was not the end product of our work. The end product of our work was ourselves and the way our development tied us into the rest of the world. I do see a difference, a greater conservativeness, in our students, but I understand. They face pressure from the practical need to survive. The world is becoming very unsure, and learning has become a way of assuring a future, so they need to work with elements that will get them jobs. Unfortunately, learning even at this level is not perceived as the acquisition of *knowledge* as Bussis defines it. The system is constructed so that students will be marketable, and marketable in what is considered the paradigmatic way of examining a discipline at that particular time.

If your own attitude is this desire for knowledge and you maintain it in the process of publication, it will eventually put you in touch with people like you, people who will nurture your process, not shame it. I keep using that word "shame" because this is a profession that makes us create public images of ourselves that are very fragile and very harshly defended. People are defensive of their image in what they write. But it is very important to realize that *it is not shameful to disagree*, though sometimes, of course, disagreement can have consequences. But the worst consequence arises if you pretend to agree, and then you forget that you're pretending: then you have created a totally false self. I think this has unfortunately happened to people in this profession: they have created a false self because they forgot what pushed them to conform, and now they simply conform.

So you have to know what you're doing and you have to be aware of what you're doing it for. And then "play the game" if you have to. We all know that in this "game" there are two kinds of works we can try to get published. There are manuscripts that are publishable, but that are not necessarily representative of you and what you intend to do with your work. They are nonetheless very valid exercises. And then there are works that *are* representative of you. If you don't see the difference between what you're doing to the best of your ability to get published, and where you're going as an intellectual, then mediocrity will set in. Your work becomes, in the worst sense of the word, academic. You must balance your existential being and saneness and your intellectual potential by maintaining your longing for deeper and deeper knowledge.

It's a very difficult task, surviving in the profession you've chosen, with all its rules of the game. There are hurdles ahead all the time. So go ahead and publish that good article you're not particularly crazy about. But try to get what you really believe in published, too. The real challenge is *growing*, not merely surviving, within the structure of the field you've chosen.

Q: Do you think the process of surviving and growing, in graduate school and beyond, has a lot to do with one's mentor?

Pianca: Yes, to an extent, but I think interlocutors are more significant because you dialogue with them, and you will have more than one. Unfortunately all institutions don't nurture internal interaction. Students become very competitive with each other; they don't know how to work collectively. I try to nurture that collective relationship in my classes by requiring three students to write a paper together, just so they learn how to talk to each other—and to share—without competing so much. They don't realize that it's not within their own department that they're competing, even though it may seem it is. If you can begin to nurture yourselves within your own department, that's great; but if you can't, then at least start finding those like-minded individuals off campus. They are the ones who will eventually help you to publish or will include you in their books because you're speaking the same language, literally. But you have to detect and nurture these relationships.

Of course, you have to be careful with the amount of time you spend on various tasks. Let me tell you about a student of mine who taught me something. He did a seminar with me and came often to my office hours. We worked closely on his paper, which he submitted for a conference. It was accepted. Then he submitted it for publication in the proceedings. We worked on it again. It was accepted, and now it's part of his dissertation. So he was able to do something in depth and use it for different needs. He didn't use the same article over and over again. Rather, he worked hard on one topic that he knew he could present orally, could then rework and submit for publication, and could relate somehow to the subject of his dissertation. Thus, instead of doing three different papers, he worked hard on one good product. That's a very good way of managing time in terms of what your needs are and how to satisfy them without driving yourself crazy.

You should really work with your professors—as much as they'll allow you. And that is all individual choice. It's not widespread that professors are particularly generous with their time. But there are some professors who believe in that nurturing process. Others don't, or can't. Speaking from the side of a professor, I must say that it's often not that we're unwilling. It's that we're being judged the most by what we publish. We're caught between the management of our needs and the management of students' needs. It's a conflict built into the current educational system that makes us unable to interact to the best of our potential. I come, for example, from an educational system in Argentina where you take an oral exam at the end of the year. And you either pass it or you don't. The teacher doesn't even know who you are. So students work very closely together because the task is passing and knowing the whole material of, say, 20th-century literature. When you go in for exams you face a table of six professors, many of whom you have never seen before, asking you anything they can possibly think of in a public forum, with all the other students behind you, watching. Where's the competition? Since everybody's trying to survive together, it's a closeknit student body.

My point is this: We're all trying to succeed within a context that is not always favorable for our survival as intellectuals, as scholars, as students, as human beings. For professors, there is an enormous world of tasks, only one of which is giving time to students. Students don't realize everything the scholarly profession can entail—producing a journal, being an editor, having to deal with readers who have limited time and resources. For a professor, all of this work counts for very little when review time comes around because it's not thought of as scholarly endeavor. It's service: I'm serving the needs of the profession, just as I do when I sit on, say, an affirmative action committee or a budget committee. None of these service-oriented tasks alone will get me a promotion. I disagree with this attitude about editorial work, by the way, not just in my case but in any case. But that's the way it is.

In the University of California system, the definition of scholarly endeavor is writing and publishing. I can see how the students would want their needs to be the professor's number one priority, but that's impossible for the professor. I wish students would realize that because then they would understand better why professors feel that they just can't do it all. One thing about this profession—and I'm sure you all recognize it—is that you never feel you've finished what you have to do. Ever. It is so monumental. You never get caught up. You'll die and you'll not have finished!

Even though this is true, possibly the best thing that can happen to you is that, twenty years down the road, you can look back and say, "This has been a good profession because I've learned to survive as a human being in it." You need to keep feeling that you still have something to discover within the profession; if not, you get tenure, and then like so many people, you find you have nothing else to say. You have a permanent job for the rest of your life. So what? You might as well be working in a factory if being here doesn't make you grow and be happy and reach out to your students to contribute the special knowledge of your discipline. If you're not here for that, then what are you here for? None of us is here for the money. This is a relatively low-paying career. But, if we're not in this for the money, then what are we in it for? Obviously for something else. We all came into this because we loved what we were doing. Or have we forgotten about that?

6

Approaching Book Publishers

Overview

The best way to approach publishers, whether in person, at a conference, or, more typically, through correspondence, is to put together a quality packet of introductory material. By providing a cover letter, a brief cv (no more than two pages), a table of contents and abstract of your proposal, and a sample chapter, you have initiated contact on a professional level. Editors will respond with either a request for the entire manuscript or a rejection. Some rejections, for whatever reason, will be only form letters; however, if your proposal is solid, chances are good that it will be read seriously, even if it is returned. Rejection letters are often very helpful, as this chapter's section of sample correspondence demonstrates.

One benefit of the large professional conference is the opportunity to visit the publishers' display booths. You can learn a good deal by simply observing what goes on. You can look over the most recently published books and publication lists. These latter are announcements of upcoming books and of the publishers' "back lists," or those books that are kept in print.

You may want to introduce yourself to the representatives of various presses, whether or not you have a book proposal ready to submit or even one in mind. You might do this by asking about one of their recent books or perhaps by discussing a book the press published that you found useful. Editors are approachable people who enjoy a good conversation. Many of them have advanced degrees or are active academics themselves. At the least, they have a strong affinity for scholarship and are probably better read in the publications of the scholar's profession, such as *The Chronicle of Higher Education, Scholarly Publishing, Profession*, and *Lingua Franca*, than you are. You can dissipate your stage fright by keeping in mind that part of their portfolio, after all, is to meet and cultivate new authors.

So do visit the publishers' booths. Visit, though; don't move in. Make your introduction impressive by its brevity and dignity; then let your packet, if you leave one, speak for itself. And at all costs, avoid this kind of introduction—even if you believe every word of it is true: "Have I got a book for you! It's innovative, interdisciplinary, multicultural, highly theoretical, revolutionary, incisive, deep, and broadly appealing. The manuscript is 985 pages; some of the corrections are in pencil; and, sorry, my spelling checker wasn't working; but here it is."

Educate yourself about publishing by consulting books such as *The Thesis and the Book* and others listed in our bibliography. If publishers give talks or appear on panels at conferences or on your campus, go to hear what they have to say. And keep pushing for that publications seminar on your campus that will make doing these things part of your credited coursework.

Most of the terminology that applies to journal publishing applies as well to book publishing. Some additional terms may need explanation:

PRESS/PUBLISHER/HOUSE/COMPANY are generally used interchangeably to designate whatever organization is ultimately responsible for publishing your book. Editors, production managers, marketing analysts, and directors of finance are some of the personnel who are employed by publishing houses.

UNIVERSITY PRESSES are funded by universities and, broadly speaking, are dedicated to scholarship as opposed to profit. They publish primarily *scholarly monographs*, those most specialized products of academic labor: books with titles like *Moby-Dick: Syntax as Sexual Ambiguity in Ishmael's Monologues* or *Rastafarian Refrains: Reggae and Reform in the Northwest Sector of Ocho Rios, May 1978– August 1978*. University presses, acknowledging the specialized and therefore typically small readership of their books, usually print high-quality, long-lasting volumes in small runs of 2,000 or less and thus must charge relatively more money for their productions. The standards for publication are favorable peer-review rather than favorable marketing reports. Some university presses have an independent status; others work closely with editorial boards composed of several of the university's professors.

Large university presses, such as Cambridge and Oxford, in addition to commitment to specialized publication, seek manuscripts of somewhat broader appeal, for example, studies of folklore or historical surveys that can compete for shelf space in book stores off campus.

ACADEMIC PRESSES are relatively small publishing houses, such as Greenwood and Peter Lang, which are not associated with universities. They produce high-quality books and have certain specialties, though often not as narrow as those of university presses. They may be primarily publishers of theses or dissertations.

TEXTBOOK PUBLISHERS are usually not associated with universities, but increasingly with large conglomerate publishers. The textbook counts less on the hierarchy of publication credit than does a substantial journal article or a university press book, since it is considered to summarize and represent accumulated knowledge in a field rather than to contribute original knowledge to it. However, producing a textbook that stays in print can be very profitable for both author and publisher. This reward must be balanced against the higher academic reward bestowed on the author of a scholarly monograph.

TRADE PRESSES are the commercial presses most of us associate, correctly, with New York City. While few academics write their way onto the bestsellers list, some in fact do. The key seems to be less subject matter than writing style, for a good writer can make almost any subject interesting. The paradox for academics is that if you use your education to write for the trade market and are actually crass enough to make money at it, it is often assumed that you have necessarily "dummied-down" your material. Yet Barbara Tuchman, Stephen Hawking, and Daniel Boorstin are a few who can hardly be accused of trivializing their own research.

SMALL OR ALTERNATIVE PRESSES often run mostly on devotion. They may produce some of the best writing and highest quality publications around, but in very small runs and for very little, if any, profit. Authors are paid in copies of the publication. Some of the larger small presses are very prestigious and may pay royalties.

TRADE PUBLICATIONS: *Writer's Market, Literary Marketplace*, and the *Publisher's Directory* are examples of guides to publishers of all kinds, from specialized university presses to small presses to giants like Simon & Schuster, whose various imprints publish trade books, reference books, children's books, and textbooks. It's worth your time to look through a book like *Writer's Market*.

MASS MARKET PRESSES are the publishers of the popular genres such as romances and science fiction that are sold on supermarket racks. If academics write for these houses, they usually use pseudonyms. Some, though, like the University of Toronto's Robertson Davies, have written literate and very popular novels.

VANITY PRESSES are often New York publishing houses, too, but unlike trade houses that seek to make a profit *with* you, vanity presses make a profit *from* you. They charge you to print your book and are capable of only perfunctory distribution. Unless you are really desperate to see your work in print, they are to be avoided. In any case, desktop publishing will likely make them obsolete.

Increasingly the borders between kinds of publishers and kinds of markets blur, for example between university presses and trade presses. And given the dominance of academic publishing as the measuring stick of the professional performance, it is not surprising that publication itself has become a substantial subject and controversial issue. "Crossover Dreams" is an article on publishing in the August 1991 *Lingua Franca*. The article is about academics who have crossed over into trade publishing success, some of them even working through literary agents, no less. The readable and professional issues–oriented *Lingua Franca* is itself a crossover, in this case between an academic journal, a slick magazine, and a provocative professional newsletter.

The academic world is nowhere livelier than in what it publishes.

It creates itself through its words, but in order to do so, it requires publication. And, to paraphrase the *Music Man*—that starts with "P," and that stands for "Publisher." Just how you create *yourself* within this world of words is partly decided by the publishers you choose to approach.

Methods for pinpointing likely publishers of your research are: (1) consult a guide to scholarly presses in your discipline, such as the *MLA Directory of Scholarly Presses in Language and Literature* (These guides are useful companion volumes to the "Directory of Periodicals" in your field, so you should invest in a personal copy as soon as possible.); (2) use your library's computerized search facility; (3) talk to reference librarians and book buyers in your specialty; (4) look around the university bookstore; (5) ask professors and your department's librarian; (6) check your own bibliography for publishers; (7) go through journals in your field and read the advertisements. Computerized cataloguing systems like the University of California's Melyvl® and the California State University's Infotrac™ enable you to scan subjects quickly for predominant publishers. In addition, your professional organization likely supplies your name to book publishers in your specialty who will send advertisements to you. Buy a packet of postcards and write to publishers, asking to be put on their mailing lists.

To get some grasp of publishing as a business, look through a standard trade reference volume such as *Writer's Market*. Study pertinent sections of these trade market sources; there are several pages in the "U" section of *Writer's Market* describing university presses. Reading over these will provide you with a good overview of academic publishing and with the varied profiles and preferences of these presses. Then reading the descriptions of trade publishers in *Writer's Market* will place scholarly publishing in context.

Don't, however, rely on the accuracy of the names of publisher's personnel listed in these hardbacks. The publishing business has a rapid turnover. As a courtesy, check names and titles; the reference librarian can aid you.

The authors of the following two essays, both editors of university presses, emphasize the importance of careful professionalism in approaching publishers. Jay Halio, Editorial Director of the University of Delaware Press, and Terence Moore, Humanities Editor at Cambridge University Press, discuss dissertationese, the stages of publication, the realities of publication, and the trust between author and editor.

Publishing Your Thesis: Some Advice to Students

JAY L. HALIO
Professor of English
University of Delaware
Editorial Director
University of Delaware Press

As the director (actually, chair of the editorial board) of a university press that publishes mainly books and not journals, I'll concern myself with books and leave journal essays for others to discuss. The first question that arises, then, is: how do I get my dissertation published as a book?

To begin at the beginning: think of your work as a book from the very outset. That is, think of your thesis as something that will be read by many more scholars than the four or five that comprise your dissertation committee. True, you must please the committee members first, and to do so you must show them that you have covered all the material pertinent to your subject. This concern naturally leads to an overabundance of citations of the literature, far more than is necessary, usually, in a published book. The "dissertationese" is the first thing, then, that has to be removed when submitting the manuscript of a revised dissertation to a publisher.

If you do your work on a word processor, revision involving the removal of inessential citations is easy. The word processor will renumber your footnotes as you remove them; moreover, it can transform footnotes to endnotes, which most publishers prefer. It will also help you rearrange sentences and paragraphs or remove them seamlessly. By all means, therefore, begin and end your work on a word processor. Some publishers may even welcome the news that you have your work on diskettes for easy further editing and possibly for printing off disk. Any of the standard software programs, such as WordPerfect®, Microsoft®, etc., may be used.

What publisher? Here you must query a number of presses. The best way is to send a short letter of inquiry along with an abstract of your work and perhaps a sample chapter. Be sure to state that your dissertation has been revised for publication as a book, since many presses will not even consider an unrevised thesis. Because there are scores of university presses as well as commercial publishers, it is useful to study their catalogs carefully before sending out your inquiries. Some presses specialize in certain fields, and if your dissertation is in one of those fields, you may have a better chance of acceptance. This is especially true of smaller presses, which make their mark in special fields and do not, like larger university presses, try to cover the whole range of scholarly pursuits. But even some larger presses have some areas of specialization. A few hours spent examining their publications may avoid frustration later on.

If you are lucky and get some nibbles, decide which press you want to consider your work first and send two clean copies of your revised manuscript. (It is not cricket to send manuscripts to two or more presses simultaneously; some presses specifically forbid it and will not consider manuscripts in multiple submissions.) Before you send off your manuscript, be sure you know the house style, and follow it as closely as possible, or at least indicate your willingness to revise your manuscript to house style. Most presses have a style sheet they will send you to help you conform to what they want. *Warning*: the surest way to get a rejection quickly is to send a manuscript that has been imperfectly proofread. Typos and other such errors irritate editors and reviewers and may prejudice them against the substance of your work.

Most presses use two or more competent scholars in the field to review submitted manuscripts. These scholars report to the press and indicate whether the manuscript is acceptable as it stands, if it needs revising before publication (and if so, how extensively), or if it is not acceptable. In many instances, the press will send the author the readers' reports, or sections of them, to help the author make revisions, whether or not the press is any longer interested in the manuscript. These comments can be very valuable, but they are to be understood as opinion, not gospel. You are free to disagree, but in that case you should explain to the editor when resubmitting your manuscript (if requested) which criticisms you do not accept and why. Most authors find comments useful and alter their manuscripts accordingly. Or they send it off, revised or not, to another press and hope for a more sympathetic reading of their work.

Do not be discouraged by one or two rejections. It may have been your bad luck to get an uncongenial reviewer. Or the press may find, for whatever reasons (e.g., they have published too many books recently on your subject, their editorial board was divided, etc.) that they cannot publish your manuscript—even though their reviewers have praised your work. A colleague of mine had the experience of finding her first book manuscript rejected by a prestigious press after rave reviews by its consultants, only to have the editor (with her permission) send it off to another equally prestigious press that published it within the year!

Note that the editor of a university press does not have the final word on accepting a manuscript for publication. He or she must present the work to an editorial board made up of scholars from the sponsoring university and win acceptance from the board by a vote of the membership. This can be a tricky business, given academic politics and the particular personalities involved, but a good editor will know how to guide a manuscript along. Again, don't allow yourself to be easily discouraged. If the editor had been seriously interested in your work, he or she may be willing to talk with you about submission elsewhere and about suggested revisions.

Finally, this word of advice: don't wait forever to get an editorial decision on your manuscript. Most presses take about two or three months to decide on a submission, longer if the work requires highly specialized consultants who may not be easily enlisted as readers. It is perfectly all right to query the press on the status of your manuscript after a reasonable period of time and ask for an approximate date on which you might expect to get a decision. You are not utterly at its mercy. Remember, too, that scholars usually receive only a small honorarium for reading manuscripts and have many other obligations; hence, they often cannot read a manuscript as soon as it arrives on their desks. But three or four months is ample time in most cases for a press to come to at least a preliminary conclusion; in any event, you are always free to withdraw your work and submit it elsewhere. You may lose valuable time by so doing, but the tradeoff is that you may gain a more efficient publisher who will expedite your work into print.

Once your book is accepted for publication, more hard work remains. The manuscript will be copyedited at the press, which will return your manuscript with many pencilled alterations of wording and sentence structure as well as a number of queries. Answer all queries fully, and make any final revisions *now*, including a careful check of your citations and especially any quoted material. Once your work is in galley proofs, changes become extremely expensive, and you may be billed for them. (It can cost over one dollar to alter or add a single punctuation mark!) At the galley proof stage, only printer's errors that must be corrected will not be charged to you. Of course, if you uncover any errors you yourself have made, by all means correct them—and accept the expense. But only errors, not stylistic niceties, should now be your concern. And do not dally over proofs. The promptness with which you return proofs (as well as the copyedited manuscript) will be a major determinant of the speed with which your book appears in print.

The final stage of publication involving an author is checking page proofs and making an index. This is your last chance to correct errors, including any printer's errors that may have been introduced between galleys and page proofs. (In correcting errors in galleys, printers have been known to make new errors!) At the same time as you read the page proofs, begin working on your index. Follow the model your press offers for indexes, or use any of the standard reference guides, such as the *Chicago Manual of Style*, which has a chapter on indexes. Some indexes include mainly proper names, but a subject index will always be useful to a reader. And throughout this process of preparation and publication, as Jacques Barzun said of freshman compositions and as I said at the start of these remarks, always remember that you are writing *to be read*. You are no longer writing simply for yourself or your committee; there is a wider audience out there who may or may not be interested in what you say according to how you say it. I know that this is sometimes difficult to bear in mind, but it is essential to the publication of a good—that is, a readable—book.

The day finally comes when bound books arrive at your door. There is scarcely any pleasure in academic life comparable to the moment when an author holds in his or her hand a first published book. But be wary of postpartum depression, with books as well as children. (For some authors, their books *are* their children.) It is wise to be well into your second book, or a series of articles, or some other absorbing research project, lest your first book be your last (as sometimes happens). You are at the start of a career that will be more or less fruitful as you are more or less prudent, industrious, and optimistic; an upbeat attitude is the best antidote to the vagaries of scholarly publication. Maintaining confidence in yourself and your work—along with the ability to take criticism productively—is the best advice anyone in academia can offer.

Taking the Long View

TERENCE MOORE, Executive Editor for the Humanities
Cambridge University Press

Scholarly publishing is quite distinct from trade publishing in many respects. One of these is the timescale of the whole process. Scholarly books take many years to write; reviewing them is a lengthy and sometimes complex procedure; there are no shortcuts in copyediting or manufacturing them. Yet all this seems appropriate, since these are books that should be in print many years (often ten or more) and whose impact on particular areas of research or study, once they have fully percolated down through them, can be profound. So it is crucially important that you, as a potential first-time author, take the long view.

Never rush into print with a book; never brush off critical reviews; do not be seduced by hopes of reaching the man or woman in the street; keep your expectations modest. The smart financial investor looks for steady and secure growth over a period of years; the first-time author, having a considerable investment in a dissertation or some other project, must do likewise and ensure that the book is placed with the right publisher and aimed at the appropriate readership.

Jay Halio has outlined the academic publishing process elsewhere in this collection. I will amplify some of the points raised in that contribution.

Choosing a Publisher

It is not difficult to find the leading scholarly publishers in a particular field. If you are active in the field yourself, it's obvious. Otherwise, a few hours in a good research library, university bookstore, or book exhibit at an academic convention will tell you what you want to know. Knowledgeable booksellers can also be a goldmine of information. But how do you decide between say, three or four university presses that seem equal candidates? There are some important considerations that you should bear in mind.

Who has the strongest lists in your particular field and in *adjacent* fields? For example, if you work in medieval literature, you may want a publisher with strong backlists in medieval history, art, or theology, as well as literature. If you are an economist, you might think about reaching political scientists, decision theorists, and sociologists. Which publisher can provide support in all these areas?

Which publisher offers the best distribution? Do certain publishers appear to be better represented in the university book stores or more active in attending your professional conventions? There is an international dimension to this, of course. Your book will be of interest in Europe, Japan, Australia, and elsewhere, so you want a publisher able to reach those markets as well.

Which publisher will keep your book in print longer? University presses will tend to be much more reliable than trade publishers in this regard, but even within the ambit of scholarly publishers you may detect differences. You should inquire about this specifically.

Where will you receive the most constructive editorial input? This may be hard to establish at the outset, but you will notice differences in reception to your letters of inquiry or even to your personal inquiries at convention exhibits. These differences in style and tone may well point to considerable differences in the willingness of editors at different presses to work with you in shaping your book.

Where do you find consistently high quality of design and production? This issue will concern some more than others, but, in general, it should be important to you.

There are some considerations that most academic authors consistently overrate; don't make the same mistake.

Do not obsess about the book's price. The size of the potential market determines print run of the book, and that market is a relatively small one. Variations in price from one publisher to another will make next to no difference (the market is simply not that sensitive). Better that your book should come out with the right publisher at five or even ten dollars more than with the wrong publisher. You will sell just as many copies (maybe more), and your royalty check at the end of the year will be a pleasant surprise.

Do not obsess about production speed. Some university presses have notorious reputations, and you may hear horror stories from colleagues. Here again, take the long view. The world has waited many years for your book; it can wait a few more months. This is particularly important if those extra months are spent constructively revising the script or scrupulously copy-editing it. In general, twelve months from delivery of the final, revised script to publication should be acceptable to you.

Do not obsess about appealing to the "general" reader. As far as you are concerned, the general reader of academic monographs has the status of a unicorn, a delightful mythological beast existing only in the minds of those who have spent too long a time closeted in libraries. In the real world, the general reader has no interest in your work, which is aimed at a purely scholarly readership. Any editor (academic or otherwise) who tries to pretend otherwise is misleading you, often in an attempt to woo you away from another press. Of course, we all want to think that we can break through the mold and address a quite different constituency. Occasionally academics do, but they are very much the exception and characteristically do so only at an advanced age. Do not use them as role models.

Do not expect significant financial returns in the form of royalties. A textbook is one thing; an academic monograph is quite another. It is not even unreasonable (on certain specialized items) for the publisher to request that you waive a royalty, at least initially.

Submissions

Jay Halio is right to suggest submitting a brief letter and synopsis of the book (including a table of contents) as the first stage. I am always very irritated when someone sends me a complete script unsolicited; it is usually dispatched back in the next mail. I have no problem with multiple submissions (though I realize that mine may be a minority view), with one condition: each publisher should be apprised of the fact; when an offer is accepted from one publisher, all the others should be informed. None of us wants to waste time and money on a project already committed elsewhere.

The letter accompanying the synopsis can go far in persuading an editor to take a closer look at your project. It is rather like applying for a job. When I first tried to enter publishing I was advised never to send a letter of inquiry stating that "I enjoyed reading or being around books." Every applicant says that; say something different, but keep it realistic.

Similarly, don't oversell your book on Ibsen's early drama by claiming that it will appeal to every member of the Modern Language Association. Don't delude yourself that it will interest the mailman or the guy who runs the local gas station. The editor at the publishing house knows exactly who it will interest and how large that market is; he or she will not be fooled by spurious claims of "accessibility" or "readability." Indeed, I'd suggest never using those particular words in a letter of inquiry.

I also strongly counsel against claims of interdisciplinary appeal. Academics always think describing a project as interdisciplinary will project a positive image that will enhance the perception of the book in question and in turn excite the publisher. More often than not, the reverse is true. While the academic thinks to himself,

"I shall sell vast quantities of the book across a range of subject areas," the publisher is saying, "This book will have limited appeal to a large body of scholars, but no substantial appeal to any single, easily defined group. I'm staying well clear of it." This is not to deny that academic research interests do often converge and that some work is genuinely "interdisciplinary." However, the word is much overused and deserves a rest.

The Review Process

University presses have different rules about the number of reports solicited on book-length scripts; the average is probably two. It has always been my experience (and many of my authors') that a good book can be transformed into a very good book through the review process. It is therefore something that should be taken very seriously by both author and publisher. Among other outcomes, the process enables the author to strengthen and buttress the arguments of the book and thereby protect it from criticisms that could be leveled against it in journal review articles once it is published. Overhasty revision and lack of serious attention to critical comments in reports are serious mistakes. A good publisher will sense when revision is inadequate and will insist on further changes. It is also a good idea to show the manuscript to colleagues for informal reactions.

Reports can often be harsh in tone, and a publisher may choose to pass on only excerpts in the interest of not causing offense. No publisher is obliged to pass on reports solicited confidentially. Do not take immediate umbrage if faced with nothing but harsh comments; they may contain invaluable advice (if only to demonstrate how you may have failed to convey your argument clearly). One day you may find yourself writing a harsh review of someone else's work.

Reviews are usually solicited under a mask of anonymity for obvious reasons. An author will often ask me for the identity of a particular reviewer (usually to include a note of thanks in the acknowledgment to the book), but this can only be revealed with the permission of the reviewer. This permission is occasionally denied, which explains the acknowledgments to anonymous reviewers in some academic books.

Rejection

No one likes rejection; even a publisher finds it painful to decline a project he or she would really have liked to publish, other things being equal. Leaving aside questions of quality, there are various other grounds upon which a publisher may decline a project. Authors should bear in mind that publishers don't allow their lists to develop at random; they have plans and projects often embodied in specific series. A series may have a quota of titles; this will act as a constraint on the number of titles that can be accepted in a given subject area. If I have published four books on Nietzsche in the past year, I might impose a temporary moratorium on Nietzsche projects. I simply would not want to upset the balance of the list.

Very often a book is rejected because the topic does not merit treatment at book length. This can be a difficult judgment call, but in the end the editor must make it. Some dissertations are real books with the trappings of dissertations. Most are not and should not be considered for publication as books. Most graduate students should be advised to quarry a couple of journal articles from their dissertations. Turning a dissertation into a book involves much more than removing layers of annotation and turgid surveys of previous literature on the topic. It should mean a complete reconception and broadening of the material, best done after the dissertation has been allowed to lie for a couple of years in a bottom drawer. By then, you can reread it from a fresh perspective.

Some authors, of course, cannot take rejection; they interpret it as part of some deep conspiracy to silence them. They will press on relentlessly, and chances are they eventually will wear down the editor at some university press and get the work published. A popular game for editors at academic conferences is to spot all the books they have turned down in the past five years at other publishers' booths. The realistic author will ponder rejection letters (if they are clearly the result of sober consideration and not just cursory rejection slips) and rethink his or her strategies. Not everyone has a book in him or her; ten years down the road an editor may turn up on the rejected author's doorstep and suggest he or she publish a collection of his/her journal articles.

Publishing, like any business, is about people, so it depends on trust. That trust on our part is rooted in providing good service and giving good advice. I encourage any budding author to exploit every opportunity to make contact with the relevant editors in his or her field. This can be done by phone, but is more easily achieved at academic conferences. You may take an instant dislike to someone (as I in my capacity as publisher might). That's an important discovery; you can't work with someone with whom you don't get on. More likely, you will find a sympathetic reception from a person with strong academic leanings (after all, if we didn't believe in what you do we'd all work for trade houses), a person keen to support academic research. Those initial contacts can develop eventually into long-term professional relationships that influence both the publishing career of the author and the direction of the publisher's list.

Forms and Formats: Queries, Proposals, and Responses

Sample Correspondence About Publishing

We began to think about this book the year before we started our dissertations, while we were taking the first Publication Workshop offered by George Slusser at UC Riverside. The need was evident enough to us: we were graduate students; we knew we needed to publish; we knew there was no class on campus. And we found out there was no book. One of us had a literary agent friend to whom the idea for the book was explained. The agent replied with some good advice:

> Dear Terri and Alida,
> Do your book proposal according to our guidelines, which I am enclosing. I am also sending one of the best proposals we have on hand for you to take a look at. An excellent proposal can make the difference in getting an editor interested in the project.
>
> Best,
> Waterside Productions

Waterside Productions' "Author's Guidelines" is printed below. Its format indicates information publishers will want from you. It is worth your study, especially in light of the remarks about submission made by editors Halio and Moore in their essays.

Consider that an editor is an employee of a publishing house who is rated on his or her performance just like the rest of us. When an editor undertakes to recommend your book for publication, he or she is initiating a process that may result in a considerable, long-term mutual relationship. Providing ample, reliable, clear information to the editor at the outset—from the first approach—is a very important initial step in accomplishing the transformation of your dissertation or book idea into a hardback reality.

Waterside Productions, Inc.
Literary Agents

NON-FICTION SUBMISSION GUIDELINES

These guidelines are designed to assist you in the preparation of your book proposal for Waterside Productions, Inc. With the information you provide, we should be able to clearly:

> a. distinguish your project from other books on the same subject,
> b. identify the audience for which you are writing, and
> c. determine the marketability of your finished book.

<u>Credentials:</u> List your previous publishing credits and credentials that are pertinent.

<u>Proposal:</u> This should be at least four or five typed pages, explaining: (a) what your book is about; (b) the problems, reasons, or situations which prompted you to write your book; (c) why your book is needed; (d) what are the unique features; anything that makes your book different from all other books in the same area; any new or fresh approach you offer; any special features you will include.

<u>Market:</u> Describe the audience at which your book will be aimed and your level of expertise, (no experience, beginner, intermediate, advanced). What are some specific applications or uses for your book (e.g. small business management; health; entertainment; education? Who would be the most likely candidates for purchasing your book and why should they buy, use, keep and talk about it?

<u>Competition:</u> List three to four books that compete directly with the project you are proposing. Briefly discuss how they compare to your book in length, depth and spectrum of topics covered, format, visual appeal. If there is no available book for the market you are addressing, cite any that seems remotely comparable, and indicate the differences among your approaches.

<u>Outline:</u> Present a brief capsule of about 100 words of the contents of each chapter. A detailed list of the key concepts to be included per chapter is also acceptable.

<u>Sample Chapters:</u> Please submit one or two sample chapters, preferably not the first one, which will provide an example of your writing style and the actual content of the book.

<u>Publishing Details:</u> (a) Proposed <u>book length</u> (an average book contains about 70,000 words; this size manuscript makes a 250 page book); (b) if there are <u>photographs</u> and/or <u>illustrations</u>, how many are there; and, (c) what amount of <u>time</u> you will need to complete the finished manuscript?

If you have any questions about this material, please contact the Acquisitions Department at Waterside Productions, Inc.

The Waterside Building
2191 San Elijo Avenue
Cardiff-by-the-Sea, CA 92007-1839
619-632-9190 Fax: 619-632-9295

What follows are examples of correspondence from stages in the process of publication for this book. First is the cover letter we wrote to introduce the book proposal. Using only one page, we tried to present our ideas and ourselves credibly. We addressed the questions of need and market, explained our contents and approach, and squeezed in additional queries about our dissertations. The complete packet we submitted followed the format of Waterside's guidelines. It was some thirty pages long and included a detailed outline of the book, notes on suggested contributors, a sample edited interview, the Assessment Sheet and two examples of its application, samples of both editors' publications, and our cvs.

We devoted considerable care to selecting potential publishers. They ranged from clearly academic university presses, such as Southern Illinois University Press, to broad-ranging academic presses, such as Cambridge University Press, to textbook and academic publishers such as St. Martin's Press, to the textbook or reference division of larger trade presses such as Harcourt Brace Jovanovich and Simon & Schuster. As the reader will note, the book in hand was published by Arco, a reference imprint of Simon & Schuster.

Cover Letter for a Book Proposal

Grammar Moses
Acquisitions Editor
University of Egghead Press
New York, NY 10019

Dear Grammar Moses,

The enclosed proposal for *The Grad Student's Guide to Getting Published* arose from a situation you're probably aware of. Certainly graduate students are aware of it: namely, we face the same pressure to publish as faculty face. Yet very few universities provide any practical training in publication. And graduate school schedules and demands leave no time for students to ferret out the information they need.

We are doctoral candidates at UC Riverside; last year, at our instigation, for the first time our department offered a Publication Workshop. The book we are proposing to you is based on the workshop, but, as our Table of Contents indicates, expands upon it considerably. *The Grad Student's Guide to Getting Published* addresses a well-defined audience experiencing an acute lack of vital information. The need for this book will grow over the next few years as publication credits become increasingly important for graduate students looking for tenure-track positions. We think you will find our proposal to be comprehensive.

While we have you on the phone, so to speak, we would like to let you know about the dissertations we have done; perhaps the topics will be of interest to the University of Egghead Press. Terri's rectifies a pervasive undervaluing of the Baroque concept of the "marvelous," based on her specialties in art and literature of the 16th and 17th centuries in Europe. Her dissertation redefines and reinterprets the theoretical underpinnings of the concept and is titled *The Aesthetics of the Marvelous: Baroque "Meraviglia" and Marino's Galeria.* Alida's dissertation is a feminist study of the major generic treatments and characterizations of Eurydice, the voiceless bride of the mythological singer Orpheus, spanning the Ur versions to the 20th century. Its title is "Eurydice: The Lost Voice."

We look forward to hearing from you. Please note that *The Grad Student's Guide to Getting Published* is a simultaneous submission.

Sincerely,
Alida Allison
Terri Frongia

Below are sample responses to our query packet. They range from polite formula rejections to thoughtful and encouraging rejections, to requests for revision, to an acceptance.

Dear Ms. Allison and Ms. Frongia:
Thank you for considering ——— as a possible publisher of your book. I am sorry this title does not fit into our present publishing plans, and therefore we will not be able to work with you on its publication.

We wish you good luck.

Sincerely,

The phrase "present publishing plans" is standard and can mean anything from "We just published a book on your subject," to "We don't publish that kind of book," to "We don't think your idea is worth pursuing."

> Dear Allison and Terri,
> I regret that I must return your proposal. I admire the thought and preparation you have put into it; however, our editors do not think it an appropriate project for our department.
> Please don't give up!
>
> Best of Luck,

This is better than the last. At least it is individualized.

> Dear Ms. Allison and Ms. Frongia,
> Thank you for sending me your proposal. I agree it would be a valuable resource for graduate students uninitiated into the ways of the publishing process. Over the past few weeks, I've thought about how we might be able to publish such a book, and I've discussed the idea with several of our editors. Finally, however, I can't see a way for us to pursue the project. We're really in the business of publishing texts for students—undergraduate students—and your proposed book is really not in our purview. So, though I think you have a good project for an identifiable audience, I must pass on the proposal, with some reluctance.
>
> Sincerely,

> Dear Ms. Allison and Ms. Frongia,
> Thank you for your proposal. I'm sure the guide would be extremely useful for graduate students, but it isn't the kind of thing —––––— publishes. We couldn't market it effectively to grad students as our direct-mail-based marketing is primarily to academic libraries. A publisher who could issue it in paperback would be your best bet.
> I have passed your names along to our dissertation editor. . . . You may want to be in touch with him directly. . . .
> Best of luck in all your endeavors.
>
> Sincerely,

Though all these replies say "no," the sting is ameliorated by the encouragement, and the practical advice is sound and genuinely useful.

The following excerpt of a detailed, perceptive reply requested revision and rethinking of our concept of the book. The editor's remarks were very helpful, and though we did not ultimately work with his publishing house, we took his criticisms seriously:

> Dear Alida Allison and Terri Frongia,
>
> . . . I am interested in the proposed publication, and I'd like to pose some questions, identify some potential problems, and determine how we might proceed from here.
>
> First, your proposal itself: Yours was thorough in a number of respects, but did not (at least upon the kind of quick perusal busy acquisitions editors can give it) reveal: (1) the estimated length of the proposed book and (2) how the transcripts will be revised for publication. Reviewers are sure to have comments and questions. Will the original presenters revise their remarks or will you? (3) Will the entire finished manuscript be in machine-readable form in a single format?
>
> Second, the contents of the book. . . . I think the utility of the book and the balance of the coverage will suffer since the author-contributors represent only the author side of the equation. No publishers are included, and I think that will limit the usefulness of the work. Finally, the proposed book appears to consider the publication process up to the point of getting something accepted for publication . . . but the book would serve . . . better if it included more information on the postcontractual steps that get the work into print. . . .
>
> Yours sincerely,

In addition to questions for you about your project, the publishing house will have many questions to ask itself before deciding on the desirability of your book. Some will be answered by the production staff: how much will your book cost to produce? Others by the marketing staff: where will the book be sold, and how will it be promoted, and how much can it sell for? Editorial staff will want to know what other books are out there. And the publisher—to come back to your role in this—will want to know who you are.

The query packet you send to the publishers should include a brief (maximum of two pages) and clear cv. Since the purpose of the cv, *in this case*, is to present your credentials to the publishing staff, you will want to tailor it to the specific qualifications and experience pertinent to the project you are proposing. Note that, because of its special function, certain categories that would otherwise be included in the professional cv are excluded. The cv you would employ in a job search, for example, would contain headings such as "Teaching Areas" and "References." Remember, you only need to tell the publisher what is revelant to this particular book proposal; any extraneous material will only detract from your presentation.

You may wish to refer to the model that follows, for which we thank Dr. Linda Nilson of UC Riverside.

Sample CV for Publication-Related Queries

LINDA NILSON, Director
Teaching Assistant Development Program
UC Riverside

NAME UNDER WHICH YOU HOLD DEGREES/PUBLISH

Institution with which affiliated   Home Address
Address at institution
Phone number   Phone number

EDUCATION (List institutions from which degrees were received)

Highest Degree conferred/in progress—Discipline, date.
 Granting institution
 Dissertation or Thesis title:
 Adviser:
Other degrees, in descending order

PROFESSIONAL EXPERIENCE (or: TEACHING AND RESEARCH PO-
SITIONS, or: TEACHING AND RESEARCH EXPERIENCE)

Note: Include only those items most pertinent to your present
purpose, and list the most *recent* experiences first.

Employer
Position, Title (e.g., Research Assistant, Teaching Assistant, Lec-
turer); when position held
Brief description of courses or project-related duties

HONORS, AWARDS, AND GRANTS

Title; year; amount awarded, if any; awarding institution (If a research grant, include topic or title of research)

PUBLICATIONS [or: PUBLISHED WORK)

Number these entries, listing the most recent first. Use your discipline's preferred citation format. "Accepted for publication,"
"forthcoming," and "in press" are used practically interchangeably. An alternative description for a not-yet-published work is
"submitted for publication" or "under review." You may identify
the journal or publisher to which you submitted your work if
you wish.

As your publications increase in number and variety, you should
identify the type of each publication. Categories include: Research Article, Book Review, Comment, Reply to Comment,
Book, Textbook, Edited Book, Chapter in Edited Book, Journal
Issue (if you edited it), Research Report, Commissioned Article
(as for a magazine or newspaper opinion section). Examples of
entries using A.P.A. format are here included for your reference.

1. L.B. Nilson, "Review of Berenice Car-   BOOK REVIEW
roll (ed.), *Liberating Women's History:
Theoretical and Critical Issues.*" *Mankind
Magazine* (September 1976). (270 words)

2. L.B. Nilson, "An Application of the Oc-   RESEARCH ARTICLE
cupational 'Uncertainty Principle' to the
Professions." *Social Problems* 26, 5 (June
1979):570–581. (12 pages)

3. L.B. Nilson, "Reply to (Donald) Light." REPLY TO COMMENT ON #2
Social Problems 2 (December 1979) 252–253. (1 page)

4. L.B. Nilson, "Disaster Nightmare: Lack of Preparation, Not Violence in the Street." *Los Angeles Times*, Monday, July 13, 1981, Part II, Opinion-Editorial Section: 5. (1,100 words; Circulated on *Los Angeles Times-Washington Post* Wire Services and reprinted in *Washington Post* and nationally)

COMMISSIONED NEWSPAPER OPINION-EDITORIAL ARTICLE

5. L.B. Nilson, "Reconsidering Ideological Lines: Beliefs About Poverty in America." *Sociological Quarterly* 22, 4 (Autumn 1981): 531–548. (18 pages)

RESEARCH ARTICLE

6. D.C. Nilson and L.B. Nilson, "Seismic Safety Planning Strategies: Lessons from California." In J.E. Beavers (ed.), *Earthquakes and Earthquake Engineering: The Eastern United States*. Vol. 2. Ann Arbor, MI: Ann Arbor Science Publishers, 1981: 1113–1136. (23 pages; I wrote one-third.)

CHAPTER IN EDITED BOOK

MAJOR DISTRIBUTED WORK

Following the same format as you use for publications, list work you have distributed widely to colleagues but have not officially published or presented at professional meetings, e.g., work you can identify only with your departmental and/or university designation. Also a report or manual that you have prepared and possibly even sold falls under this rather vague but commonly used classification. You may modify the major heading to suit your needs. Examples are included here for your reference.

L.B. Nilson, *The TA Handbook: Teaching Techniques and Self-Improvement Strategies*. TA Training Program, Department of Sociology, University of California, Los Angeles, 1981. (73 single-space pages)

TEXTBOOK/MANUAL

L.B. Nilson, *Business As Usual: A Social Scientific Assessment of Corporate Earth-quake Preparedness Plans.* University of California, Los Angeles, 1983.   MANUAL SOLD TO CORPORATIONS

INVITED LECTURES AND PAPERS PRESENTED

Again, follow the format preferred by your discipline, and list only what pertains to the project you are proposing. If you do not yet have "invited lectures" to list, shorten the heading to "PAPERS PRESENTED" or "ABSTRACTS." Here is a sample "invited lecture" designation, following the title.

Invited lecture presented at the University of California, Los Angeles, Extension Series, "Twentieth Century Landmarks Revisited," May 1991.

WORK IN PROGRESS (or: WORK IN PREPARATION)

Some examples follow for this beginner-friendly category.

Smith, J.C. The color of money: Racial discrimination in the American banking industry. PhD dissertation, completion expected August 1992.
Abstract: 100–150 wds (Abstracts are only for major works)

Smith, J.C. Racial barriers to promotion in bank boardrooms. Research article, completion expected September 1992.

PROFESSIONAL ACTIVITIES (For the *specific* purposes of a cv to send publishers, do *not* include memberships.)

This is an extremely flexible category. As such, there are few clear rules for formatting entries. If you find that you have many entries under a subcategory such as "Reviewing Activities," you may wish to list them under a separate major heading. Again, begin with the most recent activities first. Don't worry if years overlap with those in an above or subsequent entry; this is typically unavoidable. The subcategories following are probably the ones in which you'll be most involved.

Reviewer: (Name of journal or conference, etc.)

Discussant: (Name of session, conference or sponsoring association, location, date)

Organizer/Presider: (Name of session, conference or sponsoring association, location, date)

For this kind of cv, choose only those categories and specific items that indicate to the publishers why *you* as a scholar and professional are a good risk from *their* perspective. Be succinct, but clear. Give some thought to the visual presentation of your cv as well—pay attention to ease of comprehension in the format you choose. A cv on good quality white or neutral paper with dark print and an easily legible type always makes a favorable visual impression.

Of course, once you've received an expression of interest in your work, or, better yet, a contract, you'll want to immediately update your cv.

Yes!

If the response to your query is positive, the editor will request by phone or letter that you send your manuscript for review. Since you conscientiously informed all publishers to whom you submitted multiple queries that you were doing so, you can submit the complete work multiply as well, should there be interest from more than one quarter. Just *stay honest by telling the publishers you are doing so.* If you have any hesitations, call or write the editors with whom you are corresponding. As the essays by editors Halio and Moore indicated, editors are approachable and available for questions such as these.

Of course, an invitation for you to submit the complete manuscript is only the beginning. Like the journal article, the book manuscript must also be reviewed—internally, by the publishing house, and perhaps externally, by independent readers who are experts in the field—before any decisions for publication are made. The kinds of questions prospective publishers will be asking their readers about your manuscript are indicated in the forms used by leading university presses—Princeton and Johns Hopkins—reproduced below. By studying their questions, you can take a more objective and critical view of your own work before sending it out. Taking the time to assess and make needed alterations now, at this preliminary stage, may save you much time and frustration later.

PRINCETON UNIVERSITY PRESS READER'S REPORT

AUTHOR:

TITLE:

1. What are the purposes, main arguments, and conclusions of the manuscript?

2. Is it a significant contribution to the field? Why—new conceptions, data, interpretations, other?

3. To what extent will it be useful to readers outside the main field of scholarship or to general readers?

4. Is the scholarship sound? Are quotations/translations accurate? Have the proper sources been used?

5. Is the content effectively organized? Is it well written?

6. Please comment on the importance of this book in relation to other books published in its field. (Include any published by Princeton University Press.) Does it overlap with these books? Please specify how.

PLEASE WRITE ON ONLY ONE SIDE OF THE PAPER

7. My final reaction is:
   ( ) I do not recommend publication.
   ( ) I recommend publication provided the revisions suggested below are satisfactorily made.
   ( ) I recommend publication. I offer some suggestions for revision, but adoption of these should be left to the discretion of the author.
   ( ) I strongly recommend publication. I offer some suggestions for revision, but adoption of these should be left to the discretion of the author.

8. *Suggestions for revision.* Whether or not the manuscript is publishable in its present form, you would help the author and the Press by suggesting revisions. Where possible, please be specific. Attach a separate sheet if necessary.
   ( ) The manuscript can be improved by cutting.
   ( ) The manuscript can be improved by expanding.
   ( ) I offer other suggestions for revision.
   ( ) I append a list of errors.

Date: Signed: _____
                         Social Security No.: _____
Name: Home Address: _____
Title and institution: _____
(Please attach current vita) _____

Press Policy on Reader's Reports

1. The Press will not reveal the reader's name to the author without permission. Please check one of the following boxes:
   The Press may ☐ may not ☐ disclose my identity.

2. The Press reserves the right to share the report in whole or in part with the author or his foreign publisher, but will not show it to deans, department heads, foundations, other U.S. publishers, or anyone else outside the Press until the manuscript has been accepted for publication.

3. After acceptance, the Press may share a report with outside authorities or publishers (for subsidiary rights).
   The Press may ☐ may not ☐ disclose my identity.

Honorarium: I prefer cash ☐ books ☐ combination cash and books ☐

PLEASE WRITE ON ONLY ONE SIDE OF THE PAPER

America's Oldest University Press • Founded 1878

THE JOHNS HOPKINS ⓗ UNIVERSITY PRESS

701 West 40th Street, Suite 275
Baltimore, Maryland 21211

Dear Reader,

Please be completely frank in your evaluation of this manuscript. Your report will guide the editors of the Press and the faculty Editorial Board to a decision regarding publication. Although we may send your remarks to the author, we will not reveal your identity without your express permission. Please write any notes or queries on a separate sheet. Refrain from marking the manuscript itself.

These questions are of special interest to us:

1. What is the author's goal, and how well has he or she succeeded in reaching it? How original and substantial a contribution to the field is the work, and what precisely is the nature of its contribution? Is the scholarship sound?

2. What are the most important books already published in the subject area. How does this manuscript compare with them?

3. Is the manuscript organized logically and effectively? Are stylistic revisions called for?

4. Who will want to read the book? Scholars? To what extent will it appeal to interested readers outside the particular field of specialization? Is the book likely to enjoy course use? If so, in which courses?

5. In light of the above questions about content and audience, how might the manuscript be improved? Would you recommend excisions, expansions, or other kinds of alterations? (Please be as specific as possible.)

6. On balance, do you recommend publication of this manuscript? If not, can you prescribe revisions that would make it acceptable for publication?

Please feel free to comment on pertinent matters quite apart from these. We shall hope to see your report within the agreed time, and ask that you return the manuscript to us promptly.

Thank you in advance for giving us the benefit of your advice.

The Editors

PLEASE NOTE: The Press's deliberations assume a high degree of discretion and propriety on the part of all concerned. Readers are guaranteed anonymity, while authors are promised that their manuscripts will be handled in a confidential manner. Please, therefore, do not make use of the manuscript in your own work or discuss it with colleagues or students, without first requesting our permission. If you do request permission, we shall, of course, have to seek clearance from the author.

Area Code 301 • Director 338-6971 • Business Manager 338-6975 • Book Orders 338-6956 • Customer Service 338-6957
Acquisitions 338-6917 • Manuscript Editing 338-6901 • Design & Production 338-6920 • Marketing 338-6930
Journals 338-6987 • Consortium 338-6961 • Fax 301-338-6998 • Telex 510-101-2202

After reading and reviewing your entire manuscript, the publisher will come to a decision. It may well be, "Thanks but no thanks." If the response, however, is an acceptance, then you should be prepared for the additional work—negotiating the contract, doing revisions, meeting deadlines, correcting galley proofs, and so forth—that comes with success.

Find out as much as you can about contracts and the conditions of publication by reading up on the subject and asking around. Learn the terminology and the expectations so that you can negotiate intelligently and fulfill the terms of the contract with a minimum of difficulty. To prevent misunderstandings, keep records of correspondence, calls, and commitments. To help you become more informed, the bibliography of this book lists several helpful guides to publishing.

If your manuscript is not yet complete when you receive a request to review it, negotiate a reasonable time in which to complete it. Keep in mind that there will still be work to do after that point. *Most importantly:* Don't be in a rush. It's your name on the book cover. Books are highly prized in the academic world precisely because they are as close to forever as a professor can get.

The dissertation is a serious, labor-intensive endeavor; you should therefore make every effort to garner maximum benefit from it. In the essays that follow, Joan Baum offers suggestions for parlaying your dissertation into any number of possible publications, while Mercedes Jimenez describes her own struggle and success in finding a publisher who transformed her dissertation into a book.

Parlaying Your Dissertation

Excerpts from *Publishing in the Academy* by JOAN BAUM
Professor of English, York College
City University of New York

Despite publishers' warnings that 90 percent of all doctoral dissertations are unpublishable, and the fact that university presses are turning increasingly to general and popular subjects, you should try to get the thesis or a part of it published. A letter of inquiry to a book publisher or a chat with publishers' reps at national conferences is in order if you're thinking of reworking the dissertation into a book. State what you want to do, give a brief analysis of the market, show that you are aware of similar material in your discipline, and say why you think your book will make a contribution to the field. Publishers want to see proposals not only to consider their timeliness and significance, but also to see how you write. The uphill battle in getting a dissertation into print is not just because publishers have seen too much "dissertationese"; they have also read too many book proposals that seem to offer only precious elaboration. What they want is scholarship that can appeal to a wider audience, research that will sell. They point out that dissertations can be made over for a general readership, but rarely can they be published without extensive rewriting. Your sources or your treatment, for example, might need overhaul (look at the dates on your bibliography: how many references are five or more years old?). Trends move quickly in some fields, and journal editors advise studying recent issues of journals, not just the latest one on the open shelves. The point to be stressed here is that you may indeed be able to redo your thesis without succumbing to crass popularization.

An alternative to rewriting the thesis would be to create an article based on it. This would give you a chance to expand and update your thesis subject and get yourself known as a specialist in your area. You might also ask to be considered as a book reviewer for a journal in your field. Or if the journal has a letters/debate/forum section, you might write extended commentary. Theme issues are particularly worth going after because your chances of getting published in a themed issue are greater than for the general run. Theme issues are usually advertised sufficiently in advance for you to write a one-page letter of inquiry that contains a brief summary of your work, asking if it's suitable.

Writing as well for a popular audience need not conflict with writing for colleagues in your discipline. There can be mutual benefits. Writing for a popular audience helps dispel dissertationese and encourages a relaxed and fluid style of discourse. Besides, one good way of testing a scholarly work for significance is to make research widely accessible at the same time you are writing for a scholarly publication. Try to write about your specialty for a newspaper, for public t.v., or for radio. Popular writing can also be intellectually profitable; when you write for the media, you're forced into presenting a strong rationale, evoking interest, and adopting a conversational style. The important point is not to get stuck in the dissertation field and think that is all there is.

A Quest for a Publisher

MERCEDES JIMENEZ, Lecturer,
Department of Spanish and Portuguese
UC Riverside

After two long and exhausting years of reading, rereading, writing, rewriting, and more rewriting, and after thousands of hours in front of the computer—the same computer that pitilessly erased several dozen hard-worked pages—the end of an era had arrived: I had finished my dissertation, and it had been approved by my committee.

The job had been so absorbing, that, at that supposedly happy moment, I could feel nothing but an enormous sensation of emptiness. On my desk, the thick bundle of pages containing my dissertation was lying lazily. What could I do with it? All the effort, the enthusiasm, the time . . . just to decorate my desk? No. The work had been so praised by its readers: could not I try to publish it? But . . . how? Where? How does a brand-new doctor publish a dissertation?

A new quest had started.

Many professors have published their dissertations, so I asked them. The question was easy enough, but the answer was not what I expected to hear.

"I think it a great idea. You must publish it."

"How?"

"Well, write to different publishers."

"Could you give me some names?"

"There are so many."

"Just a few of them. Please."

"Go to the library and look in the books there."

As a graduate student, I did not want to insist, so I left with all the "information" provided. Graduate students, as we all know, sometimes confront a professorial attitude that seems to say, "Don't worry. You have been through so much already that a little more suffering won't affect you."

I went to the library and looked at the books I had been using during those two years of solitude.

"How can I dare write to the publishers of Damaso Alonso or Francisco Rico?" I asked myself. I needed to find other, less renowned publishers. An anonymous reference librarian guided me around the labyrinth of books and showed me those that contained the precious information for which I was so desperately looking. The users of the libraries around the world hardly give enough credit to the selfless help and generous advice that librarians offer!

At least two books are basic: the *Publishers Directory*, containing the names and addresses of all the publishers in the United States, and the *International Literary Market Place*, containing the names, addresses, and specialties of publishers in 160 countries and a list of literary prizes. This latter book is of special significance for those authors who use foreign languages. My dissertation, for example, was written in Spanish.

No sooner had I targeted several publishers whose specialties included my topic than a new question arose: "What should I send them? Should I send the whole manuscript? Part of it? Which part?" I went back to one of my old professors, one of the two who had helped me the most since my arrival in this country. My friend told me I should submit the table of contents and excerpts of what I considered the best of some chapters to give a general and precise idea of the work.

With all of the pieces of the puzzle apparently uncovered, I started the selection, copying, and sending of my dissertation. I wrote the publishers a cover letter asking for an indication of interest and conditions of the publication. At that point, I had done everything I could. Patience, an important quality for a scholar, is especially necessary for an apprentice. Letters take time to arrive at their destination, especially if it is a foreign country. Reading the selections—which you do not want to take too long but which you do want to be thorough and sympathetic—is slow for readers who do not know you and may not share your enthusiasm.

Finally, the answers, polite but painful, start to arrive. Readers seem to agree on how interesting your subject appears to be, but whether the publishers say you wrote too soon or too late or that their publishing load for quite some time has already been decided, rejection is still rejection. Nevertheless, most publishers will encourage you to keep trying somewhere else. Here comes patience again. You write more letters and . . . one day you are taken by surprise: a publisher asks you to send your whole manuscript. At last your work has been rewarded.

But the process is far from over, and you may still be disappointed. Your manuscript may be returned with a note of thanks and a courteous excuse. The story will likely be repeated two or three times until, one day, you find a letter in the mail that looks like many others you have already received, but this time the content is very different: "The board of readers unanimously has recommended the publication of your manuscript."

The words are magic.

Some publishers ask the author to contribute financially to publication; some do not. Regardless of how eager you are, it is important to wait and study the conditions for publication, the number of books to be printed and their quality, the publisher's distribution network, etc. Once you have all the details, you can choose whether to sign the contract or to keep looking for another publisher.

The *International Literary Market Place*, as I mentioned before, has a list of literary prizes. Most prizes consist of a stipend plus the publication of the winning work. Thinking of it as a door to knock at, I presented my dissertation to the "Letras de Oro" contest in the essay category, a literary prize organized by the University of Miami. Though I did not win the coveted prize, I was selected as one of the finalists. This item I naturally added to my cover letter: "finalist for the literary prize 'Letras de Oro' " definitely made my work more attractive. You are, after all, selling a product, and since the market is full of wonderful books, yours benefits greatly by special attributes.

As a summary of all my struggles, I learned several lessons:

- From the outset of your dissertation, write a book, not a long paper.
- Select several publishers according to the language and subject of your work. Find books they have published and assess them.
- Send a copy of the table of contents and excerpts of the best chapters together with an introductory letter.
- Be patient and keep trying.
- If the publishing companies are not interested in your book, there are still other possibilities. In some countries, for example, local governments publish works on native people and native subjects. If your dissertation topic seems suitable, contact them.
- Let colleagues know what you are attempting; solid information sometimes comes from unexpected quarters.

7

Using Your University Fully

Educating Yourself About Your University
Terri Frongia, PhD and Alida Allison, PhD

Library Resources: Using a University Library to Aid in Your
  Research and Your Search for a Publisher
Peter Bliss, MLS

Two Rudiments of Proposal Writing
Robert A. Lucas, PhD

Educating Yourself About Your University

As an institution, the University seeks prestige. This prestige largely stems from the quality of its faculty, staff, and students, and on the quality of the facilities and support the University makes available to them. To further its reputation and vitality, it is in the University's own interest to provide the most conducive environment possible to facilitate and encourage research and study. This environment constitutes the university in its largest sense—as purveyor of information and technology (e.g., the library and media resources), as financial institution (e.g., the grants/fellowships office), as professional training ground (e.g., instructor training programs, resumé writing workshops, job interview sessions), and as arena for mutual exchange (e.g., the collegial coffee bar). It is in *your* best interest to become educated about the training programs and facilities available on your campus.

187

Among the (few) "perks" of graduate school, besides the thrilling access to department stationery, is the substantial bonus of highly professional free training. The practical knowledge you can acquire is of both immediate and long-lasting value. For example, you can receive instruction in matters such as using your library's state-of-the-art research tools, incorporating media technology into your classroom, constructing and tailoring your cv, taming your dissertation, and giving a commendable job interview. Depending on the amount of time you have—and even more fundamentally, on what your particular campus offers—take as much of this important practical training as you can. The information may be presented in various formats; credited courses, workshops, and seminars are preferred.

Although preparation for the realities of the academic vocation is one of the most important areas of the graduate school experience, it is often neglected by the very people whom it would benefit most. On the one hand, you, the graduate student or new faculty member, may feel too overwhelmed by more pressing needs to fill gaps within your professional education. On the other, your institution, although largely responsible for your educational and professional welfare, may overlook this aspect of its mission. The oversight may be the result of unavailability of resources; more probably, though, it will be a consequence of the unsystematic presentation and inadequate promotion of those resources that in actuality *are* available. Professors and graduate departments—knowing that the necessary information is out there somewhere—will typically assume that somehow you will encounter it on your own, just as they assume you will somehow come by the skills necessary for getting your research papers published in professional journals.

Some campuses are very diligent in publicizing their resources and making them easily available to students and faculty. But many universities aren't. You should, therefore, take responsibility for practical training. Moreover, you should urge your professors—and your department—to organize, enlarge, and publicize the scope of *their* involvement in these crucial aspects of your education. Not only is this sound policy from the graduate student perspective, but the wise investment of already available resources in their students' future success offers potentially high dividends for the department and campus as well: stellar products reflect glory on their producers and nurturers.

Approach your professors and department staff to inquire about what your program offers or knows about in these areas. You should take advantage of whatever may be available and useful. If you don't find what you need within your own department, seek out information through the student newspaper or special service groups, such as Career Services, Women's Outreach, Reentry Student Services, etc., where announcements and schedules for resumé-writing workshops, job interview workshops, dissertation requirement seminars, and other such services are likely to be publicized. Read posted announcements and circulars which often advertise career training available on campus. A final source of information is your network. Good relations with department staff, peers, and friends in other departments can serve you well, for they may call to your attention what you may have overlooked.

After you find out what resources are available to you, work these special offerings into your schedule, just as if they were regular classes or other serious obligations. You need this resolve because this training *is* an educational requirement—not for the degree, but for *you*—and you are the only one who can make sure you know as much as you need to know.

If, for example, you are a graduate student uncomfortable with your level of expertise in research methodologies, then look to your professors *and* to your library's staff for assistance in building these skills. Professors may be willing to set aside some time for intensive personal instruction, or, perhaps even better, to facilitate an impromptu workshop or a special study session for you and other like-minded students. If interest is sufficient, you and your peers may wish to actively encourage your department to institute a credited course on research methods if one is not already offered.

Sometimes, though, it is not possible for the department to fulfill your needs, and you will be constrained to look elsewhere. If (to continue with the same example) you need help with research methods, then you will probably turn to the place you will be doing most of your research anyway—the campus library. Some campuses offer credited courses on using today's computerized library. Courses like these offer an invaluable service to the novice and to the veteran alike, chiefly because the complex and rapidly changing university library houses more information than ever before, and the explosion in technology has altered radically the what, how, and where of research. Even if you only audit a course on library use, the explanations, demonstrations, and exercises will sharpen your own research techniques; without doubt, the effort and time invested in such a course will be amply rewarded.

Through courses such as these, you will also discover other significant—and useful—aspects of the world behind the circulation desk. Library personnel often hold advanced academic degrees and receive tenure and promotion as do departmental faculty; like faculty as well, they specialize in certain fields. As University of California Reference Librarian Peter Bliss indicates in this chapter's first essay, reference librarians enjoy working with graduate students whose projects require advanced research skills and technology and long-term library use. Start making it a habit to check in at the reference desk for assistance on short-term projects like research papers, for every seminar paper is a potential journal article or conference presentation. Long-term endeavors like the dissertation will benefit from even more frequent contact: throughout your research, the reference librarian can direct your efforts and, once aware of your interests, can keep alert for pertinent material. Additionally, with their intimate knowledge of reference materials, reference librarians can guide you in locating research sources in other geographical areas—an important consideration when you want to locate (and perhaps, with the aid of a grant, travel to) data or collections you will want to consult for your work.

Your contacts with these highly trained professionals should also be made with an eye to the larger perspective: this is an excellent opportunity to create connections for your career network. As specialists, librarians are personally acquainted with the journals and publishers in your field; they can therefore prove invaluable for your own publication success. Through their databases they can access important information on journals to which you are considering sending a submission. They can tell you, for example, about the contents of the journal's most current issue or what the forthcoming issue is supposed to contain. They can also give you information on the journal's current editorial staff or its regularity of publication. Knowing that a journal you have targeted is already long overdue or is working from a substantial backlog might persuade you to readdress the envelope of that article you were about to mail.

The reference librarian can also direct you to other resources important to your sanity and survival, such as references like the *Directory of American Scholars*. By familiarizing yourself with the interests, publications, achievements, and institutions of the people who are about to interview you for a job or whom you are considering contacting in a professional context, you are likely to feel more at ease. Not only may they be flattered by the attention, but your own poise and knowledge will no doubt positively affect their opinion of you.

The reference desk is not the only place in the library where you may want to establish professional contacts. There are, for example, the specialists who order the books in your field. These individuals are very up-to-date on scholarly publishers and their particular emphases—useful information if you want to submit a book proposal. Being current on important topics, trends, and authors, they may be able to direct you to the publisher most likely to be receptive to your dissertation manuscript or to other book-length projects, such as translations, anthologies, critical editions, annotated bibliographies, and so forth.

Your library may also house any number of special collections. If any of these has holdings in areas of interest to you, by all means take the initiative and introduce yourself to the collection's curator and staff. Besides comfortably conducting your own research there, you may also be able to meet visiting scholars and lecturers—an economical, painless way to network with the biggest, best, or most interesting personalities in that field. Since many of these collections are connected to research centers or other such scholarly organizations, you may also discover opportunities to acquire funding for your research or other related professional pursuits. As a graduate student you may also want to vector yourself toward any predoctoral and postdoctoral fellowships the research center may offer or about which it has information. The journals you subscribe to in your discipline are important information sources for these opportunities as well.

Having located research centers, collections, or museums in your field, you next need to research those grants and fellowships that will fund your travel to and research in those institutions. Remember—grants fund research can lead to publication. Here again, your valuable self-education in academic savvy can start on your own campus. Maintaining and staffing service and research facilities is only part of the university's role. As grants specialist Dr. Robert Lucas points out in his essay, the university provides its own grants and fellowships to support faculty and students with special interests, projects, or qualifications. In addition, through the specialists in its graduate school or division and through its faculty development program, the university offers you access to information on regional, national, government, and private sources for graduate student and faculty funding. The informational services available may even include computer searches for identifying likely grants for your project, as well as practical instruction in the application process. The seminars some universities offer in targeting and applying for grants can be of great benefit to you, even if you have not yet formulated your research project clearly. While a definite research, travel, or publication project is ultimately crucial, attending a seminar simply to acquaint yourself with the world of grants and its relationship to your publication pursuits can help you define and tailor your ideas. By learning what grant-funding agencies look for in the proposals they receive from applicants, you will become that much closer to putting together a successful application.

While research has many intrinsic rewards, it goes without saying that receiving a grant or fellowship for research or travel is tremendously satisfying. It also has the added springboard benefit of looking very good on your cv. Extrinsic rewards such as these make important statements about you and your work. From the perspective of future donors, each grant you have secured in the past represents a persuasive reason for offering *you* additional funding for additional research and therefore additional publication. From the perspective of your colleagues, prospective employers, and potential publishers, the fact that your research has been deemed important and substantial enough to merit funding greatly enhances your overall value and appeal. Both you and your work are proven investments. The grant you successfully apply for can fund research and writing far beyond its actual time limit; a year's grant from the National Endowment for the Humanities, for example, can open onto a decade's worth of publication spinoffs. Contacts made on grant-funded research trips can develop in unexpectedly beneficial ways. These contacts can begin with the simple act of introducing yourself to the appropriate grant officers on your campus.

Before others will invest in your future as a professional, however, you need to invest in yourself. And that means taking the time to discover and utilize the myriad resources available to you on your own campus. The two essays completing this chapter can help you maximize your contact with those resources. Peter Bliss's "Library Resources: Using a University Library to Aid in Your Research and Your Search for a Publisher" explains the strategies and latest resources available for your research. Robert Lucas's "Two Rudiments of Proposal Writing" explains skills you'll need to locate and successfully approach grant programs to help fund your research for publication.

Library Resources: Using a University Library to Aid in Your Research and Your Search for a Publisher

PETER BLISS
Reference Librarian, Education Services Librarian
Tomás Rivera Library
Adjunct Lecturer, College of Humanities and Social Sciences
UC Riverside

When you consider writing for publication, your university library is an essential resource. First, quite obviously, the library is an essential component of the research process itself, the starting point for your background work and your guide to what has already been written on your topic. The second reason you should get to know your library may not immediately occur to you. When your research is finished and you're investigating publishing possibilities, a university library, particularly an academic research library, will provide you with samples of the professional literature in books, journals, conference papers, and proceedings. You should be able to browse dozens of journals in your field and get a feeling for the type of article they publish, in addition to checking their guidelines for the submission of manuscripts. The library probably owns the style manuals that journals designate for the format of submitted manuscripts. Through your library you can identify and obtain materials you may need from other libraries and save yourself the time and expense of traveling to get them.

Get to Know Your Reference Librarians

Your academic library will have a reference desk where you can ask for assistance in your library research. Most university libraries staff these desks with professional reference librarians who have a Master of Library Science degree and frequently a second master's degree in their field of specialization. Generally speaking, reference librarians *like* to deal with graduate students. The more complex and in-depth questions that masters and doctoral students ask challenge reference librarians to utilize their full knowledge of the resources in a particular field in a way that undergraduate queries rarely do. The ongoing nature of graduate research enables reference librarians to work with graduate students over a period of time, whereas undergraduates usually have more short-term goals.

Get to know the reference staff at your library. Find out if there is a librarian who has special expertise in your field. Ask if there is a course in library usage or if there are specialized workshops on library resources in your area of interest. Remember that librarians were graduate students at one time, too, and that many of them have published. They could be among your more valuable contacts at your university.

The Tools of Research: Catalogs, Indexes, and Abstracts

Academic libraries are undergoing tremendous changes brought about by automation. Anyone returning to an academic library after an absence of more than a year will find *some* degree of difference in the tools used to conduct research. Automation has changed nearly every library function, from the cataloging of library materials to the way those materials are charged out, but what concerns you the graduate student most is the way in which *reference tools* such as indexes have been changed. Upon entering the library and seeing the many computer terminals in the reference section, you may think that you should use one of these systems in your research, perhaps to the exclusion of other types of resources. But which one should you begin with, and how will you know if you're not missing another vital resource?

This early point in the research process is an excellent time to consult a reference librarian. The reference sources in every field are different; some fields have automated indexes and others may not. Among the automated sources, there are many variables that you need to be aware of, such as years of coverage or the existence of abstracts. A reference librarian can tell you about the sources in your field, automated or otherwise, steer you toward the best sources, and warn you about the shortcomings of others.

When doing graduate-level library research, especially research that will lead to publication, there is a real need to be comprehensive, to uncover all the written materials relevant to your topic. If you limit your research to books and journals, for instance, you could be embarrassed to discover at a late stage in the research process that there is a dissertation that matches your topic exactly. What follows is a brief discussion of each kind of library resource and the reference tools that allow you to access them.

Books

In spite of the increasing importance of academic journals in graduate research, books retain an important place also, particularly in fields such as history, art history, literatures and languages, and philosophy, where currency of information is not of such overwhelming urgency as it is in the sciences. With their time-consuming publication process, books cannot match the currency of journals, but they have obvious advantages of comprehensiveness that are invaluable in gaining background knowledge. Many university libraries at research institutions now have online catalogs for the books in their collections, supplementing or replacing their card catalogs. It is *very* important that you understand the coverage of the catalogs when looking for books. If the card catalog has been "closed," then cards are no longer being added, and you will have to look in the online catalog to find recently published books and other recent acquisitions. If there is an online catalog, find out how far back the coverage goes; some online catalogs lack listings for books added to the collection before a certain date. Another important point to consider about online catalogs is that they are sometimes *union catalogs,* or catalogs of books from more than one institution or library. Examples of union catalogs would be Illinet, an online catalog of Illinois public and academic libraries, and the MELVYL® system, which is an online catalog of books in the nine University of California libraries.

A card catalog entry:

Getting into Print

Z479
P68   Powell, Walter W.
1985   Getting into Print : the decision-making process in
       scholarly publishing
       / Walter W. Powell. — Chicago :
       University of Chicago Press, 1985.
       xxxi, 260 p. ; 23 cm.
       Bibliography: p. 233-250
       ISBN 0-226-67704-4
       1. Scholarly publishing—United States—Decision
       making. 2. Book Industries and trade—United States—
       Decision making. 3. Editing—Decision making.
       4. Authors and publishers—United States. 5. Organization.
       I. Title
CU-Riv 850916 ha*   CRUGnt 84-23962

The entry for the same book, from the MELVYL® system, the online catalog of the University of California libraries:

1. Powell, Walter W.
    Getting into print: the decision-making process in scholarly publishing/Walter W. Powell. Chicago: University of Chicago Press, 1985.
    UCR Rivera Z479 .P68 1985

Journals

In fields where currency of information is vital, journals have replaced books as the primary medium of scholarly communication. This is particularly true in the sciences, and to a lesser extent it applies to such social science disciplines as psychology, sociology, economics, and anthropology. In all fields, of course, journals cannot be overlooked.

As the importance of journals to academic research has grown, so has the number of indexes that organize journal articles and list them by subject. There is such a bewildering array of indexes available in book and automated formats that it is wise to consult with a reference librarian when beginning to search for articles on your topic.

Print Indexes

When you think of a periodical index, the *Reader's Guide to Periodical Literature* may come to mind. This venerable publication has been indexing popular magazine articles since the turn of the century and is the best-known index published. Its usefulness for graduate research is negligible, however, since it covers such non-scholarly titles as *Ladies Home Journal, Road and Track,* and *Popular Science* in addition to news and commentary magazines. There are literally hundreds of indexes that *do* cover scholarly journals, such as the *Social Sciences Index,* the *Art Index, Psychological Abstracts, Women's Studies Abstracts,* the *Philosopher's Index,* and *Biological Abstracts.* Some provide just the basic information about a periodical article, as in the entries below from the *Social Sciences Index*:

Neoclassical economics
   The impossibility of fiscal policy [neoclassicists vs. institutionalists] W. Waller. *J Econ Issues* 23:1047-58, D '89
   Market-like forces and social stratification: how neoclassical theories of wages can survive recent sociological critiques. S. Cohn. bibl *Soc Forces* 68:714-30 Mr '90

Most journal indexes abbreviate extensively in order to save space. The two articles above are from the *Journal of Economic Issues*, volume 23, December 1989 and from *Social Forces*, volume 68, March 1990.

Other indexes provide an *abstract*, or short summary of the article, as in this entry from *Psychological Abstracts*:

> 30430. Lindemann, Carol. (New York Psychological Ctr) "Relaxation-induced panic (RIP): When resting isn't peaceful": Commentary. A. *Integrative Psychiatry*, 1987 (Jun), Vol 5 (2), 109-110. —In response to the article by C.M. Adler et al (see PA, Vol 75:30404) on RIP and anxiety, the present author comments that this line of research has clinical applicability and that organizing the clinical observation under the concept of interoceptive conditioning brings a new dimension to the phenomenon. (0 ref)

The usefulness of abstracts in your research should not be underestimated. An abstract can tell you whether or not it is worth your trouble to actually locate the journal, which can be time-consuming in an academic library with thousands of journal subscriptions and even more time-consuming if you have to obtain the article through Interlibrary Loan. With an index that does not provide abstracts, you must decide from the title of the article alone whether or not the article is worth investigating.

Automated Journal Indexes

Journal indexes have been changed considerably by the advent of automated systems. The powerful capabilities of automated indexing add considerably to the usefulness of all kinds of periodical indexes. Most traditional periodical indexes are constructed so that one year of coverage is contained in one book, and therefore if you want to search through six years of art journals, you have to search six different volumes of the *Art Index*. With automated indexing, it has now become possible to search those six years all at once, if you so desire, or to limit your search to the most recent year.

Until a few years ago, utilizing a computerized journal index meant making an appointment with a librarian, explaining the subject you were searching, and watching while the librarian typed in the search using somewhat complicated protocol. It also frequently involved waiting up to a week to get a printout with the search results. In most academic libraries this is no longer the case; many automated indexes can be directly accessed by you, the library user.

The technology that has made this possible is called CD-ROM, or Compact Disk Read Only Memory.

CD-ROMs, which resemble audio compact discs, hold data instead of sound. Over 550 million bytes of data, or over 200,000 pages of typed information, can be stored on a disk. In libraries that have CD-ROMs, you will see a workstation consisting of a personal computer, monitor, CD player, and printer. Depending on the library, you may be able to access one index or several indexes from the same workstation. The introductory screen that you first see should tell you the name of the database and the years of coverage. For instance, PsycLIT is a CD-ROM index that is the equivalent of the print index *Psychological Abstracts*, with coverage for the years 1974 to the present.

The search below used PsycLIT to find articles on health attitudes of the middle aged. The subject terms "health attitudes" and "middle aged" have been entered and combined; the system then searches for all articles that are indexed under both terms. The result in this case is six articles, one of which is printed below.

SilverPlatter 2.00		*PsycLIT Disc 2 (1/83–6/91)*
No.	Records	Request
1:	553	HEALTH-ATTITUDES
2:	961	MIDDLE-AGED
3:	6	HEALTH-ATTITUDES AND MIDDLE-AGED

TI: Marriage and the psychological consequences of a heart attack: A longitudinal study of adaptation to chronic illness after 3 years.
AU: Waltz, -Millard; Badura, -Bernhard; Pfaff, -Holgar; Schott, -Thomas
IN: U Oldenburg Inst of Sociology, Oldenburg Longitudinal Study, Fed Rep Germany
JN: Social-Science-and-Medicine; 1988 Vol 27(2) 148–158
AB: Surveyed almost 400 *middle-aged* males who suffered a myocardial infarction (MI) and their wives to assess the role of patient health cognitions and marital factors on Ss' recovery. Ss were surveyed at several time points over 5 years following MI. Negative appraisals of threat and loss due to cardiac impairment/ disability were found to be the best predictors of anxiety and depressions at 3–4 yrs after hospitalization. High intimacy marriages appeared to provide adequate social support, and the level of intimacy between spouses was inversely related to depressed mood. Findings suggest that a social support system provides a buffering effect for MI Ss. (PsycLIT Database Copyright 1989 American Psychological Assn, all rights reserved)
DE: *HEALTH ATTITUDES*; MARITAL-RELATIONS; SOCIAL-SUPPORT-NET-WORKS; ADJUSTMENT-; MYOCARDIAL-INFARCTIONS; ANXIETY-; MAJOR DEPRESSION; *MIDDLE-AGED*; LONGITUDINAL-STUDIES; ADULTHOOD-
AN: 76-16258

The great advantage of the automated journal index is *speed*; the computer can search extensive databases of articles and locate those that meet your specifications with amazing rapidity. The search above, for instance, would probably take less than five seconds from the time you entered it to the time the six articles were identified.

Dissertations

Keeping in mind that graduate research aims to be comprehensive, you shouldn't neglect to check up on what dissertations have been written in your subject area. This will be especially important if you're considering publication. You may not have found any books or journal articles that cover the same ground that you plan to cover, but there could be a dissertation out there that is an exact match to your topic. The sooner you know what's been written, the better, so checking up on dissertations is *very* important.

Dissertation Abstracts International (DAI) is the source to use when researching dissertations. Your library's card and online catalogs will most likely list only dissertations written at that institution. There may be a smattering of dissertations from other schools, but only a tiny percentage of all the dissertations written will be covered. DAI, while not listing all American dissertations, is far closer to comprehensive than any other source. DAI is available at many libraries in CD-ROM form, which brings the advantages of automated searching to your search for dissertations.

The resurrection of Richard Nixon: A case study of the media's effect on collective memory. Johnson, Thomas J., Ph.D. *University of Washington*, 1989. 256pp. Chairperson: Gladys Engel Lang
Order Number Da9006967
Researchers have established that the media have an important influence on what present events people consider important and how they view those events. But researchers have all but ignored how media use affects how individuals view the past. This dissertation used surveyed University of Washington School of Communications alumni to investigate how retrospective media use influenced recollections of Richard Nixon's political life. More specifically, this study looked at whether those who clearly remembered events in Nixon's political life have different images of Nixon than those who learned about them through retrospective communication.
This study found significant differences between those who clearly remembered Watergate and those who learned about it through retrospective communication. Those who learned about Watergate through

retrospective communication were less likely to judge Nixon guilty of Watergate crimes and rate him an honest man than those who directly experienced the scandal. Ideology proved a stronger predictor of Nixon images than whether individuals learned of Nixon through direct experience or retrospective communication, but the relationship between Nixon memories and images of Nixon remained significant on most measures after controlling for important intervening variables.

This study delineated how retrospective media use influences our images of the past. How individuals learn of events (direct experience or retrospective media use) only affects like attitudes. For instance, how individuals learned about Watergate events only affected attitudes about Watergate. Second, the event itself must have had an important impact on people's outlook on life for it to affect images.

This study provided an important conceptual link missing from most works in collective memory by joining the study of collective memory with the Theory of Generations and found that different age groups did view Nixon differently.

Citation Indexes: Who's Cited Whom and Where

The purpose of a citation index is to enable the user to locate sources where a particular work has been cited. This is particularly useful when you know the name of a leading authority in your area of interest and want to know what other scholars have cited that person's work over a particular period of time. The example below, from the *Social Sciences Citation Index*, shows authors citing the various works of M. Fine in 1989 and 1990. For instance, Fine's 1988 article, which appeared in the *Journal of Social Issues*, volume 44, page 3, was cited by C. Baxter in the *Journal of Mental Deficiency*, volume 33, page 455, 1989.

```
FINE M
81 J SOCIOLOGY SOCIAL W          8     233
   PHILLIPS MJ     SOCIAL SC M                   30    849
90
   WESTBROO.MT   WOMEN HEAL              15    93    89
83 IMAGINATION COGNITTIO         3           249
   BELLE D         AM PSYCHOL              45    385   90
   MCCAUL KD       J APPL SO P             20    1     90
85 PSYCHOL WOMEN QUART           9     167
   CRAWFORD M    PSYCHOL                   13    477   89
R
   KAHN AS                        "        13    417   89
```

MARCEK J		"	13	367	89
E					
PEPLAU LA		"	13	379	89
TALBOTTG.M		"	16	253	89
85 WOMEN DISABILITY DOU	6				
MEEKOSHA H. AUST J SOC			24	249	89
86 ADV APPLIED SOCIAL P	3	103			
CRAWFORD M PSYCHOL WO			13	477	89
R					
86 TEACH COLL REC 87	89				
CAIRNS RB CHILD DEV			60	1437	89
88 J SOC ISSUES 44 3					
BAXTER C J MENT DEF			33	455	89
88 WOMEN DISABILITIES E					
SAXTON M J HEALTH P			15	235	90
B					
88 WOMEN DISABILIITIES E					
CRAWFORD M PSYCHOL WO			13	477	89
R					
LERMAN H CONT PSYCHO			35	268	90
B					
LEVIN BW SOCIAL SC M			30	901	90
MARECEK J PSYCHOL WO			13	367	89
E					
89 GENDER THOUGHT PSYCH					
MARECEK J PSYCHOL WO			13	367	89
E					
89 GENDER THOUGHT PSYCH	146				
CRAWFORD M PSYCHOL WO			13	477	89
R					

There are three citation indexes that you can probably locate in the Reference Department of your University Library: the *Science Citation Index*, the *Social Sciences Citation Index*, and the *Arts and Humanities Citation Index*. As a way of searching the journal literature in your field, they offer distinct advantages: the aforementioned citation searching capability and their coverage of *thousands* of journals, as opposed to hundreds in most journal indexes. A drawback of citation indexes is their lack of subject indexing: no subject headings have been assigned to the articles. A rough kind of subject indexing is available through the volume entitled *Permuterm Subject Index*, however. This volume arranges the articles covered by key words in their titles. Using this volume, you could locate all articles in a particular time period with the word "semantics" in the title, or match up "semantics" with another key word, such as "arabic." While this is not a foolproof method of indexing, it does provide a certain amount of subject access to the thousands of journals indexed.

Staying Current with *Current Contents*

Now that you've covered indexes to books, journals, and dissertations and have looked at citation indexes, you may feel that you've covered every index in the library that could possibly lead you to material on your topic. All of the above indexes have a time lag, however; it takes a certain amount of time, perhaps two weeks, perhaps three months, for indexing to appear. Such a small gap in indexing may not seem important, but during such short periods of time a lot of material is published, and a graduate student needs to check this material in order to be comprehensive.

To cover this time lag, there is a weekly publication called *Current Contents*, which reproduces the tables of contents of journals right at the time they are published, or sometimes even ahead of that time. This publication allows readers to browse the contents of the most recent issues of important journals in their field well before the articles are indexed in standard journal indexes. In addition to the contents listings, *Current Contents* arranges each issue's articles by author and by title word.

Interlibrary Loans

No matter how impressive the library collections are at your university, no graduate student will ever find all the materials she or he needs in a single library, or even in a single library *system* at a very large research institution. Interlibrary loan departments have been created to deal with the needs of students and faculty to gain access to materials at other libraries, and it is highly advisable that graduate students "learn the ropes" of interlibrary loans early on in the research process.

While the process may seem simple at first glance, there are many variables to the use of interlibrary loans. First and foremost is the matter of turnaround time, which in turn is dependent on a host of other variables: what libraries own the desired materials and how cooperative they are, the distance of the lending library, the speed of the mail, etc. Will the library lending a journal send the actual whole issue, or a photocopy of the article requested? If an item is in the Special Collections department or rare books collection of a library, that library may be reluctant to lend it. The same may be true of items that are only available in microfilm or microfiche formats.

Using the Library to Locate Publishing Opportunities

Academic libraries, particularly those at research-oriented institutions, are great places to review the literature of a field and generate ideas for publishing opportunities. Browsing the stacks of books in your area of interest can give you an idea of the kind of books being published and which publishers are publishing them; a trip to the reference department can probably give you an address and phone number for a publisher you may be interested in contacting. Similarly, among the thousands of journals to which academic research libraries subscribe, there may be dozens, perhaps hundreds, of titles that might accept articles in your area of interest.

While academic journals differ in the amount of useful information they provide in each issue to prospective authors, the *most* helpful will have a section entitled "Information for Authors" or "Notes to Contributors" or "Guidelines for Authors." This section will describe that journal's policy regarding the submission of manuscripts, its requirements for the format and/or length of manuscripts, and its process for selecting submitted manuscripts for publication. Other useful information might include the waiting period for an answer after you've submitted your manuscript.

INFORMATION FOR AUTHORS

Sociological Spectrum is a refereed interdisciplinary social science journal that publishes theoretical, methodological, quantitative and qualitative substantive research, and applied articles in the areas of sociology, social psychology, anthropology, and political science. Generally, it does not publish book reviews or comments.

Submission of a manuscript to this journal is understood to imply that it or substantial parts of it have not been published or accepted for publication elsewhere and that it is not under consideration for publication elsewhere.

Submission of manuscripts. Original and three copies of the manuscripts should be submitted to one of the editors. All accepted manuscripts, artwork, and photographs become the property of the publisher. With the manuscript please include a $10.00 fee payable to the Mid-South Sociological Association to help defray processing costs.

Transfer of copyright. All papers accepted for publication must be accompanied by a copyright release form signed by the author. This form will be provided by the editors.

Preparation of Manuscripts. All manuscripts must be typed double-spaced on 8½" × 11" paper with 1" to 1½" margins all around. Manuscripts that do not conform to these requirements may be returned to the authors for corrections and thus be delayed in publication.

References. Should be listed on separate pages following the text and should be typed double-spaced and refer only to material cited in the manuscript. They should be listed in alphabetical order and otherwise follow the current *American Sociological Review* style. In text, reference citations should include author, year of publication, and, where needed, page numbers (Brown 1978, p. 54). Identify subsequent citations of the source in the same way as the first, not using *ibid., op. cit.,* or *loc. cit.* Give both last names for dual authors; for more than two use "et al." in the text. When two authors have the same last name, use identifying initials in the text. For institutional authorship, supply minimum identification from the beginning of the complete citation (U.S. Bureau of the Census 1963, p. 117).

The reference list must be complete and include all references in the text. The use of "et al." is not acceptable in the reference list; provide the names of all authors. If there is more than one reference to the same author and year, distinguish them by the letters a,b, etc. added to the year (Levy 1963a, p 12). The first letter of each word in an article title should be capitalized. Titles of books and journals will be printed in italics, so each word of the title should be underlined. Give the publisher's name in as brief a form as is fully intelligible. For example, *John W. Wiley & Sons* should be *Wiley*. If the cited material is unpublished, use "Forthcoming" with the name of journal or publisher, otherwise use "Unpublished."

Even after you've talked with faculty and wandered through the journal stacks, you still may get a nagging feeling that you've missed some journals that might be promising. You may want to ask the reference librarian to see if there is a directory of publishing opportunities in your field. These directories list periodicals in a particular discipline and provide information similar to that contained in the "Information for Authors" section of an academic journal, namely the policies and procedures regarding the submission of material for publication. Some of these directories will also include general advice on writing articles, preparing and submitting manuscripts, and dealing with acceptance and rejection.

Some of the most useful and current directories of publishing opportunities are listed here:

MLA Directory of Periodicals. Scholars in the fields of literature, languages, and folklore have in the *MLA Directory of Periodicals* one of the most comprehensive and up-to-date directories of publishing opportunities available. This directory is a companion volume to the *MLA International Bibliography*, the most comprehensive index of journals in literature and languages, and is published biennially. The 1990/91 edition contains listings for 3,225 journals from around the world, each providing an address and information on subscriptions and advertising. Of primary interest to prospective authors is the section entitled "Editorial Description," which describes the scope of the coverage, the languages, and whether or not the journal reviews books, and the section entitled "Submission Requirements," which states the guidelines for manuscripts and the policies for acceptance and rejection.

English Record

Thomas J. Reigstad, Editor
English Dept.
SUNY College at Buffalo
1300 Elmwood Ave.,
Buffalo, NY 14222

First Published: 1950
Sponsoring organization: New York
State English Council
ISSN: 0013-8363
MLA *acronym: EngR*

SUBSCRIPTION INFORMATION

Frequency of publication: 4 times/yr
(Fall, Winter, Spring, Summer)
Circulation: 1,500
Available in microform: No

ADVERTISING DESCRIPTION

Advertising accepted: Yes

EDITORIAL DESCRIPTION

Scope: General articles of interest
to English teachers on all levels of instruction are invited.
Reviews books: Yes
Publishes notes: No
Languages accepted: English
Prints Abstracts: No

SUBMISSION REQUIREMENTS

Author pays submission fee: No
Author pays page charges: No
Length of articles: 1,500-2,000 words
Length of book reviews: 350 words
Style: None
Number of copies required: 2
Rejected manuscripts: Returned;
enclose return postage
Time before publication decision: 6-8
weeks
Articles submitted per year: 150
Articles published per year: 28
Book reviews published per year: 2-4

Refereed and Nonrefereed Economic Journals: A Guide to Publishing Opportunities (Greenwood Press, 1988). For prospective authors seeking to publish in economics journals, this guide lists over two hundred journals that accept manuscripts in English. The main body of the work is a directory of these journals, with each entry divided into three parts: (1) a brief sketch of the journal, showing the date it began, its circulation, its affiliation, and a brief statement of its editorial policy (i.e., "To provide a forum for creative and scholarly work in agricultural economics" is one of the more vague editorial statements, others include such specifics as " . . . Topicality, comprehensibility for foreign readers, and novelty are preferred"); (2) a guide to the reviewing process, including information on the acceptance rate for manuscripts, the average time a review will take, and the time it will probably take to get published; (3) information regarding the length, style, and other essential information about the manuscript itself.

Journals in Psychology: A Resource Listing for Authors (American Psychological Association, 1989). In the 1989 second edition of this directory, there are 232 journals listed. The criteria for inclusion are that the journal must be in English and that psychology must comprise "at least a substantial portion of the journal's editorial domain." Each entry includes the address of the publisher, the name and address of the editor, the number of articles the journal publishes each year, the number of subscribers, and the frequency with which the journal is published. Perhaps of most interest to prospective authors, however, are two sections entitled *Editorial Policy* and *Selective Notes on Submissions.* As you can see from the example below, the Editorial Policy section defines the scope of the journal and lists any special considerations, such as the acceptability of interdisciplinary articles, the language requirements for manuscripts, and whether the journal accepts empirical, theoretical, or review articles. The "Selective Notes on Submission" section gets more into the details of the manuscript: what style manual to follow, how many copies to submit, etc.

> Editorial Policy: *Adolescence* is an international quarterly devoted to the physiological, psychological, psychiatric, sociological, and educational aspects of the second decade of human life.

> Selective Notes on Submissions: Instructions to authors included in each issue of the journal. Authors to prepare manuscripts according to the *Publication Manual of the American Psychological Association* (3rd ed.). Submit two (2) copies of the manuscript to the editor, c/o the publisher.

A Guide to 100 Publishing Opportunities for Business Faculty. From *Journal of Business Ethics* to the *Journal of Accountancy* to the *Labor Law Journal*, one hundred journals in which business faculty might be able to publish are listed; essential information on manuscript submission is included for each. Many titles are from outside the narrow definition of business and management, from such areas as applied psychology, law, economics, etc. While the title implies that these are publishing opportunities for business *faculty*, there is no stipulation that graduate students cannot submit manuscripts as well. Entries can be up to five pages long and will describe the journal's publishing format in great detail, e.g., "*Economica* strongly discourages the use of footnotes."

The Annotated Bibliographies of Serials series (Greenwood Press). This series is primarily designed to assist librarians in selecting serials for their collections. By serials, the editors of this series mean any publication appearing at least once per year. This series does not include all the detailed information on manuscript submission that you may find in other directories described here, but it can nevertheless be very helpful in identifying titles that might accept your manuscript. Each volume in the series provides "comprehensive coverage of the English-language serials in one subject area with extensively annotated entries for each serial." For each serial listed, you can find the publisher's address, the name(s) of the editor(s), the date the title was founded, the price, the circulation, the target audience, where the title is indexed, and the way in which manuscripts are selected. In addition, there is a short annotation, usually no more than two paragraphs, describing the scope of the serials' coverage, as seen below in an example from *History Journals and Serials; An Analytical Guide*:

> 295. *The Journal of American History.* DATE FOUNDED: 1914. TITLE CHANGES: *Mississippi Valley Historical Review.* (1914-1964). FREQUENCY: q. PRICE: $40/yr. institutions. PUBLISHER: Organization of American Historians, 112 N. Bryan St, Bloomington, IN 47401. EDITOR: Lewis Perry. INDEX. ADVERTISEMENTS. CIRCULATION: 12,000. MANUSCRIPT SELECTION: Blind refereed. MICROFORMS: MIMC, UMI. BOOK REVIEWS. INDEXED/ABSTRACTED: AmerH, BoRv, CurrCont, HumI, SSCI. TARGET AUDIENCE: AC.

All periods and topics in American history are covered in this excellent journal. Editorial policy is to seek articles that either make a significant advance in scholarship on a topic or problem of general interest or survey recent specialized scholarship so as to make it accessible to a wider readership. Each issue contains five articles, up to 100 signed reviews of about 500 words, book notes, news and comments (which includes material about archives and bibliographies and research guides), communications, and lists of recent articles and recent dissertations. The extensive reviews and other bibliographical features make it particularly valuable to librarians.

Here follows a list of titles from the *Annotated Bibliographies of Serials* series:

Library and Information Science Journals and Serials: An Analytical Guide. Mary Ann Bowman, compiler.
Philosophy Journals and Serials: An Analytical Guide. Douglas H. Ruben, compiler.
Dentistry Journals and Serials: An Analytical Guide. Aletha A. Kowitz, compiler.
Agricultural and Animal Science Journals and Serials: An Analytical Guide. Richard D. Jensen, Connie Lamb, and Nathan M. Smith, compilers.
Economics Journals and Serials: An Analytical Guide. Beatrice Sichel and Werner Sichel, compilers.
Financial Journals and Serials: An Analytical Guide to Accounting, Banking, Finance, Insurance, and Investment Periodicals. William Fisher, compiler.
Marine Science Journals and Serials: An Analytical Guide. Judith B. Barnett, compiler.

History Journals and Serials: An Analytical Guide. Janet
  Fyfe, compiler.
Serials on Aging: An Analytical Guide. Shirley B. Hesslein,
  compiler.
Anthropology Journals and Serials: An Analytical Guide.
  John T. Williams, compiler.
Cancer Journals and Serials: An Analytical Guide. Pauline
  M. Vaillancourt, compiler.
Education Journals and Serials: An Analytical Guide. Mary
  Ellen Collins, compiler.
Religion Journals and Serials: An Analytical Guide. Eugene
  C. Fieg, Jr., compiler.

As you can see, for almost every field in which a journal is
published, there is at least one guide to journals. Some of these
guides will offer very specific guidelines on how to submit manuscripts for publication, others may not provide this but can still be
useful in your search for a publisher.

The examples listed above are merely a sampling of the dozens
of potentially helpful directories available. To find out what your
library has, ask your reference librarian, or check your online catalog or card catalog under some of the following headings (insert
any subject in place of "psychology"):

PSYCHOLOGY—PERIODICALS—BIBLIOGRAPHY
PSYCHOLOGY—AUTHORSHIP
PSYCHOLOGY—PERIODICALS—DIRECTORIES
PSYCHOLOGY—PERIODICALS—AUTHORSHIP
PSYCHOLOGY—PERIODICALS—PUBLISHING

Two Rudiments of Proposal Writing

ROBERT A. LUCAS
Associate Vice President
Graduate Studies and Research
California Polytechnic State University
San Luis Obispo

Writing for publication unquestionably challenges the graduate student. But those who write for journals have an advantage that those

who write proposals for grants do not have: they have seen copious examples of what an article looks like. Anyone exposed to writing research papers for seminars has already perused innumerable articles in print. Not so the beginning writer of grant proposals.

The World of Proposals Is Mysterious

Compared to scholarly publication, the world of proposals and grants seems shrouded in mystery largely because few scholars see examples of funded proposals. Proposals are considered proprietary. As a result, they aren't available to the public. Once a grant is made, you may have to invoke the Public Information Act to see one, if you know what to ask for in the first place.

To make matters worse, graduate programs offer no instruction in or orientation to the practice of writing proposals. Although more and more universities are adding instruction in the skills of proposal writing to the graduate program as part of a seminar in research methods, writing for grants is still one of the least-studied tools of the profession.

The World of Proposals Is Not Mysterious

Seeing examples of a proposal or two will go a long way to removing much of the mystery about the business. One way to do this without invoking the Public Information Act is to scan the list of local awards published by your campus grants office, find one of interest to you, and then stop by the grants office and ask to see it. If the office believes you have good reason to look and are not simply asking to rifle through the files indiscriminately, the staff will probably be cooperative.

There are also a few published collections of proposals. Any of the three editions of *The Proposal Writer's Swipe File* prints numerous examples of professionally written proposals. The proposals, though, focus on statements written for nonprofits like alcohol and drug rehabilitation programs and rape crisis centers and are therefore less appropriate in an academic setting. Similar to the swipe file is Pam Moore's *Models for Success, A Look at Grant-Winning Proposals*, published in 1990. A collection more appropriate to academic audiences is *Grant Proposals That Succeeded*, edited by Virginia White. This compendium prints proposals written in a university setting and offers a helpful analysis of each. The discussion reviews how the proposal was developed, how it was improved through iteration, what happened when the grant was negotiated, and what can be learned specifically from each case. More current examples of proposals are printed in "The Grants Clinic" section of *Grants Magazine*.

Once you've seen a proposal or two, a lot of the mystery disappears. Your first look may even be a bit of a letdown. "Oh, is that all it is? I thought it was a big deal." Writing a grant will begin to seem oddly doable. All that's required is a sound idea, some documentation, a bit of forethought, and a workable plan of attack.

Caution: In the humanities, in contrast to the world of the social sciences, a great number of awards are made for fellowships. These are personal awards rather than grants; that is, the check has the name of the faculty member on it rather than that of the university. Thus, the grants office will not see these, and you won't be able to ask for sample copies to view. In this case, it's best to ask the agency making the award if there are any copies of exemplary fellowship proposals you could see.

Fear of Failure Is a Great Impediment

If an article is turned down for publication, the author will often assume it was because it was at the wrong journal. He or she will usually have the patience to find the right place to which to send it. But if a proposal is turned down, the message is often received differently.

By definition, you can't prove conclusively that a proposal is good until you've gotten the grant and tested the idea. So added to the fear of failure we all have when we write something for publication is the uncertainty that the idea may be no good at all. At any point along the way, it's easy for someone to undermine your confidence. The writer is left to think, worry, suspect, grieve that the proposal was really worthless after all. It takes conviction to write, to put it out there, to be rejected, and to continue to believe in your idea.

Fear of failure adds to the anxiety of proposal writing and thins out the ranks of those willing to take a chance. The good news is that if you do choose to write, the thinned ranks increase your odds for success.

What Grants Are Made For

Grants are made for a variety of purposes, some obvious, some not so. They can include the following:

- a grant for research;
- a grant for a summer fellowship at the home institution;

- a grant for released time from teaching for research or for new course development;
- a grant to pay for an undergraduate or graduate student as a research assistant in a mentor relationship;
- a grant to travel to a collection;
- a grant to do research while at a collection;
- a grant to travel to another research site and collaborate with an established researcher on something you can't do at your institution;
- a grant for research equipment;
- a grant for innovative instructional equipment;
- a grant to demonstrate a promising technique or concept in your field;
- a grant to offer a training program in a new area, with additional funds to develop new and innovative training materials.

Why Grants Are Made

Proposals are funded because they propose a good idea and because they are in the right place at the right time. Both halves of this equation can be equally valid. Only those grant proposals in writing and on the sponsor's desk can be funded. Sponsors are not like textbook sales representatives. They do not visit campus and ask if you've got any good ideas for a grant the way the salespeople will root around looking for the next Samuelson's *Economics*. What they do do is sit around in offices hundreds or thousands of miles from where you are, reading stacks of proposals written by hundreds of researchers who propose a vast variety of ideas for support. If yours isn't in that stack, it hasn't a chance of being funded.

So Secret Rule #1 is: Proposals that are written are more likely to be funded than proposals that are not.

A Reasonable Success Rate

In the world of article writing, the success rate for publication is high. As long as one has a decent article and the patience to keep revising it and sending it out until the right journal is found, it is likely that it will be published. A prolific scientist might publish as much as 90 percent of what he or she writes.

For grants, a reasonable success rate is much lower. The actual rate depends on the sponsor and the competition. Usually the competition guidelines will tell you how much money is available, how many proposals were received in the previous year, and how many awards were made. Depending on the stiffness of the competition, funding rates can run from 5 to 35 percent.

A reasonable overall goal for a beginner is a 20- to 25-percent success rate. Many hold a higher standard for themselves. They also suffer a lot of needless frustration and stress. It is better to assume that in the beginning you'll get a lot of turndowns, and that you'll learn a lot, too.

Start by Getting Something in Writing
The best way to get started on one of these proposals is to write before you are ready. If you have ever thought about writing a proposal to a program for which you're eligible, then start today. You probably already know enough to write 70 percent of this proposal, and the other 30 percent will be easier to manage once you have something concrete in writing so you can see what it is you don't know.

Don't waste time wondering whether you should try, or whether you should wait until the perfect grant program comes along, or whether you're the type, or whether your department will value it, or whether there will be a place on the tenure and promotion checklist to enter grants received. Just do it.

Writing a proposal with the goal of familiarizing yourself with the process the first time through is plenty enough to do without worrying about whether you'll actually get the money. Just getting the feel of shaping an idea, finding a sponsor, drafting a proposal, creating a budget, and meeting the deadline is an important experience. If you do get a grant the first time out, consider that a bonus.

Finding Sponsors
Once you have decided to write a proposal, if you're unsure about where to send it, there are a number of books that catalog sponsors. Most of the sources that summarize grant opportunities, like the *Annual Register of Grant Support*, are organized according to field. You can use the index or the table of contents, or just skim the major sections on social science or the humanities. It's like looking through the *Whole Earth Catalog*. You'll find all sorts of possibilities for grants that had never occurred to you.

A good overview of what's available for the social scientist is the *Guide to Federal Funding for Social Scientists*, edited in 1990 by Anne Mantegna. Sponsored by the American Political Science Association, this volume describes over 300 federal programs and summarizes their funding priorities and guidelines.

For the humanist, there is the *Directory of Grants in the Humanities*. It covers competitions ranging from the Swann Foundation Fellowship for the Study of Caricature and Cartoon to the American Council of Learned Societies Fellowships for Dissertation Research Abroad Related to China.

If you prefer computers and databases, check with your library or campus grants office to see if they subscribe to a computerized sponsor database system like IRIS from the University of Illinois or SPIN from the State University of New York. These systems offer data printout and information fast. Although the entries have no more information than those in the printed books, changeable data like the names of the contact people and the amounts available will be more up-to-date.

Don't assume that a one-paragraph description from the books or computer programs will be enough for you to write a proposal, though. After all, how much can you learn in one paragraph? Remember the time you answered a singles ad from a one-paragraph description that seemed perfect? Do you recall what that character was like in person?

Let's face it. You've got to know a whole lot more about a program to be sure that it's the one for your proposal. So how do you find out?

Get the Guidelines and Read Them

The basic rule for winning grants is guidelines, guidelines, guidelines. You can get them by writing the sponsor at the address listed in the books. Or you can ask your campus grants office. That's one of the reasons it's in business—to keep up-to-date guidelines in its sponsor files. If it doesn't have this year's guidelines, last year's will give you some direction to move in until the new ones arrive.

Read the guidelines thoroughly and believe everything they say. They have got to be read and digested. No program officer at a granting agency is going to want to read a proposal that hasn't been written to those specific guidelines.

Talk to the Program Officer

Once you've read the guidelines and think you know what they say, tell yourself you don't, because you really don't, and call the program officer at the sponsor. This step is the second most critical one in the proposal writing process.

So Secret Rule #2 is: Talk to the program officer before you move on to completing the draft of your proposal for that sponsor.

No matter how clear the guidelines are, they will not tell you everything you need to know to write a good proposal. So you must read them carefully, and then assume you don't know the whole story because you don't, and then call the program officer. This step is not optional. That's why it's been repeated.

When you call, tell the Program Officer that you are writing a proposal for the BLOP competition, that you've read the guidelines, and that your idea seems to fit, but you wanted to make sure (for example, you're not clear about the scope of a statement in the eligibility requirements).

Then describe your idea in one paragraph. (*Hint:* A paragraph usually has a topic sentence, three or four sentences amplifying it, and a summary sentence. Don't spend any more time on your description. You made the call to listen, not to lobby.) Once you have made your brief statement, activate all your listening skills to learn what this person, who may be responsible for the allocation of millions of dollars each year, has to say. You'll be amazed at what you can learn. The ten minutes on the phone will be invaluable.

Learning More About the Parts of a Proposal

The guidelines for a competition will tell you what you should put into your proposal. If they don't, or if you just want to know more about the kinds of things that are usually included, say, in the section on methods, a number of books describe this phase of proposal development fully. One is Robert Lefferts's book called *Getting a Grant in the 1990s*. It focuses on the university context even though the one example of a proposal given describes a social service program.

For the person in the social sciences, David R. Krathwohl's *How to Prepare a Research Proposal: Guidelines for Funding Dissertations in the Social and Behavioral Sciences* is helpful for both graduate school dissertations and for writing proposals for external sponsorship. In its third edition in 1988, it's a classic.

The Role of the Grants Office

As a new academic it is wise to get in touch with the grants officers on your campus. Unlike the IRS, it is there to help. Like the IRS, it'll cost, in the indirect costs the grants office adds to the budget you send in with your grant proposal. But like taxes, you probably

216 • The Grad Student's Guide to Getting Published

won't be able to avoid overhead on your grant anyway, so you should take advantage of the services your money is intended to provide. The staff in the research administration office is particularly adept at helping you budget your grant.

Special Advantages for the New Professor

Another incentive to writing proposals before you achieve full professorship is the fact that early in your career, your very inexperience works in your favor, giving you an advantage. The new professor—that is, the person within five years of the conferral of the terminal degree—receives special consideration for peer review in some competitions by being grouped only with other beginners. Take advantage of this edge, because all too soon you'll be a tenured, first-rung, associate professor in competition with people who have fifteen years of experience at the full-professor level.

Internal Grants

If your campus has a well-developed internal seed grant program that makes released-time awards or minigrants of less than $10,000 or summer fellowships, you should plan on applying for these and figure that you are entitled to one, two, or maybe even three seed grants. The benefit of applying for inside funds is that the competition is less stiff, and as a graduate student or a new faculty member, your chances of being funded should be high—maybe one out of two.

The best use of these small grants is to get you started on a project that will lead to outside sources of support for your research. Look for larger grants or fellowship awards from federal agencies or foundations. That's what your department, the committee, or administrator who gave you the grant will expect you to do with the grant.

What To Do When Your Proposal Is Turned Down

If you get turned down, don't act surprised. And above all don't get incensed, at least not in front of the people who said "no." Assume it will happen, and that the event presents you with another opportunity to improve your idea. Ask the program officer at the sponsor for the peer reviews. If these are not available, ask for general comments about areas for improvement. Use these to revise the proposal. The success rate for resubmitted proposals is higher than it is for proposals submitted the first time.

Last Words, Coda, End Note, Footsection, Final Thoughts
The books about proposal writing give a lot of detail about writing proposals. But the best advice is to start by writing a proposal and not worrying about whether it's perfect. A proposal is by definition a trial balloon. Unlike a journal article, it doesn't have to have all the parts perfectly in place, all the edges sanded, all the pockmarks filled in, all the paint matching. But it does have to be written in order to be funded.

Do yourself a favor and develop the skill and habit of writing proposals early in your career. It's the gift that keeps giving.

8

Shaping the Future

Conclusion
Alida Allison, PhD and Terri Frongia, PhD

The Shape of the PhD: Past, Present, and Future (excerpt)
Theodore Ziolkowski, PhD

Shaping the Future of the Profession Through Publication
Alida Allison, PhD and Terri Frongia, PhD

Conclusion

This book began by stating the fact that most of us receive little training in the practical aspects of our profession during our increasingly long years in graduate school. Throughout the pages of *The Grad Student's Guide to Getting Published*, we have attempted some remedy by offering crucial information on publishing not only in its particulars, but in the broadest sense as scholarly exchange and scholarly self-identity. The point has been often repeated that it is largely up to you to find out what your university may indeed offer in terms of practical training, up to you to learn what you can within that context, and up to you to agitate for more training, such as a publication workshop on your campus. You've been encouraged to publish and to present at conferences, and to begin establishing a network of peers, professors, mentors, interlocutors, and friends.

Along with many contributors, we have emphasized the fundamental obligation to determine and define the purpose of our re-

219

search and publication: to whom do we address our scholarship—to each other, to our students, to the general public? How do we assess each other's value when the rewards of an academic's life are handed round? And how do we explain the nature of the rewards and punishments themselves: Is the reward research time and is the punishment teaching?

As we approach the millennium, the highly specialized training in research we receive in graduate school may be less and less applicable to the real world most of us will live in as professional academics. Except for a relative few, increasing numbers of us will work on nonresearch-oriented campuses where the broad-based educational mission of the institution, the real work load, and the needs of the student constituency require more from us as teachers than as researchers. Few of us will receive time off from teaching to pursue publication. And even when we do publish, much of the scholarly work we actually perform will be undervalued, including editing or reading for a journal, translating, publishing collaboratively, or writing for the generally literate world that exists outside the university. This imbalance between essential facets of academic endeavor—such as serving the profession, educating the public, or even teaching—and publication as the primary assessment for academic acclaim and reward is at the crux of the crisis of identity in the profession.

In *The Grad Student's Guide to Getting Published*, you've heard different voices speaking from many perspectives. To these, to the information they've imparted and the issues they've raised, we now add one more voice, that of Theodore Ziolkowski, Dean of Princeton's Graduate School. In his speech to the Association of Departments of English, Dean Ziolkowski addresses fundamental questions about the doctorate in terms broadly applicable to both the humanities and the social sciences: questions about both the process of getting the degree and questions about using it. Like George Slusser, whose essay opened this book, Ziolkowski critiques the disjuncture between what we are trained to do in graduate school and what most of us will actually be doing once we are employed.

Like other contributors, Dean Ziolkowski also raises concerns about the erosion of ethics and the escalation of self-interest and scholarly entrepreneurship in both faculty and students. This escalation is largely in response to the disproportionate rewards for certain kinds of publication in the academic market. The demands on professors to publish tend to conflict with their role in training graduate students for the profession. While recognizing this conflict, Dr. Ziolkowski points out that the increasing need for professional flexibility and the growing diversity of the student population are potentially invigorating sources of scholarship, for example, through interdisciplinary research or through translation. The academic world, in its highest sense, is a unifying network that more than ever needs to include rather than exclude.

The Shape of the PhD: Past, Present, and Future

Excerpts from an address to the Association
of Departments of English
THEODORE ZIOLKOWSKI
Dean, Princeton Graduate School
Professor of Comparative Literature

... In 1964 the Association of Graduate Schools and the Council of Graduate Schools issued a joint statement summarizing their view that the entire course of study for the PhD should normally involve no more than four years beyond the baccalaureate. Reality, of course, has veered sharply away from this ideal. In 1970 only 12 percent of graduate students completed their PhDs within four years of the baccalaureate. The average registered time to earn the degree steadily increased from 5.2 years in 1958–60 to 5.4 years in 1967 and, without a break in the curve, to 6.9 years in 1988. But these scandalous figures do not have to be accepted as an unalterable pattern.

Various factors have been cited to account for the lengthening time required for the PhD—ranging from the rise in the number of part-time students to the sources of support (personal funds, teaching, other jobs, research assistantships, or fellowships). But these considerations are less important than shifts in disciplinary expectations. Almost all the other conditions can be changed by external adjustments, but disciplinary expectations can be transformed only from within the individual departments.

Frequently, as exciting new avenues of scholarship open up, we simply add to the existing requirements—and accordingly to the period of study before the general examination—instead of making decisions and tailoring our expectations to a rational program. Instead of thinking about the program that will benefit our students, we think of our own special interests. We insist that every student should be exposed to our own period or genre or theoretical mode. We have a cumulative theory of doctoral education rather than a representative one. Our colleagues in the sciences have generally displayed a sharper sense of the state of their arts and have shaped their requirements accordingly. Indeed, science departments nationally tend to move their students as quickly as possible through the year or two of preliminary courses in order to involve them in full-time research.

The sciences have in general done a much better job of accommodating their theses to the practices of the discipline: the dissertations, parts of which have often already been presented at conferences and published in journals, are prepared according to current publication standards. In the humanities, in contrast, many of us still permit or even encourage theses that stand in no apparent relation to the expectations of book publishers or journals. In a day when most university presses are reluctant to look at manuscripts of more than 400 pages encumbered with the standard bibliographic review and the usual excessive footnotes, it is almost unethical of us as advisers to tolerate such work from our students. How many of us have never known the student who had to spend a year padding out a thesis to our satisfaction, only to spend another year taking it all out again so that a publisher will look at it? Indeed, as I scan the readers' reports from various departments that pass across my desk, I am constantly astonished at the admonitions that otherwise acceptable dissertations will require substantial revisions before they can be published. Who, after all, should be counseling the student on these matters if not the faculty advisers? Why was the dissertation permitted to become so long and unruly in the first place?

... we can help [our students] by rethinking the doctoral program, by cutting our expectations back to a reasonable norm, and by insisting that the dissertation be not a lifework—a *Habilitationsschrift* or *thèse d'état*—but simply a demonstration of scholarly competence. For what kinds of careers, after all, are we preparing our students?

... the facts do suggest that we need to prepare students for teaching careers in which flexibility will be a high priority. In many of our graduate programs today we accustom our students to expect to teach mainly advanced courses or seminars on highly specialized topics. Indeed, many departments suffer from a plethora of thinly populated courses on a variety of esoteric subjects that do not constitute a thoughtful, coherent program for either undergraduate or graduate students. . . .

. . . let me share with you a few more personal opinions—you may wish to call them biases or even prejudices. I have spoken of the need to change the departmental ethos to accommodate the expectations of the PhD to the realities of publication and teaching. But I want to add a word about ethics as well. It has been my own depressing experience, during a decade in the dean's office, that academic fraud has been, if not necessarily increasing among students, then certainly more often detected in their work—the delicts ranging from plagiarism to computer fraud. We can no longer take for granted that the standards of academic ethics will be absorbed osmotically by students or by junior colleagues. Just as both graduate students and instructors have learned from the highly publicized cases of academic highfliers to attempt to negotiate the terms of their fellowships and assistantships, so too a few of them have apparently learned from their tenured role models that the end justifies the means and that entrepreneurship is an adequate alternative to scholarship. When we restore the old-fashioned mentoring relationship—what used to be called the apprenticeship—that is necessary for training in the skills of scholarship and teaching, we should also pay explicit attention to the ethics of the academic profession—the ethics of footnotes as well as the ethics of collegial responsibility.

I return now finally to the notion of flexibility: if many of our current graduate students are likely to spend most of their careers teaching nonhumanists in comprehensive institutions and nonmajors in liberal arts colleges, that does not imply a sacrifice of the mind. Certainly they should be encouraged to pursue their research wherever their imaginations may lead them. As far as their teaching is concerned, however, we are obliged to prepare them for the trends they are likely to encounter. . . . So we must prepare our students for accommodation—that is, we must help them develop the flexibility to accept new developments into their thinking and teaching and to expose their students to the variety of approaches that characterize the humanities. This goal is doubly important because many of our students will be teaching in institutions where they cannot afford to be mere specialists.

Following a century of departmentalization, every field—from the physical and life sciences to the social sciences and humanities—has entered a new era of interdisciplinary enrichment. Our students can turn this trend to their teaching advantage if they are prepared, when dealing with students whose major interests lie in seemingly remote areas, to think creatively about whatever subject is under study—indeed, to remember that it *is* a subject and not just a method, that it is substance, not theory. Again, the approach should not be legislated; students should be encouraged to follow their own inclinations. But the interdisciplinary movement in literary studies has in the past decade alerted us to the possibilities of many combinations that extend beyond departmental boundaries: gender studies, or law and literature, or medicine and literature . . . .

Let me conclude by summarizing my views as theses.

1. There will be a need, in the late nineties and the following decades, for steady and even slightly larger cohorts of PhDs in the MLA fields. . . .

2. This need should be addressed . . . by enabling students to obtain their degrees more smoothly and by reducing the cases of attrition caused by faculty neglect.

3. This goal can be accomplished, first, by applying new monies from federal, corporate, or university sources to the support of current enrollment levels and resisting the temptation to spread these funds more widely and thinly.

4. It can be expedited, second, by a thoughtful reassessment of our PhD programs, which should accommodate our academic expectations to the realities of our changing disciplines and the real world of scholarship and publication.

WORKS CITED

Bowen, William G., and Julie Ann Sosa. *Prospects for Faculty in the Arts and Sciences: A Study of Factors Affecting Demand and Supply, 1987 to 2012*. Princeton: Princeton UP, 1989.

Council of Graduate Schools. *The Doctor of Philosophy Degree: A Policy Statement*. Washington: CGS, 1990.

Shaping the Future of the Profession Through Publication

Our concluding advice is this: although the leap from student to faculty member is an enormous one, don't forget your graduate school experience ... or lack of experience. Change is not only possible and necessary, for better or worse it is inevitable. The inadequacies of graduate school training, the imbalances in professional recognition, and the decline of academic ethics can—and should—be redressed. Certainly preferable to passively perpetuating the deficiences of the vocation you have worked so long to enter is to actively participate in shaping its future. And one of the most enduring ways to participate, of course, is to publish.

NOTES ON CONTRIBUTORS

Editors

Alida Allison received her BA and her MA from San Diego State University; in 1990 she received her PhD in Comparative Literature from UC Riverside. She is an Assistant Professor in the Department of English and Comparative Literature at San Diego State University where she specializes in children's literature and contemporary fiction. Her interest in mythology and women's studies was expressed in her dissertation "Eurydice: The Lost Voice," a study of the changing depictions of Eurydice. Her first academic publication was a seminar paper that the course professor submitted on her behalf to the *Dictionary of Literary Biography*. She has subsequently published many articles, presents often at conferences, and serves as the director of the SDSU-based community group, the Children's Literature Circle. Her book *Isaac Bashevis Singer: His Stories for Children* is due out in 1993 for Twayne's American Children's Authors series. She is also a freelance writer and editor and the author of four children's books.

Terri Frongia, who studied in Italy for several years and earned a BA in Art History, received her PhD in 1990 in Comparative Literature from UC Riverside. She is currently a freelance writer, translator, and interpreter. Before receiving her MA, she was approached by her mentor, Dr. Jean-Pierre Barricelli, to collaborate on an article for his book *Melopoiesis: Approaches to the Study of Literature and Music*; it was her first academic publication. Along with Alida Allison, she conducted interviews with science fiction writers at a conference in Leeds, England; the result appears in *Fiction 2000: Cyberpunk and the Future of Narrative* (University of Georgia Press).

She has completed a monograph, "The Aesthetics of the Marvelous," and has written several reference book articles. Her scholarly interests include 17th-century aesthetics (the subject of her dissertation), contemporary Italian fantasy, and children's literature. By approaching these seemingly disparate realms through the concept of "meraviglia" (the marvelous, wonder), she finds much material for reflection, conference presentations, and publications.

Contributors

Robert Apatow received his BA in Philosophy from UC Santa Barbara. He is currently working on his dissertation concerning Plato's *Meno*, and will soon receive his PhD in Philosophy from UC Riverside.

Jean-Pierre Barricelli, Professor of Romance Languages and Comparative Literature, received his PhD from Harvard; he is currently Chair of the Department of Literatures and Languages at UC Riverside. Author of numerous books and articles on the Renaissance, romanticism, interart theory, and interdisciplinary studies involving literature and music/visual arts/law, his most recent publications include *Teaching Literature and Other Arts* (which he co-edited for the MLA's "Options for Teaching" series), *Manzoni*, and *Dante's Vision and the Artist*.

Joan Baum, who received her PhD from Columbia, is Professor of English at York College, City University of New York. She is editor and author of the booklet *Publishing in the Academy*, which grew out of a university-supported seminar in faculty development.

Peter Bliss, who also holds a degree in History, received a Master of Library Science from the University of Washington. He is presently Reference Librarian and Head of the Education Services unit at the Rivera Library, UC Riverside.

Diane Buckles, a graduate student and teaching assistant (GTA) specializing in composition and rhetoric at San Diego State University, is currently completing her thesis, which examines the gendered space of composition in the academy. She has also worked as an editor, nationally syndicated food columnist, and travel writer.

Susan E. Cayleff, who received her PhD from Brown University, is Associate Professor of Women's Studies at San Diego State University, where she teaches culturally diverse U.S. women's history, women and the history of medicine, women's sexuality, women in sports, and biography/autobiography. The founder of Graduate Women Scholars of Southern California (an academic/social network), her most recent publications include *The "Golden Cyclone":* *The Life and Legend of 'Babe' Didrikson Zaharias* (University of Illinois Press).

Joseph Childers, who holds a PhD from Columbia University, is an Assistant Professor of English at UC Riverside. A recent recipient of an American Council of Learned Societies (ACLS) fellowship, he has authored articles on Victorian culture and society, literary theory, cultural theory, and the English novel, and has recently completed the monograph "Interpretive Strategies: Language, Politics, and the Early Victorian Novel."

Brian Copenhaver received his PhD from the University of Kansas. He has been Professor of History and Philosophy and Dean of Humanities and Social Sciences at UC Riverside since 1988. He teaches and writes about the history of philosophy and science in early modern Europe.

Robert Griffin, who received his PhD from Yale University, is a Professor of French and Comparative Literature at UC Riverside. A specialist in Comparative Mythology and French and Italian literatures of the Middle Ages and Renaissance, he has authored over forty scholarly articles on Greek, Roman, French, Italian, and English literature and culture. His most recent books include *Flaubert's Early Writings* (University of Nebraska Press).

Jay L. Halio received his PhD from Yale and has been a Professor of English at the University of Delaware since 1968. Associate Provost for Instruction from 1975 to 1981, he founded the University's Center for Teaching Effectiveness and its publication *About Teaching*; in 1985 he was appointed Chair of the Board of Editors of the University of Delaware Press. His publications include old-spelling critical editions of works from the English Renaissance, as well as numerous journal articles and reviews. He is currently preparing a book on the comedy of Philip Roth.

Roberta A. Hobson is an MA candidate in the Department of History at San Diego State University. Her thesis is entitled " 'At the End of Her Rope': Women Murderers in Southern California, 1880–1910."

Patricia Huckle, who received her PhD from the University of Southern California, is a Professor in the Women's Studies Department and Associate Dean of the College of Arts and Letters at San Diego State University. Her publications include articles on affirmative action issues and a political biography, *Tish Sommers, Activist, and the Founding of the Older Women's League* (University of Tennessee Press).

Mercedes Jimenez, a native of Madrid, Spain, received her PhD from UC Riverside, where she is presently a Spanish instructor and teaching assistant supervisor. She has published several articles on contemporary Spanish literature, and her dissertation was published as the book *Carmen Martín Gaite y la narración: teoría y práctica.*

Robert A. Lucas, who received a PhD in English from the University of Illinois, is currently Associate Vice-President for Graduate Studies and Research at Cal Poly, San Luis Obispo. Author of over forty articles, he serves on the editorial boards of *Grants Magazine* and *Research Management Review*, writes regularly for *Grants Magazine*, and is nationally known for his tongue-in-cheek column, "Ask Ann Granters." In addition to numerous grant-writing and publications workshops, he has also produced a book, *The Grants World Inside Out* (University of Illinois Press).

Larry McCaffery received his PhD from the University of Illinois and is a Professor of English at San Diego State University. Co-editor of *Fiction International, Critique: Studies in Contemporary Fiction*, and *American Book Review*, he has authored numerous books on postmodern fiction, including most recently *Storming the Reality Studio: A Casebook of Cyberpunk and Postmodern Science Fiction* (Duke University Press).

Terence Moore, recipient of an MA from St. John's College, Cambridge, joined Cambridge University Press in 1976 and was for several years responsible for much of the literary criticism list. He moved to the United States in 1987 to take up his present position as Executive Editor responsible for Humanities publishing at the New York branch of the University Press.

Max Neiman, who received his doctorate from the University of Wisconsin, Milwaukee, is a Professor of Political Science at UC Riverside whose research focuses on public policy, urban planning politics, and urban political theory. A reader for such journals as the *Journal of Politics* and the *Urban Affairs Quarterly*, he has published in a variety of political science journals.

Linda Nilson received an MS and PhD from the University of Wisconsin, Madison, and is presently the Director of the Teaching Assistant Development Program (TADP) at UC Riverside. On the faculty of the Department of Sociology at UCLA for ten years, she developed and administered her department's TA training program and was twice nominated for a campuswide Distinguished Teaching Award.

Marina Pianca, who received a PhD from UCLA and has taught at various institutions in the United States, Argentina, and Panama, is presently an Associate Professor of Spanish and Portuguese, and Chair of Latin American Studies at UC Riverside. She has published widely on the subject of Latin American Theater, and her most recent books include *Popular Theatre in Latin America: Continuities and Transformations* (ATINT research collective, University of New Mexico Press).

Robert N. Pollin holds a PhD in Economics from the New School for Social Research and is Associate Professor of Economics at UC Riverside. He has published widely in his specialty areas (money and credit, macroeconomics, and political economy), including several coauthored articles with graduate students. He is on the national steering committee of the Union for Radical Political Economics, is an Editorial Associate of *Dollars and Sense* magazine, and has worked with the Joint Economic Committee of the U.S. Congress, the United Nations Development Program, and the Economic Policy Institute in Washington, D.C.

Roberta J. Schmitz is an MA candidate in the Department of History at San Diego State University. Her thesis is titled "Florence Hagen Prybylla: Eighty Years in the Life of a German Catholic Minnesotan; A Biographical Study."

Jacqueline S. Senteney, who has an MA in Educational Technology, is completing her MA in Rhetoric and the Teaching of Writing at San Diego State University. A former high school English teacher and Senior Editor for Harcourt Brace Jovanovich, she and Patricia Westheimer have published *The Executive Style Book*.

George Slusser, who holds a PhD from Harvard, is Professor of Comparative Literature, Curator of the Eaton Collection, and Director of the Center for Bibliographic Studies' Eaton Program for Science Fiction and Fantasy Studies at UC Riverside. Recipient of the Science Fiction Research Association's Pilgrim Award for lifetime achievement in scholarship in the field of science fiction and fantastic literature in 1986, he has written over sixty articles and authored or edited seventeen books. His most recent publications include *Ursula Le Guin: Between Worlds* (Borgo Press) and *Fiction 2000: Cyberpunk and the Future of Narrative* (editor; University of Georgia Press).

Jonathan H. Turner, who received a PhD from Cornell University, is Professor of Sociology at UC Riverside. Author of over twenty books on a wide range of topics in sociology, he has published over one hundred articles in all of the principal sociology journals.

Theodore Ziolkowski, who received his PhD from Yale and joined Princeton's Department of Germanic Languages and Literatures in

1964, is currently a Professor in the Department of Comparative Literature. Appointed to Princeton's Class of 1900 Professorship of Modern Languages in 1969, from 1979 to 1992 he was Dean of Princeton's Graduate School. His scholarly works include several edited volumes and books on the works of Herman Hesse, as well as the prize-winning study *Fictional Transfigurations of Jesus* (Princeton University Press). He has served on the editorial boards of several journals and of Princeton University Press and in 1978 received the Howard T. Behrman Award for Distinguished Achievement in the Humanities.

Jack Zupko, who received his PhD from Cornell University, is an Assistant Professor of Philosophy at San Diego State University whose research and teaching interests include contemporary metaphysics and epistemology. He has publications on medieval philosophy, is currently working on a book-length manuscript on psychological explanation in the later Middle Ages, and is collaborating on the critical Latin edition of a 14th-century psychological treatise.

BIBLIOGRAPHY

Achtert, Walter, and Joseph Gibaldi. *The MLA Style Manual*. New York: Modern Language Association, 1985.

Anderson, Worth, Alycia Best, Cynthia Best, John Hurst, Brandt Miller, and Susan Miller. "Cross-Curricular Underlife: A Collaborative Report on Ways with Academic Words." *College Composition and Communication* (1990): 11–36.

Annual Register of Grant Support. Chicago: Marquis Academic Media, annual.

Anson, Chris M. "A Computerized List of Journals Publishing Articles in Composition."

Arnaudet, Martin L., and Mary Ellen Barrett. *Approaches to Academic Reading and Writing*. Englewood Cliffs, NJ: Prentice-Hall, 1984.

Bailey, Herbert Smith. *The Rate of Publication of Scholarly Monographs in the Humanities and Social Sciences, 1978–88*. New York: Association of American University Presses, 1990.

Barzun, Jacques. *On Writing, Editing, and Publishing: Essays, Explicative and Hortatory*. 2nd ed. Chicago: University of Chicago Press, 1986.

Baum, Joan, coordinator, and members of the CUNY Faculty Development Program. "On Publishing in the Academy." New York: Instructional Resource Center, City University of NY, n.d.

Becker, Howard S. *Writing for Social Scientists: How To Start and Finish Your Thesis, Book, or Article*. Chicago: University of Chicago Press, 1986.

Bennett, Hal Zina, with Michael Larsen. *How to Write with a Collaborator*. Cincinnati, OH: Writer's Digest Books, 1988.

Bernard, Jessie Shirley. *Academic Women*. University Park: Pennsylvania State University Press, 1964.

Biguenet, John, and Rainer Schulte. *The Craft of Translation*. Chicago: University of Chicago Press, 1989.

Boice, Robert. *Professors as Writers: A Self-Help Guide to Productive Writing*. Stillwater, OK: New Forums Press, Inc. 1990.

Books in a Series: Original, Reprinted, In-Print, and Out-of-Print Books, Published or Distributed in the U.S. in Popular, Scholarly and Professional Series. 3rd ed. New York: Bowker, 1980.

Brodkey, Linda. *Academic Writing as Social Practice*. Philadelphia: Temple University Press, 1987.

Budd, Louis J. "On Writing Scholarly Articles." *The Academic's Handbook*. Ed. A. Leigh DeNeef, Crauford D. Goodwin, and Ellen Stern McCrate. Durham, NC: Duke University Press, 1988. 201–15.

Cambra, Ann, Nancy Schluntz, and Susan Cardoza. *Graduate Students' Survival Guide*. Jefferson, NC: McFarland and Co., 1984.

Cargill, Oscar, William Charvat, and Donald D. Walsh. *The Publication of Academic Writing*. New York: MLA, 1986.

Carver, Ronald P. *Writing a Publishable Research Report: In Education, Psychology, and Related Disciplines*. Springfield, IL: Charles C. Thomas, 1984.

Cheney, Theodore A. Rees. *Getting the Words Right: How to Revise, Edit, and Rewrite*. Cinncinnati: Writer's Digest Books, 1983.

Cook, Claire Kehrwald. *Line by Line: How To Improve Your Writing*. New York: MLA, 1985.

Davis, Gordon B., and Clyde Parker, *Writing the Doctoral Dissertation: A Systematic Approach*. Woodbury, NY: Barron's, 1979.

Dawsey, James M. *A Scholar's Guide to Academic Journals in Religion*. Metuchen, NJ: Scarecrow Press, 1988.

DeNeef, A. Leigh, Crauford D. Goodwin, and Ellen Stern McCrate, eds. *The Academic's Handbook*. Durham, NC: Duke University Press, 1988.

Directory of American Scholars. Eighth edition. Lancaster, PA: Science Press, 1982.

Directory of Grants in the Humanities. Phoenix, AZ: Oryx Press, 1986.

Dorn, Fred J. *Publishing for Professional Development*. Muncie, IN: Accelerated Development Inc., 1985.

Downes, Robin, ed. *Computing, Electronic Publishing, and Information Technology: Their Impact on Academic Libraries*. New York: Haworth Press, 1988.

Dukelow, David C., and Grace Joely Beatty. *Dissertation Proposal Guidebook: How to Prepare a Research Proposal and Get It Accepted*. Springfield, IL: Charles C. Thomas, 1980.

Elbow, Peter. *Writing with Power: Techniques for Mastering the Writing Process*. New York: Oxford University Press, 1981.

Erkut, Sumru, and Janice R. Mokros. "Professors as Models and Mentors for College Students." Working Paper 65. Wellesley, MA: Center for Research on Women, Wellesley Coll., 1981.

Ezell, Susan, et. al, eds. *The Proposal Writer's Swipe File III: 15 Professionally Written Grant Proposals ... Prototypes of Approaches, Styles, and Structures*. Washington, D.C.: Taft Corp., 1981.

Fischel, Daniel N. *A Practical Guide to Writing and Publishing Professional Books: Business, Technical, Scientific, Scholarly*. New York: Van Nostrand Reinhold, 1984.

Foley, Frank. *The Market for English-Language Academic Publications in Japan*. Canberra, Australia: Research School of Pacific Studies, Australian National University, 1988.

Forester, John. *Notes on Writing In and After Graduate School*. Ithaca, NY: Dept. of City and Regional Planning Publications, Cornell University, 1984.

Foo, Mary Frank, ed. *Scholarly Writing and Publishing: Issues, Problems, and Solutions*. Boulder, CO: Westview Press, 1985.

Fulton, Len, ed. *International Directory of Little Magazines and Small Presses*. Paradise, CA: Dustbooks, annual.

Harman, Eleanor, and Ian Montagnes, eds. *The Thesis and the Book*. Toronto: University of Toronto Press, 1976.

Harner, James L. *Literary Research Guide: A Guide to Reference Sources for the Study of Literatures in English and Related Topics*. New York: MLA, 1989.

————, ed. *MLA Directory of Scholarly Presses in Language and Literature*. New York: MLA, 1991.

Hashimoto, Irvin. "Toward a Taxonomy of Scholarly Publishing." *College English* 45 (1983): 500–05.

Howard, V.A., and J.H. Barton. *Thinking on Paper*. New York: William Morrow, 1986.

Joliffe, David A., ed. *Writing in Academic Disciplines*. Norwood, NJ: Ablex Publishing Corporation, 1988.

Katz, Bill, and Linda Sternberg Katz. *Magazines for Libraries*. New York: R.R. Bowker, 1986.

Keller, Evelyn Fox, and Helene Moglen. "Competition and Feminism: Conflicts for Academic Women." *Signs* 12 (1987): 493–511.

Kennedy, Mary Lynch, and Hadley M. Smith. *Academic Writing: Working with Sources Across the Curriculum*. Englewood Cliffs, NJ: Prentice Hall, 1988.

Krathwohl, David R. *How to Prepare a Research Proposal: Guidelines for Funding and Dissertations in the Social and Behavioral Sciences*. Syracuse, NY: Syracuse University Press, 1988.

Kronik, John W. "On Mentoring Women: Then and Now." *Profession 90*: 52–56.

Kurtz, David L,, and A. Edward Spitz. *An Academic Writer's Guide to Publishing in Business and Economic Journals*. Ypsilanti: Bureau of Business Services and Research, Eastern Michigan University, 1972.

Larson, Michael. *How To Write a Book Proposal*. Cincinnati, OH: Writers Digest Books, 1985.

Lefferts, Robert. *Getting a Grant in the 1990s: How to Write Successful Grant Proposals*. New York: Prentice Hall Press, 1990.

Leki, Ilona. *Academic Writing: Techniques and Tasks*. New York: St. Martin's Press, 1989.

Lunsford, Angela, Helene Moglen, and James Slevin, eds. *The Future of Doctoral Studies in English*. New York: MLA, 1989.

Markland, Murray. "Taking Criticism—and Using It." *Scholarly Publishing* 14 (February 1983): 139–47.

Martin, Roy. *Writing and Defending a Thesis or Dissertation in Psychology and Education*. Springfield, IL: Charles C. Thomas, 1980.

McCartney, Eugene Stock. *Recurrent Maladies in Scholarly Writing*. Ann Arbor: University of Michigan Press, 1953.

Merriam, Sharan. "Mentors and Proteges: A Critical Reivew of the Literature." *Adult Education Quarterly* 33 (1983): 161–73.

MLA Directory of Periodicals: A Guide to Journals and Series in Languages and Literatures. New York: MLA, annual.

Nash, Walter, ed. *The Writing Scholar: Studies in Academic Discourse*. Newbury Park, CA: Sage Publications, 1990.

Powell, Walter W. *Getting into Print: The Decision-Making Process in Scholarly Publishing*. Chicago: University of Chicago Press, 1985.

Reitt, Barbara. "An Academic Author's Checklist." *Scholarly Publishing* 16 (October 1984): 65–72.

Rodman, Hyman. "Some Practical Advice for Journal Contributors." *Scholarly Publishing* 9 (April 1978): 235–41.

Rosovsky, Henry. *The University: An Owner's Manual*. New York: W.W. Norton, 1990 (Grad student 131–156).

Ross, Mary Bucher, et al., eds. *Directory of Publishing Opportunities: A Guide to Academic, Business, Research, Scientific, and Technical Publishing Opportunities*. 2nd ed. Orange, NJ: Academic Media, 1973.

Rowson, Richard C. "The Scholar and the Art of Publishing." *The Academic's Handbook*. Ed. A. Leigh DeNeef, Crauford D. Goodwin, and Ellen Stern McCrate. Durham, NC: Duke University Press, 1988. 226–37.

Shaffer, Susan E. *Guide to Book Publishing Courses: Academic and Professional Programs*. Princeton, NJ: Peterson's Guides, 1979.

Staff of the University of Chicago Press. *Chicago Guide to Preparing Electronic Manuscripts for Authors and Publishers.* Chicago: University of Chicago Press, 1987.

Sternberg, David. *How to Complete and Survive a Doctoral Dissertation.* New York: St. Martin's Press, 1981.

Stott, Bill. *Write to the Point.* New York: Columbia University Press, 1991.

Sugden, Virginia M. *The Graduate Thesis: The Complete Guide to Planning and Preparation.* New York: Pitman Publishing Corp., 1973.

Symposium On Scholarly Communication: Papers Delivered at the Symposium Held in Ottawa in October 1980 by the Aid to Scholarly Publications Programme of the CFH/SSFC Under the Auspices of the Social Sciences. Ottawa, Ont.: Aid to Scholarly Publications Programme, 1981.

The Standard Periodical Directory. New York: Oxbridge Communications, Inc., annual.

Tuckman, Howard P. *Publication, Teaching, and the Academic Reward Structure.* Lexington, MA: Lexington Books, 1976.

Turabian, Kate L., and Bonnie Birtwistle Honigsblum. *A Manual for Writers of Term Papers, Theses, and Dissertations.* Chicago: University of Chicago Press, 1987.

Ulrich's International Periodicals Directory. New York: R.R. Bowker, annual.

Van Leunen, Mary-Claire. *A Handbook for Scholars.* New York: Alfred Knopf, 1979.

Van Maanen, John. *Tales of the Field: On Writing Ethnography.* Chicago: University of Chicago Press, 1988.

Van Til, William. *Writing for Professional Publication.* Boston: Allyn and Bacon, 1986.

Ward, Adrienne Marie, compiler. *A Guide to Professional Organizations for Teachers of Language and Literature in the United States and Canada.* New York: MLA, 1990.

Watson, George, *The Literary Thesis: A Guide to Research.* London: Longman Group, 1970.

Webb, William, et. al. *Sources of Information in the Social Sciences: A Guide to the Literature*. Chicago: American Library Association, 1986.

Westmeyer, Paul. *A Guide for Use in Planning and Conducting Research Projects*. Springfield, IL: Charles C. Thomas, 1981.

Wolper, Roy S. "On Academic Reviewing: Ten Common Errors." *Scholarly Publishing* 16 (April 1985): 269–75.

Wyche-Smith, Susan, and Shirley K. Rose. "One Hundred Ways to Make the Wyoming Resolution a Reality: A Guide to Personal and Political Action." *College Composition and Communication* 41.3 (October 1990): 318–24.

Yates, Brian T. *Doing the Dissertation: The Nuts and Bolts of Psychological Research*. Springfield, IL: Charles C. Thomas, 1982.

Zinsser, William. *On Writing Well: An Informal Guide to Writing Nonfiction*. New York: Harper and Row, 1980.

——. *Writing with a Word Processor*. New York: Harper and Row, 1983.

Other fine books from
Prentice Hall General Reference

The New York Public Library Desk Reference: A researcher's dream, a browser's delight, these pages are chock-full of important, useful, offbeat, and interesting facts in twenty-six subject areas. Destined to take its place next to your dictionary and thesaurus.

The New York Public Library Book of Chronologies: The ultimate collection of dates, events, people, places, and pastimes. Cross-references, a comprehensive index, and a selected bibliography make this a superior timeline reference work.

The New York Public Library Book of How and Where to Look It Up: This reference shows you how to access information stored in directories, libraries, special collections, electronic databases, photographic archives, museums, and more! An indispensable guide for students, librarians, journalists, public relations professionals, lawyers, activists, and anyone in the fact-finding business.